U·X·L Encyclopedia of World Mythology

VOLUME 1: A–B

U·X·L Encyclopedia
of World Mythology

VOLUME 1: A–B

U·X·L
A part of Gale, Cengage Learning

GALE
CENGAGE Learning™

Detroit • New York • San Francisco • New Haven, Conn • Waterville, Maine • London

GALE
CENGAGE Learning™

U·X·L Encyclopedia of World Mythology

Product manager: Meggin Condino

Project editor: Rebecca Parks

Editorial: Jennifer Stock, Kim Hunt

Rights Acquisition and Management: Kelly A. Quin, Scott Bragg, Aja Perales

Composition: Evi Abou-El-Seoud

Manufacturing: Rita Wimberley

Imaging: Lezlie Light

Product Design: Jennifer Wahi

© 2009 Gale, Cengage Learning

For product information and technology assistance, contact us at Gale Customer Support, 1-800-877-4253.
For permission to use material from this text or product, submit all requests online at cengage.com/permissions.
Further permissions questions can be emailed to permissionrequest@cengage.com.

Cover photographs reproduced by permission of Purestock/Getty Images (picture of Statue of Poseidon); Voon Poh Le/Dreamstime.com (drawing of paper cut dragon); Werner Forman/Art Resource, NY (picture of an incense burner of a sun god); Charles Walker/Topfoto/The Image Works (photo of a papyrus drawing of Anubis weighing the heart); and The Art Archive/Richard Wagner/Museum Bayreuth/Gianni Dagli Orti (photo of a drawing of a valkyrie).

LIBRARY OF CONGRESS CATALOGING-IN-PUBLICATION DATA

U*X*L encyclopedia of world mythology
  p. cm.
  Includes bibliographical references and index.
  ISBN 978-1-4144-3030-0 (set) -- ISBN 978-1-4144-3036-2 (vol. 1) -- ISBN 978-1-4144-3037-9 (vol. 2) -- ISBN 978-1-4144-3038-6 (vol. 3) -- ISBN 978-1-4144-3039-3 (vol. 4) -- ISBN 978-1-4144-3040-9 (vol. 5)
  1. Mythology—Encyclopedias, Juvenile. I. Title: UXL encyclopedia of world mythology. II. Title: Encyclopedia of world mythology.

BL303.U95 2009
201'.303—dc22   2008012696

Gale
27500 Drake
Farmington Hills, MI 48331-3535

ISBN-13: 978-1-4144-3030-0 (set)   ISBN-10: 1-4144-3030-2 (set)
ISBN-13: 978-1-4144-3036-2 (Vol. 1)   ISBN-10: 1-4144-3036-1 (Vol. 1)
ISBN-13: 978-1-4144-3037-9 (Vol. 2)   ISBN-10: 1-4144-3037-X (Vol. 2)
ISBN-13: 978-1-4144-3038-6 (Vol. 3)   ISBN-10: 1-4144-3038-8 (Vol. 3)
ISBN-13: 978-1-4144-3039-3 (Vol. 4)   ISBN-10: 1-4144-3039-6 (Vol. 4)
ISBN-13: 978-1-4144-3040-9 (Vol. 5)   ISBN-10: 1-4144-3040-X (Vol. 5)

This title is also available as an e-book.
ISBN-13: 978-1-4144-3846-7 ISBN-10: 1-4144-3846-X
Contact your Gale, a part of Cengage Learning sales representative for ordering information.

Printed in the United States of America
1 2 3 4 5 6 7 12 11 10 09 08

Table of Contents

Table of Contents by Culture

Reader's Guide

The *U·X·L Encyclopedia of World Mythology* examines the major characters, stories, and themes of mythologies from cultures around the globe, from African to Zoroastrian. Arranged alphabetically in an A–Z format, each entry provides the reader with an overview of the topic as well as contextual analysis to explain the topic's importance to the culture from which it came. In addition, each entry explains the topic's influence on modern life, and prompts the reader with a discussion question or reading/writing suggestion to inspire further analysis. There are five different types of entries: Character, Deity, Myth, Theme, and Culture. The entry types are designated by icons that are shown in a legend that appears on each page starting a new letter grouping so that you can easily tell which type of entry you are reading.

Types of Entries Found in This Book

Character entries generally focus on a single mythical character, such as a hero. In some cases, character entries deal with groups of similar or related beings—for example, Trolls or Valkyries. Deities (gods) are found in their own unique type of entry.

Deity entries contain information about a god or goddess. An example would be Zeus (pronounced ZOOS), the leader of the ancient Greek gods. Deities are very similar to other mythical characters, except that they often appear in many different myths; each Deity entry provides a summary of the most important myths related to that deity.

Myth entries focus on a specific story as opposed to a certain character. One example is the entry on the Holy Grail, which tells the legend of the vessel's origins as well as the many people who sought to locate it. In some cases, the myth is primarily concerned with a single character; the entry on the Golden Fleece, for example, features Jason as the main character. Like the Holy Grail entry, however, this entry focuses on the legends surrounding the object in question rather than the character involved.

Theme entries examine how one single theme, idea, or motif is addressed in the mythologies of different cultures. An example would be the Reincarnation entry that examines different cultural depictions of this eternal cycle of death and rebirth.

Culture entries contain a survey of the myths and beliefs of a particular culture. Each entry also provides historical and cultural context for understanding how the culture helped to shape, or was shaped by, the beliefs of other cultures.

Types of Rubrics Found in This Book

Each entry type is organized in specific rubrics to allow for ease of comparison across entries. The rubrics that appear in these entries are: *Character/Myth/Theme Overview*; *Core Deities and Characters*; *Major Myths*; *[Subject] in Context*; *Key Themes and Symbols*; *[Subject] in Art, Literature, and Everyday Life*; and *Read, Write, Think, Discuss*. In addition, the character, deity, and myth entries all have key facts sections in the margins that provide basic information about the entry, including the country or culture of origin, a pronunciation guide where necessary, alternate names for the character (when applicable), written or other sources in which the subject appears, and information on the character's family (when applicable).

Character Overview offers detailed information about the character's place within the mythology of its given culture. This may include information about the character's personality, summaries of notable feats, and relationships with other mythological characters. *Myth Overview* includes a summary of the myth being discussed. *Theme Overview* provides a brief description of the theme being discussed, as well as a rundown of the major points common when examining that theme in different mythologies.

Core Deities and Characters includes brief descriptions of the main deities and other characters that figure prominently in the given culture's mythology. This is not a comprehensive list of all the gods or characters mentioned in a particular culture.

Major Myths features a brief summary of all the most important or best-known myths related to the subject of the entry. For example, the entry on Odin (pronounced OH-din), chief god of Norse mythology, includes the tale describing how he gave up one of his eyes in order to be able to see the future.

[Subject] in Context provides additional cultural and historical information that helps you understand the subject by seeing through the eyes of the people who made it part of their culture. The entry on the weaver Arachne (pronounced uh-RAK-nee), for instance, includes information on the importance of weaving as a domestic duty in ancient Greece.

Key Themes and Symbols outlines the most important themes in the tales related to the subject. This section also includes explanations of symbols associated with the subject of the entry, or which appear in myths related to the subject. For example, this section may explain the meaning of certain objects a god is usually shown carrying.

[Subject] in Art, Literature, and Everyday Life includes references to the subject in well-known works of art, literature, film, and other media. This section may also mention other ways in which the subject appears in popular culture. For example, the fact that a leprechaun (pronounced LEP-ruh-kawn) appears as the mascot for Lucky Charms cereal is mentioned in this section of the Leprechauns entry.

Read, Write, Think, Discuss uses the material in the entry as a springboard for further discussion and learning. This section may include suggestions for further reading that are related to the subject of the entry, discussion questions regarding topics touched upon in the entry, writing prompts that explore related issues and themes, or research prompts that encourage you to delve deeper into the topics presented.

Most of the entries end with cross-references that point you to related entries in the encyclopedia. In addition, words that appear in bold within the entry are also related entries, making it easy to find additional information that will enhance your understanding of the topic.

Other Sections in This Book

This encyclopedia also contains other sections that you may find useful when studying world mythology. One of these is a "Timeline of World Mythology," which provides important dates from many cultures that are important to the development of their respective mythologies. A glossary in the front matter supplements the definitions that are included within the entries. Teachers will find the section on "Research and Activity Ideas" helpful in coming up with classroom activities related to the topic of mythology to engage students further in the subject. A section titled "Where to Learn More" provides you with other sources to learn more about the topic of mythology, organized by culture. You will also encounter sidebars in many of the entries; these sections offer interesting information that is related to, but not essential to, your understanding of the subject of the entry.

Comments and Suggestions

We welcome your comments on the *U•X•L Encyclopedia of World Mythology* and suggestions for other topics to consider. Please write to Editors, *U•X•L Encyclopedia of World Mythology,* Gale, 27500 Drake Rd., Farmington Hills, Michigan, 48331-3535.

Introduction

On the surface, myths are stories of gods, heroes, and monsters that can include fanciful tales about the creation and destruction of worlds, or awe-inspiring adventures of brave explorers in exotic or supernatural places. However, myths are not just random imaginings; they are cultivated and shaped by the cultures in which they arise. For this reason, a myth can function as a mirror for the culture that created it, reflecting the values, geographic location, natural resources, technological state, and social organization of the people who believe in it.

Values

The values of a culture are often revealed through that culture's myths and legends. For example, a myth common in Micronesian culture tells of a porpoise girl who married a human and had children; after living many years as a human, she decided to return to the sea. Before she left, she warned her children against eating porpoise, since they might unknowingly eat some of their own family members by doing so. Myths such as these are often used to provide colorful reasons for taboos, or rules against certain behaviors. In this case, the myth explains a taboo among the Micronesian peoples against hunting and eating porpoises.

Geography

Myths often reflect a culture's geographic circumstances. For example, the people of the Norse culture live in a region that has harsh, icy winters. It is no coincidence that, according to their myths, the being whose death led to the creation of the world was a giant made of frost. By contrast, the people of ancient Egypt lived in an dry, sunny land; their most important gods, such as Ra, were closely associated with the sun. Geographic features are also often part of a culture's myths, or used as inspiration for mythological tales. Spider Rock, a tall peak located at Canyon de Chelly National Monument in Arizona, is said by the Hopi people to be the home of the creation goddess Spider Woman. The Atlas mountains in northern Africa took their name from the myth that the Titan Atlas (pronounced AT-luhs) had once stood there holding up the heavens, but had been transformed to stone in order to make his task easier.

Natural Resources

Myths can also reflect the natural resources available to a culture, or the resources most prized by a certain group. In Mesoamerican and American Indian myths, maize (commonly referred to as corn) often appears as a food offered directly from gods or goddesses, or grown from the body of a deity. This reflects not only the importance of maize in the diets of early North and Central American cultures, but also the ready availability of maize, which does not appear as a native plant anywhere else in the world. Similarly, the olive tree, which is native to the coastal areas along the Mediterranean Sea, is one of the most important trees in ancient Greek myth. The city of Athens, it is said, was named for the goddess Athena (pronounced uh-THEE-nuh) after she gave its citizens the very first domesticated olive tree.

Sometimes, myths can reflect the importance of natural resources to an outside culture. For example, the Muisca people of what is now Colombia engaged in a ceremony in which their king covered himself in gold dust and took a raft out to the middle of a local lake; there he threw gold trinkets into the water as offerings to the gods. Gold was not commonly available, and was prized for its ceremonial significance; however, when Spanish explorers arrived in the New World and heard of this practice, they interpreted this to mean that gold must be commonplace in the area. This led to the myth of El Dorado, an entire city made of gold that many Spanish explorers believed to exist and spent decades trying to locate.

Technology

A culture's state of technological development can also be reflected in its myths. The earliest ancient Greek myths of Uranus (pronounced

YOOR-uh-nuhs) state that his son Cronus (pronounced KROH-nuhs) attacked him with a sickle made of obsidian. Obsidian is a stone that can be chipped to create a sharp edge, and was used by cultures older than the ancient Greeks, who relied on metals such as bronze and steel for their weapons. This might suggest that the myth arose from an earlier age; at the very least, it reflects the idea that, from the perspective of the Greeks, the myth took place in the distant past.

Social Order

Myths can also offer a snapshot of a culture's social organization. The Old Testament tale of the Tower of Babel offers an explanation for the many tribes found in the ancient Near East: they had once been united, and sought to build a tower that would reach all the way to heaven. In order to stop this act of self-importance, God caused the people to speak in different languages. Unable to understand each other, they abandoned the ambitious project and scattered into groups across the region.

Besides offering social order, myths can reinforce cultural views on the roles different types of individuals should assume in a society. The myth of Arachne (pronounced uh-RAK-nee) illustrates a fact known from other historical sources: weaving and fabric-making was the domestic duty of wives and daughters, and it was a skill highly prized in the homes of ancient Greece. Tales of characters such as Danaë (pronounced DAN-uh-ee), who was imprisoned in a tower by her father in order to prevent her from having a child, indicate the relative powerlessness of many women in ancient Greek society.

Different Cultures, Different Perspectives

To see how cultures reflect their own unique characteristics through myth, one can examine how a single theme—such as fertility—is treated in a variety of different cultures. Fertility is the ability to produce life, growth, or offspring, and is therefore common in most, if not all, mythologies. For many cultures, fertility is a key element in the creation of the world. The egg, one of the most common symbols of fertility, appears in Chinese mythology as the first object to form from the disorder that previously existed in place of the world. In many cultures, including ancient Greece, the main gods are born from a single mother;

in the case of the Greeks, the mother is Gaia (pronounced GAY-uh), also known as Earth.

For cultures that relied upon agriculture, fertility was an important element of the changing seasons and the growth of crops. In these cases, fertility was seen as a gift from nature that could be revoked by cruel weather or the actions of the gods. Such is the case in the ancient Greek myth of Persephone (pronounced per-SEF-uh-nee); when the goddess is taken to the underworld by Hades (pronounced HAY-deez), her mother—the fertility goddess Demeter (pronounced di-MEE-ter)—became sad, which caused all vegetation to wither and die.

For the ancient Egyptians, fertility represented not just crop growth and human birth, but also rebirth into the afterlife through death. This explains why Hathor (pronounced HATH-or), the mother goddess of fertility who supported all life, was also the maintainer of the dead. It was believed that Hathor provided food for the dead to help them make the long journey to the realm of the afterlife.

For early Semitic cultures, the notion of fertility was not always positive. In the story of Lilith, the little-known first wife of Adam (the first man), the independent-minded woman left her husband and went to live by the Red Sea, where she gave birth to many demons each day. The myth seems to suggest that fertility is a power that can be used for good or evil, and that the key to using this power positively is for wives to dutifully respect the wishes of their husbands. This same theme is found in the earlier Babylonian myth of Tiamat (pronounced TYAH-maht), who gave birth to not only the gods but also to an army of monsters that fought to defend her from her son, the hero Marduk (pronounced MAHR-dook).

These are just a few of the many ways in which different cultures can take a single idea and interpret it through their own tales. Rest assured that the myths discussed in this book are wondrous legends that capture the imagination of the reader. They are also mirrors in which we can see not only ourselves, but the reflections of cultures old and new, far and near—allowing us to celebrate their unique differences, and at the same time recognize those common elements that make these enchanting stories universally beloved and appreciated by readers and students around the world.

Timeline of World Mythology

c. 3400 BCE Early Sumerian writing is first developed.

c. 3100 BCE Egyptian writing, commonly known as hieroglyphics, is first developed.

c. 2852–2205 BCE During this time period, China is supposedly ruled by the Three Sovereigns and Five Emperors, mythical figures that may have been based on actual historical leaders.

c. 2100 BCE Earliest known version of the *Epic of Gilgamesh* is recorded in Sumerian.

c. 1553–1536 BCE Egyptian pharaoh Akhenaten establishes official worship of Aten, a single supreme god, instead of the usual group of gods recognized by ancient Egyptians.

c. 1250 BCE The Trojan War supposedly occurs around this time period. Despite the war's importance to Greek and Roman mythology, modern scholars are not sure whether the war was an actual historical event or just a myth.

c. 1100 BCE The Babylonian creation epic *Enuma Elish* is documented on clay tablets discovered nearly three thousand years later in the ruined library of Ashurbanipal, located in modern-day Iraq.

c. 800 BCE The Greek alphabet is invented, leading to a flowering of Greek literature based on myth.

c. 750 BCE The Greek epics known as the *Iliad* and the *Odyssey* are written by the poet Homer. Based on the events surrounding the

Trojan War, these two stories are the source of many myths and characters in Greek and Roman mythology.

c. 750 BCE The Greek poet Hesiod writes his *Theogony*, which details the origins of the Greek gods.

c. 563–480 BCE According to tradition, Gautama Buddha, the founder of Buddhism, is believed to have lived in ancient India and Nepal during this time.

525–456 BCE The Greek dramatist Aeschylus writes tragedies detailing the lives of mythical characters, including *Seven Against Thebes*, *Agamemnon*, and *The Eumenides*.

c. 500–100 BCE The oldest version of the *Ramayana*, the Hindu epic about the incarnation of the god Vishnu named Rama, is written.

c. 496–406 BCE Ancient Greek playwright Sophocles creates classic plays such as *Antigone* and *Oedipus the King*.

c. 450 BCE The Book of Genesis, containing stories fundamental to early Christianity, Judaism, and Islam, is collected and organized into its modern form.

c. 431 BCE Greek builders complete work on the temple of Athena known as the Parthenon, one of the few ancient Greek structures to survive to modern times.

c. 150–50 BCE The Gundestrup cauldron, a silver bowl depicting various Celtic deities and rituals, is created. The bowl is later recovered from a peat bog in Denmark in 1891.

c. 29–19 BCE Roman poet Virgil creates his mythical epic, the *Aeneid*, detailing the founding of Rome.

c. 4 BCE**–33** CE Jesus, believed by Christians to be the son of God, supposedly lives during this time period.

c. 8 CE Roman poet Ovid completes his epic work *Metamorphoses*. It is one of the best existing sources for tales of ancient Greek and Roman mythology.

c. 100 CE The *Mahabharata*, a massive epic recognized as one of the most important pieces of literature in Hinduism, is organized into its modern form from source material dating back as far as the ninth century BCE.

c. 570–632 CE The prophet Muhammad, founder of Islam, supposedly lives during this time.

c. 800–840 CE The oldest surviving remnants of *The Book of One Thousand and One Nights*, a collection of Near Eastern folktales and legends, are written in Syrian.

c. 1000 CE The Ramsund carving, a stone artifact bearing an illustration of the tale of Sigurd, is created in Sweden. The tale is documented in the *Volsunga* saga.

c. 1010 CE The oldest surviving manuscript of the Old English epic *Beowulf* is written. It is recognized as the first significant work of English literature.

c. 1100 Monks at the Clonmacnoise monastery compile the *Book of the Dun Cow*, the earliest written collection of Irish myths and legends still in existence.

c. 1138 Geoffrey of Monmouth's *History of the Kings of Britain* is published, featuring the first well-known tales of the legendary King Arthur.

c. 1180–1210 The *Nibelungenlied*, a German epic based largely on earlier German and Norse legends such as the *Volsunga* saga, is written by an unknown poet.

c. 1220 Icelandic scholar Snorri Sturluson writes the Prose Edda, a comprehensive collection of Norse myths and legends gathered from older sources.

c. 1350 The *White Book of Rhydderch*, containing most of the Welsh myths and legends later gathered in the *Mabinogion*, first appears.

1485 Thomas Malory publishes *Le Morte D'Arthur*, widely considered to be the most authoritative version of the legend of King Arthur.

c. 1489 *A Lytell Geste of Robin Hode*, one of the most comprehensive versions of the life of the legendary British character of Robin Hood, is published.

c. 1550 The *Popol Vuh*, a codex containing Mayan creation myths and legends, is written. The book, written in the Quiché language but using Latin characters, was likely based on an older book written in Mayan hieroglyphics that has since been lost.

1835 Elias Lonnrot publishes the *Kalevala*, an epic made up of Finnish songs and oral myths gathered during years of field research.

1849 Archeologist Henry Layard discovers clay tablets containing the Babylonian creation epic *Enuma Elish* in Iraq. The epic, lost for centuries, is unknown to modern scholars before this discovery.

1880 Journalist Joel Chandler Harris publishes *Uncle Remus, His Songs and Sayings: the Folk-Lore of the Old Plantation*, a collection of myths and folktales gathered from African American slaves working in the South. Many of the tales are derived from older stories from African myth. Although the book is successful and spawns three sequels, Harris is accused by some of taking cultural myths and passing them off as his own works.

Words to Know

benevolent: Helpful or well-meaning.

caste: A social level in India's complex social class system.

cauldron: Kettle.

chaos: Disorder.

chivalry: A moral code popularized in Europe in the Middle Ages that stressed such traits as generosity, bravery, courtesy, and respect toward women.

constellation: Group of stars.

cosmogony: The study of, or a theory about, the origin of the universe.

deity: God or goddess.

demigod: Person with one parent who was human and one parent who was a god.

destiny: Predetermined future.

divination: Predicting the future.

dualistic: Having two sides or a double nature.

epic: A long, grand-scale poem.

fertility: The ability to reproduce; can refer to human ability to produce children or the ability of the earth to sustain plant life.

hierarchy: Ranked order of importance.

hubris: Too much self-confidence.

immortal: Living forever.

imperial: Royal, or related to an empire.

indigenous: Native to a given area.

Judeo-Christian: Related to the religious tradition shared by Judaism and Christianity. The faiths share a holy book, many fundamental principles, and a belief in a single, all-powerful god.

matriarchal: Female-dominated. Often refers to societies in which a family's name and property are passed down through the mother's side of the family.

mediator: A go-between.

monotheism: The belief in a single god as opposed to many gods.

mummification: The drying and preserving of a body to keep it from rotting after death.

nymph: A female nature deity.

omen: A mystical sign of an event to come.

oracle: Person through whom the gods communicated with humans.

pagan: Someone who worships pre-Christian gods.

pantheon: The entire collection of gods recognized by a group of people.

patriarchal: Male-dominated. Often refers to societies in which the family name and wealth are passed through the father.

patron: A protector or supporter.

pharaoh: A king of ancient Egypt.

polytheism: Belief in many gods.

primal: Fundamental; existing since the beginning.

prophet: A person able to see the plans of the gods or foretell future events.

pyre: A large pile of burning wood used in some cultures to cremate a dead body.

resurrected: Brought back to life.

revelation: The communication of divine truth or divine will to human beings.

rune: A character from an ancient and magical alphabet.

seer: A person who can see the future.

shaman: A person who uses magic to heal or look after the members of his tribe.

sorcerer: Wizard.

syncretism: The blending or fusion of different religions or belief systems.

tradition: A time-honored practice, or set of such practices.

underworld: Land of the dead.

utopia: A place of social, economic and political perfection.

Research and Activity Ideas

Teachers wishing to enrich their students' understanding of world mythologies might try some of the following group activities. Each uses art, music, drama, speech, research, or scientific experimentation to put the students in closer contact with the cultures, myths, and figures they are studying.

Greek Mythology: A Pageant of Gods

In this activity, students get to be gods and goddesses for a day during the classroom "Pageant of the Gods," an event modeled after a beauty pageant. Each student selects (with teacher approval) a deity from Greek mythology. Students then research their deity, write a 250-word description of the deity, and create costumes so they can dress as their deity. On the day of the pageant, the teacher collects the students' descriptions and reads them aloud as each student models his or her costume for the class.

Materials required for the students:

Common household materials for costume

Materials required for the teacher:

None

Optional extension: The class throws a post-pageant potluck of Greek food.

Anglo-Saxon Mythology: Old English Translation

Students are often surprised to learn that *Beowulf* is written in English. The original Old English text looks almost unrecognizable to them. In this activity (which students may work on in the classroom, in the library, or at home), the teacher begins by discussing the history of the English language and its evolution over the past one thousand years (since the writing of *Beowulf*). The teacher then models how a linguist would go about translating something written in Old English or Middle English (using an accessible text such as *The Canterbury Tales* as an example), and makes various resources for translation available to the students (see below). The class as a whole works on translating the first two lines of *Beowulf*. The teacher then assigns small groups of students a couple lines each of the opening section of *Beowulf* to translate and gloss. When each group is ready with their translations, the students assemble the modern English version of the opening of *Beowulf* and discuss what they learned about the various Old English words they studied.

Materials required for the students:

None

Materials required for the teacher:

Copies of an Old English version of the first part of *Beowulf* for distribution to students.

There are multiple Old English dictionaries available online, so student groups could work on this activity in the classroom if a sufficient number of computer workstations with Internet access are available. There are also many Old English dictionaries in print form. If none is available in the school library, some can be checked out from the public library.

Egyptian Mythology: Mummify a Chicken

The ancient Egyptians believed preserving a person's body ensured their safe passage into the afterlife. The process of Egyptian mummification was a secret for many centuries until ancient Greek historian Herodotus recorded some information about the process in the fifth century BCE. Archaeologists have recently refined their understanding of Egyptian mummification practices. In this activity, students conduct their own mummification experiment on chickens.

The teacher contextualizes the activity by showing students a video on mummies and asking them to read both Herodotus's account of mummification and more recent articles about mummification that center on the research of Egyptologist Bob Brier.

Once students understand the basics of mummification, groups of five or six students can begin their science experiment, outlined below. The teacher should preface the experiment with safety guidelines for handling raw chicken.

Materials required for students:

Scale

One fresh chicken per group (bone-in chicken breast or leg may substitute)

Disposable plastic gloves (available at drugstores)

Carton of salt per group per week

Spice mixture (any strong powdered spices will do; powdered cloves, cinnamon, and ginger are good choices)

Extra-large (gallon size) air-tight freezer bags

Roll of gauze per group (available at drugstore)

Disposable aluminum trays for holding chickens

Cooking oil

Notebook for each group

Materials required for the teacher:

Video on mummies. A good option is: *Mummies: Secrets of the Pharaohs* (2007), available on DVD.

Reading material on mummies, including Herodotus's account. See: http://discovermagazine.com/2007/oct/mummification-is-back-from-the-dead; http://www.nationalgeographic.com/tv/mummy/; http://www.mummytombs.com/egypt/herodotus.htm

Plenty of paper towels and hand soap.

Procedure

1. All students put on plastic gloves.

2. Weigh each chicken (unnecessary if weight printed on packaging) and record the weight in a notebook. Record details of the chicken's appearance in the notebook.

3. Remove chicken organs and dispose of them. Rinse the chicken thoroughly in a sink.

4. Pat the chicken dry with paper towels. Make sure the chicken is completely dry, or the mummification process might not work.

5. Rub the spices all over the chicken, both inside and outside, then salt the entire chicken and fill the chicken cavity with salt.

6. Seal the chicken in the air-tight bag and place it in the aluminum tray.

7. Remove gloves and wash hands thoroughly with soap and water.

8. Once a week, put on plastic gloves, remove the chicken from the bag, dispose of the bag and accumulated liquid, and weigh the chicken. Record the weight in a notebook and make notes on changes in the chicken's appearance. Respice and resalt the chicken, fill the chicken cavity with salt, and seal it in a new bag. Remove gloves and wash hands. Repeat this step until no more liquid drains from the chicken.

9. When liquid no longer drains from the chicken, the mummy is done! Wipe off all the salt and rub a light coat of cooking oil on the mummy. Wrap it tightly in gauze.

Optional extension: Students can decorate their mummies using hieroglyphics and build shoebox sarcophagi for them.

Near Eastern Mythology: Gilgamesh and the Cedar Forest

The story of Gilgamesh's heroics against the demon Humbaba of the Cedar Forest is one of the most exciting parts of the *Epic of Gilgamesh*. In this activity, students write, stage, and perform a three-act play based on this part of the epic. Necessary tasks will include writing, costume design, set design, and acting. The teacher can divide tasks among students as necessary.

Materials required for the students:

Household items for costumes

Cardboard, paint, tape, and other materials for sets

Copy of the *Epic of Gilgamesh*

Materials required for the teacher:

None

Hindu Mythology: Salute the Sun

The practice of yoga, an ancient mental and physical discipline designed to promote spiritual perfection, is mentioned in most of the Hindu holy texts. Today, the physical aspects of yoga have become a widely popular form of exercise around the world. In this activity, the students and teacher will make yoga poses part of their own daily routine.

The teacher introduces the activity by discussing the history of yoga from ancient to modern times, by showing a video on the history of yoga, and by distributing readings from ancient Hindu texts dealing with the practice of yoga. After a class discussion on the video and texts, the teacher leads students through a basic "sun salutation" series of poses with the aid of an instructional yoga video (students may wish to bring a towel or mat from home, as some parts of the sun salutation involve getting on the floor). Students and the teacher will perform the sun salutation every day, preferably at the beginning of class, either for the duration of the semester or for another set period of time. Students will conclude the activity by writing a summary of their feelings about their yoga "experiment."

Materials required for the students:

Towel or mat to put on floor during sun salutations.

Materials required for teacher:

A DVD on the history of yoga. Recommended: *Yoga Unveiled* (2004), an excellent documentary series on the history of yoga.

An instructional yoga video that includes the "sun salutation" sequence (many available).

Handouts of ancient Indian writings on yoga. See *The Shambhala Encyclopedia of Yoga* (2000) and *The Yoga and the Bhagavad Gita* (2007).

African Mythology: Storytelling

Anansi the Spider was a trickster god of West African origin who was known as a master storyteller. In this activity, students work on their own storytelling skills while learning about the spread of Anansi stories from Africa to the Americas.

The teacher begins this activity by discussing the ways that oral traditions have helped the African American community preserve some part of their West African cultural heritage. The spread of stories about Anansi around Caribbean and American slave communities is an example, with the Uncle Remus stories of Joel Chandler Harris being a good demonstration of how the Anansi tales have evolved. The class then conducts a preliminary discussion about what the elements of a good spoken story might be, then watches or listens to models of storytelling. After listening to the stories, the class discusses common elements in the stories and techniques the storytellers used to keep the audience's attention and build interest.

Students then read a variety of Anansi and Uncle Remus stories on their own. With teacher approval, they select one story and prepare it for oral presentation in class (several students may select the same story). After the presentations, students can discuss their reactions to the various oral presentations, pointing out what was effective and ineffective.

Materials required for the students:

Optional: props for story presentation

Materials required for the teacher:

Background reading on West African oral traditions.

Recordings or videos of skilled storytellers. See *The American Storyteller Series* or the CD recording *Tell Me a Story: Timeless Folktales from Around the World* (which includes an Anansi story).

Optional extension: The teacher may arrange for students with especially strong oral presentations to share their stories at a school assembly or as visiting speakers in another classroom.

Micronesian and Melanesian Mythology: Island Hopping

The many islands that make up Micronesia and Melanesia are largely unfamiliar to most students. In this activity, students learn more about these faraway places.

The teacher introduces this activity by hanging up a large map of the South Pacific, with detail of Micronesian and Melanesian islands. The teacher explains that, during every class session, the class will learn the location of and key facts about a particular island. Each day, one student is given the name of an island. It is that student's homework assignment that night to learn the location of the island, its population, and its key industries. The student must also learn two interesting facts about the island. The next day, the student places a push pin (or other marker) on the map showing the location of his or her island. The student presents the information to the class, writes it down on an index card, and files the index card in the class "island" box. In this way, the students learn about a new Micronesian or Melanesian island every day and build a ready resource of information about the islands.

Materials required for the students:

> None

Materials required for the teacher:

> Large wall map with sufficient detail of Micronesia and Melanesia
> Index cards
> Box for island index cards
> Push pins, stickers, or other markers for islands

Northern European Mythology: The Scroll of the Nibelungen

The *Nibelungenlied* is an epic poem set in pre-Christian Germany. The tale contains many adventures, fights, and triumphs. In this activity, students prepare a graphic-novel version of the *Nibelungenlied*.

To introduce this activity, the teacher gives students a synopsis of the *Nibelungenlied* and describes the various interpretations of the saga (including Richard Wagner's opera and J. R. R. Tolkien's *Lord of the Rings* triology). The teacher then explains that the class will create a graphic novel of the *Nibelungenlied* on a continuous scroll of paper. The teacher shows models of various graphic novels and discusses the conventions of graphic novel representations.

Students are divided into groups of three or four, and each group receives one chapter or section of the *Nibelungenlied* as its assignment.

After reading their sections, the groups meet to discuss possible graphical representations of the action in their chapters and present their ideas to the teacher for approval. After gaining approval, student groups work, one group at a time, to draw and color their chapters on the scroll. When the scroll is finished, each group makes a short presentation explaining what happens in their chapter and how they chose to represent the action. The final scroll can be displayed around the classroom walls or along a school hallway.

Materials required by the students:

None

Materials required by the teacher:

Easel paper roll (200 feet)

Markers, colored pencils, and crayons

Copies of *Nibelungenlied* chapters for students (or refer students to http://omacl.org/Nibelungenlied/)

Inca Mythology: Make a Siku

A siku is an Andean pan pipe. Pipes such as these were important in Inca culture, and remain a prominent feature in Andean music. In this activity, students will make their own sikus.

The teacher begins this activity by playing some Andean pan pipe music, showing students the Andes on a map, and discussing the ways in which Inca culture remains part of the lives of Native Americans in countries like Peru. The teacher shows a picture of a pan pipe (or, ideally, an actual pan pipe) to the students and explains they will build their own.

Students need ten drinking straws each (they can bring them from home, or the teacher can provide them) and a pair of scissors. To make the pipe:

1. Set aside two of the straws. Cut the remaining straws so that each is one-half inch shorter than the next. The first straw is uncut. The second straw is one-half inch shorter than the first. The third is one inch shorter than the first, and so on.

2. Cut the remaining straws into equal pieces. These pieces will be used as spacers between pipe pieces.

3. Arrange the straws from longest to shortest (left to right) with the tops of the straws lined up.

4. Put spacer pieces between each part of the pipe so they are an equal distance apart.

5. Tape the pipe in position, making sure the tops of the straws stay in alignment.

6. The pipe is finished. Cover in paper and decorate if desired. Blow across the tops of straws to play.

Materials required by the students:

Ten drinking straws

Scissors

Tape

Materials required by the teacher:

Andean pipe music

Pictures of a pan pipe or an actual pan pipe

Picture of the Andes on a map

U·X·L Encyclopedia
of World Mythology

VOLUME 1: A–B

A

 **Character**

 Deity

Myth

Theme

Culture

Nationality/Culture
Greek

Pronunciation
uh-KILL-eez

Alternate Names
None

Appears In
Homer's *Iliad*, tales of the Trojan War

Lineage
Son of Peleus and the nymph Thetis

Achilles

Character Overview

Achilles (pronounced uh-KILL-eez) is one of the most important warriors in **Greek mythology**. He had strength, bravery, military skills, pride, and honor—all qualities that the ancient Greeks prized as manly virtues. Yet his behavior was also shaped by anger, stubbornness, and revenge. The conflict between Achilles' larger-than-life virtues and his all-too-human weaknesses plays an important part in the heroic tragedy of the *Iliad*.

Like many mythological **heroes**, Achilles was part human and part supernatural being. His parents were Peleus (pronounced pe-LAY-uhs), a king of Thessaly in northern Greece, and a sea nymph named Thetis (pronounced THEE-tis). According to Homer, Thetis raised both Achilles and his closest friend and companion, Patroclus (pronounced pa-TROH-kluhs).

According to legend, Achilles' mother Thetis tried to make her infant son invulnerable (incapable of being wounded, injured, or harmed) by dipping him into the river Styx, which flowed through the **underworld**, or land of the dead. Afterward, no sword or arrow could pierce Achilles wherever the Styx's water had touched him. However, the water did not touch the heel by which Thetis held Achilles, so this remained the only vulnerable spot on his body. This myth is the source of the term *Achilles' heel*, which refers to a person's most notable weakness.

1

Achilles' strength and athletic superiority emerged early. At age six, he could run fast enough to catch deer. Some myths say that Achilles learned to run from the centaur Chiron (pronounced KYE-ron), who also taught him music, medicine, and the skills of warfare. According to some legends, Achilles was destined from birth to suffer one of two fates: a long life without glory, or a glorious death in battle.

The Trojan War Achilles played a central role in the Trojan War. The Trojan War was a ten-year conflict between the Greeks and the Trojans. The war began when the Trojan prince Paris kidnapped a beautiful Greek queen named **Helen**. Her husband, King Menelaus, pulled together a large army and chased Paris and Helen, tracking them to the city of Troy. The Greek army camped outside of the city walls and laid siege (engaged in a persistent attack against the city) to Troy for ten years.

When the Trojan War began, Achilles' parents tried to keep him from joining the Greek forces against the Trojans in order to prevent the prophecy regarding his death in battle from coming true. But the Greeks felt they needed Achilles to fight with them because they had received a prophecy that they could not defeat the Trojans without him. They therefore sent the Greek leader **Odysseus** (pronounced oh-DIS-ee-uhs) to persuade Achilles to join the war. Achilles agreed to fight with them—even though he knew his choice might cost him his life—because he valued glory in battle more than a quiet existence in peace.

Achilles did indeed earn great glory in battle against the Trojans. Throughout the ten-year siege he killed many Trojans and struck fear into the hearts of the Trojan forces. The Trojans were helpless against his mighty strength and his invulnerability to weapons. He was, however, an extremely proud warrior; when he felt that he had been insulted by the leader of the Greek forces, **Agamemnon**, he refused to fight for the Greeks. He only returned to the fight when his friend Patroclus died at the hands of the great Trojan warrior **Hector**.

Achilles rushed into battle in a furious desire to avenge the death of Patroclus. He chased Hector around the walls of Troy three times before killing the Trojan prince in one-on-one combat. He then dragged the body behind his chariot for nine days, which prevented the Trojans from holding a proper funeral. The gods forced Achilles to surrender the body of Hector to his grieving father, King Priam of Troy. Soon after,

Achilles was killed on the battlefield when he was struck in his vulnerable heel by an arrow fired by Hector's brother, Paris.

Achilles in Context

The Trojan War in which Achilles fought was a struggle between two different groups—the Greeks and the Trojans—over Helen, who was a symbol of Greek pride as the most beautiful woman in the world. Modern-day scholars do not know for sure just how much of the story of the Trojan War is fiction, but the story reflects the reality of living in a time period when the ancient Greeks were frequently in conflict with nearby regions for control of land and resources. The warrior culture of ancient times arose from the need to protect land used for farming or keeping animals. Warriors also conquered more land when poor farming conditions or conflict with other peoples made moving necessary. Young men were trained in warrior skills as well as in the warrior code of honor and glory. Under the command of Alexander the Great, the Greeks succeeded on the battlefield and spread their empire across much of what is now the Middle East and western Asia. In an oral culture such as ancient Greece, the tales of battles and heroism passed on from generation to generation highlighted the importance of heroic deeds and glory.

The glory Achilles achieves does not make him a perfect example of a Greek man, however. His pride causes him to put himself above that of the army in which he fights, and results in both heavy Greek losses in battle and the death of his own best friend Patroclus. This flaw in the character of Achilles reflects the importance of the group over that of an individual to the ancient Greeks. In ancient Greek society, life was so difficult that people relied heavily on their social relationships in order to survive; one person acting for his or her own interests rather than that of the group could bring about the downfall of everyone.

Key Themes and Symbols

Achilles represents the ultimate warrior, seeking glory through his skills as a soldier. He chooses to die on the battlefield, knowing his heroic deeds will be remembered forever, rather than live a long, unremarkable life away from battle.

Another theme of the story of Achilles is revenge. After having an argument with Agamemnon, Achilles gets his revenge on the king by refusing to fight. This leads to the death of Patroclus, which prompts Achilles to seek revenge against his friend's killer, Hector. After Achilles kills Hector, Paris seeks revenge against Achilles for the death of his brother.

Achilles in Art, Literature, and Everyday Life

Achilles and his story have appeared in many forms over the centuries. In addition to being the main character of Homer's *Iliad*, he was the subject of several plays written by Greek dramatists Aeschylus (pronounced ES-kuh-lus) and Sophocles (pronounced SOF-uh-kleez). During the Renaissance, he was featured as a character in Shakespeare's *Troilus and Cressida*, and appears in modern works such as Disney's animated television series *Hercules* (1998).

Read, Write, Think, Discuss

Achilles is faced with a choice between two destinies: he can die young but with great glory, or he can live long but be forgotten when he is gone. Achilles chooses glory. In the modern world, some terrorists—such as suicide bombers—are willing to **sacrifice** their lives for great glory and rewards they believe they will receive in the **afterlife**. How do you think these terrorists are different from or similar to Achilles?

SEE ALSO Agamemnon; Greek Mythology; Heroes; *Iliad, The*; *Odyssey, The*

Adam and Eve

Character Overview

According to the monotheistic religions (those religions that believe there is only one god) of the Middle East, the first man and woman that God created were the couple named Adam and Eve. Genesis, the first book of the Bible, contains two accounts of how Adam and Eve came into being. The first version, which most likely dates from 600 to 400 BCE, says that God created all living things, including a man and woman "in his own image," on the sixth day of creation. According to the second version,

Nationality/Culture
Judeo-Christian

Pronunciation
AD-uhm and EEV

Alternate Names
None

Appears In
The Old Testament, Holy Bible

Lineage
Created by God

A Sumerian Version of Adam's Rib

The story of God making Eve out of Adam's rib may have come from an ancient legend from Mesopotamia, a region located in southwest Asia between the Tigris and Euphrates rivers, in modern-day Iraq. After the Sumerian god Enki ate eight plants belonging to his wife, the goddess Ninhursag, she cursed him so that eight parts of his body became diseased. When he was nearly dead, the gods persuaded Ninhursag to help him, and she created eight healing goddesses. The goddess who cured Enki's rib was Ninti, whose name means "lady of the rib" and "lady of life." In Hebrew mythology, Adam names the woman created from his rib Hawwah, which means "life." The Sumerian story probably influenced the Hebrew one, which became the basis for the version of Eve's creation found in the Bible.

which is longer and probably several centuries older, God made Adam from dust and breathed "the breath of life" into his nostrils. God then created animals so that Adam would not be alone. However, God saw that Adam needed a human partner, so he put Adam to sleep, took a part of him (traditionally, his rib), and created Eve from it.

The Garden of Eden and the Fall Adam and Eve lived in a garden called **Eden**, from which four rivers flowed out into the world. Like other earthly paradises in mythologies of the dry Near East, Eden was a well-watered, fertile place that satisfied Adam and Eve's every need. God imposed only one rule about life in this paradise: the two were told to never eat the fruit of the "tree of knowledge."

A clever serpent in the garden persuaded Eve to eat the forbidden fruit, then Adam tasted the fruit as well. Immediately upon tasting the fruit, Adam and Eve lost their innocence. Ashamed of their nakedness, they covered themselves with leaves. God saw that they had disobeyed him and drove them from the Garden of Eden.

When Adam and Eve left Eden, human history began. The two worked long and hard to survive. Eventually, they grew old and died, but not before they had children. The first two were their sons, **Cain and Abel**. According to Jewish, Christian, and Islamic tradition, all the people of the world are descended from the sons and daughters of Adam and Eve.

As punishment for disobeying God, Adam and Eve were driven out of Eden. "THE EX-PULSION FROM EDEN," FRES-CO BY MASACCIO, 1427, THE BRANCACCI CHAPEL OF S. MARIA DEL CARMINE, FLOR-ENCE, ITALY, PHOTOGRAPH.

Adam and Eve in Context

The Jewish, Christian, and Islamic traditions each have their own versions of the story of Adam and Eve as well as their own ideas about what it means. In Christian thought and belief, three important parts of the story are the serpent, the Fall, and the idea of original sin.

Christians believe the serpent was identified with **Satan**, a rebellious fallen angel and the force behind all evil. In the Christian tradition, it was Satan's pride in thinking he could be the equal of God that caused him to be cast out of **heaven**. He then persuades Eve to commit the very same sin by telling her that she can be like God if she eats of the fruit of the tree of life. Pride, therefore, is a serious sin in the Christian tradition, for no one should think of himself as the equal of God.

The Fall refers to the expulsion, or the forcing out, of Adam and Eve from the Garden of Eden into the world of ordinary, imperfect human life, sometimes called the fallen world. Some people interpret the Fall to mean that in the original state of existence before the beginning of history, people lived in harmony with each other, God, and the natural world. Closely related to the idea of the Fall is the idea of original sin. This idea came from the writings of the Christian leader St. Paul, whose work appears in the New Testament of the Bible, and of later Christian thinkers whom he influenced. According to this idea, the sin that Adam and Eve committed when they ate the forbidden fruit marks every human being descended from them. As a result, no one is born completely innocent and free from sin.

Eve being made from Adam's rib is sometimes used as a way to explain why men are more important than women. In this view, the original woman was just a rib made as a companion to Adam, and therefore not of equal status. However, this idea seems to have been based on a wrong translation of the Hebrew text. The word translated as "rib" is actually the Hebrew word for "side." Some biblical scholars believe that Adam was androgynous—both male and female—and the story of the creation of Eve is about the separation of the female "side" of the first human from the male side. Ribs do not play any part in the story at all. The fact that Eve brings about Adam's downfall by getting him to share the fruit has supported negative attitudes towards women as tempters of men.

Key Themes and Symbols

Adam and Eve are typically shown as naked in the Garden of Eden, showing their innocence and purity while living in a world without sin. Once they introduce sin into the world, however, they feel they should clothe themselves with animal skins, indicating that they feel ashamed. This shame is made even worse when God orders them to leave Eden.

The importance of obedience to God is an important theme. The perfect life that Adam and Eve led in Eden is ruined by the fact that they did not listen to God when he told them not to eat the fruit of the tree of life. Even worse, their sin dooms the rest of mankind to live in an imperfect world. In both literature and art, the apple is almost always portrayed as the fruit Eve took from the tree of life, even though the Bible did not name a specific fruit.

Adam and Eve in Art, Literature, and Everyday Life

During the many centuries when European art dealt mostly with religious ideas, the story of Adam and Eve was a favorite subject. Among the famous images of the couple are the paintings in the Sistine Chapel in Rome by Italian artist Michelangelo. Completed in the early 1500s, they show the creation of Adam and Eve and the Fall. Another well-known painting of Adam and Eve comes from German artist Albrecht Dürer, which was done in 1504. In general, artists of all periods have used fruit and snakes as symbols of temptation and evil.

Aside from the story of creation and the Fall in the book of Genesis, the Bible contains little information about Adam and Eve. Other writings, however, have added details to their story. One such work, the *Life of Adam and Eve*, was presented in the form of a biography. Written sometime between 20 BCE and 70 CE, it provides an interesting account of the Fall and the sufferings of Adam and Eve after leaving Eden. The most famous literary treatment of the story of Adam and Eve is the book-length poem *Paradise Lost*, written by English poet John Milton and published in 1667.

Further modern interpretations of the Adam and Eve myth have also been created, which build upon popular knowledge of the original story. *Eve's Diary* by Mark Twain, written in 1906, is a humorous retelling of the familiar events. Since the 1940s, numerous science fiction stories offered a new twist on the traditional tale, usually involving some type of disaster that wipes out the human race and a pair of survivors (sometimes actually named Adam and Eve) upon whom the fate of the species depends.

The story of Adam and Eve is the source of the common phrase "forbidden fruit"—referring to something that is tempting because one is not supposed to have it. Although there was plenty of other fruit she could have eaten in the garden, Eve chose the fruit from the tree of life specifically because God told her she could not have it.

Read, Write, Think, Discuss

Adam and Eve first lived in the Garden of Eden, which is described as an earthly paradise. Imagine your own idea of an earthly paradise. What would it be like? Write a detailed description of your own personal paradise. How different is it from the Garden of Eden?

SEE ALSO Creation Stories; Fruit in Mythology; Lilith; Semitic Mythology; Serpents and Snakes

Nationality/Culture
Greek/Roman

Pronunciation
uh-DON-is

Alternate Names
None

Appears In
Ovid's *Metamorphoses*, Hyginus's *Fabulae*

Lineage
Son of Theias and Myrrha

Adonis

Character Overview

In **Greek mythology** Adonis (pronounced uh-DON-is) was an extremely handsome young man who died and was reborn. Like many other mythological figures who are resurrected, or brought back to life, Adonis became associated with the annual cycle of the seasons in which plants die in the fall and grow back again in the spring. Adonis's counterpart in Akkadian mythology was the god Tammuz (pronounced TAH-mooz).

U•X•L Encyclopedia of World Mythology

Beauty Lost and Regained

Many other cultures have stories similar to that of Adonis and Aphrodite, all of which seem to explain the changing of the seasons as a temporary loss of a beautiful youth. Tammuz and Astarte of Babylon and Isis and Osiris of ancient Egypt are examples. The Bible (in the book of Ezekiel) describes Babylonian women "weeping for Tammuz" as part of a ritual mourning for his loss.

Major Myths

According to tradition, Adonis was the son of Myrrha (pronounced MER-uh) and her father, Theias (pronounced THEE-us), the king of Assyria. So attractive was the infant Adonis that the goddess **Aphrodite** fell in love with him. She hid the baby in a box and gave him to **Persephone**, goddess of the **underworld**, for safe keeping. When Persephone saw Adonis, however, she also fell in love with him and refused to return him to Aphrodite.

Zeus, the supreme ruler of the gods who lived on Mount Olympus, settled the argument by ordering Adonis to divide his time between the two goddesses. During spring and summer, the time of fertility and fruitfulness, Adonis stayed with Aphrodite. He spent fall and winter, the period of barrenness and death, with Persephone.

Adonis adored hunting. While out on a chase one day during his time with Aphrodite, he was killed by a wild boar. Some stories say that the boar was **Hephaestus** (pronounced hi-FES-tuhs), Aphrodite's husband, in disguise, or perhaps it was **Ares** (pronounced AIR-eez), the god of war and Aphrodite's jealous lover. Both stories maintain that beautiful red flowers called anemones (pronounced uh-NEM-uh-neez) grew and bloomed where Adonis's blood fell on the soil.

Adonis in Context

In ancient Greece, as in many ancient societies, the changing of the seasons was a mystery. For this reason, seasons were often seen as evidence of the gods at work. Since Adonis was considered a god of plants and vegetation, his months-long stay in the underworld explained why flowers and other greenery failed to grow during winter. Each year in ancient Greece, Adonis worshippers, who tended to be mostly women, mourned his death by wailing and beating their breasts, and also

celebrated his rebirth by planting "gardens of Adonis" for festivals held in his honor.

Key Themes and Symbols

As a god of vegetation, Adonis is a symbol of fertility and growth. Because he spent half of each year in the world of the living and half in the world of the dead, he is closely identified with the seasons of the year. He is also often identified with seasonal plants that sprout and die in a short period of time. The god has become a symbol of male beauty, and in modern times a handsome young man is sometimes called an "Adonis."

Adonis in Art, Literature, and Everyday Life

Because of his famous beauty and rather tragic love affairs with goddesses, Adonis has been the subject of many works of art. He is often paired with Aphrodite, called Venus in **Roman mythology**, as in the painting *Venus and Adonis*, created around 1555 by Titian. The story of the couple is also the subject of Shakespeare's 1593 poem "Venus and Adonis," as well as the John Blow opera of the same name, composed in the 1680s. While use of the term "Adonis" to refer to an attractive young man is common, the mythological Adonis appears only rarely in contemporary art. Adonis was featured in an episode of the animated Disney series *Hercules* in 1998.

Read, Write, Think, Discuss

The poem "Adonais" (1821) by Percy Bysshe Shelley is both a reflection of the Adonis myth and a memorial to Shelley's recently deceased friend, poet John Keats. Using your library, the Internet, or other resources, find a copy of the poem and read it. How is Adonis portrayed in the poem? Do you think the poem tells the same story as the Greek myth?

SEE ALSO Aphrodite; Ares; Greek Mythology; Persephone

Aeneas

Character Overview

The hero Aeneas (pronounced i-NEE-uhs) appears in both Greek and **Roman mythology**. He was a defender of Troy, the city in Asia Minor that the Greeks destroyed in the Trojan War. After the war, Aeneas led the surviving Trojans to the land now called Italy. According to Roman versions of the myth, after Aeneas and his followers founded Rome, he became its first great hero and legendary father.

Nationality/Culture
Greek/Roman

Pronunciation
i-NEE-uhs

Alternate Names
None

Appears In
Homer's *Iliad*, Virgil's *Aeneid*

Lineage
Son of Aphrodite and Anchises

Like many legendary **heroes**, Aeneas was a demigod, meaning he had one parent who was human and one parent who was a god. His father was Anchises (pronounced an-KY-seez), a member of the royal family of Troy. One day **Aphrodite**, the Greek goddess of love (called Venus by the Romans), saw Anchises on the hills of Mount Ida near his home. The goddess was so overcome by the handsome youth that she seduced him and bore him a son, Aeneas.

Mountain **nymphs** (minor nature goddesses represented as beautiful maidens) raised Aeneas until he was five years old, when he was sent to live with his father. Aphrodite had made Anchises promise not to tell anyone that she was the boy's mother. Still, he did so and was struck by lightning. In some versions of the legend, the lightning killed Anchises; in others, it made him blind or lame. Later variations have Anchises surviving and being carried out of Troy by his son after the war.

When the Greeks invaded Troy, Aeneas did not join the conflict immediately. Some versions of the myth say that he entered the war on the side of his fellow Trojans only after the Greek hero **Achilles** (pronounced uh-KILL-eez) stole his cattle. Aeneas's reluctance to join the fighting partly came from the uneasy relationship he had with King Priam of Troy. Some sources say that Aeneas disliked the fact that Priam's son **Hector** was supreme commander of the Trojan forces. For his part, Priam disliked Aeneas because the sea god **Poseidon** (pronounced poh-SYE-dun) had predicted that the descendants of Aeneas, not those of Priam, would rule the Trojans in the future. Nevertheless, during the Trojan War, Aeneas married Creusa (pronounced kree-OO-suh), one of Priam's daughters, and they had a son named Ascanius (pronounced ass-KAN-ee-us).

The Greek Tradition Aeneas appears as a character in the *Iliad*, the epic by the Greek poet Homer that tells the story of the Trojan War. The *Iliad* and other Greek sources provide a number of details about Aeneas's role in the war. According to Greek tradition, Aeneas was one of the Trojan leaders, their greatest warrior after Hector. An upright and moral man, Aeneas was often called "the pious" because of his respect for the gods and his obedience to their commands. In return, the gods treated Aeneas well. Some of the most powerful gods, including **Apollo**, Poseidon, and Aphrodite, Aeneas's mother, gave him their protection.

There are various accounts of the last days of the Trojan War. One story relates that Aphrodite warned Aeneas that Troy would fall, so he left the city and took refuge on Mount Ida, where he established a new kingdom. In later years, several cities on the mountain boasted that they had been founded by Aeneas. Another version states that Aeneas fought bravely to the end of the war and either escaped from Troy with a band of followers or was allowed by the victorious Greeks—who respected his honor and religious devotion—to leave.

The Roman Tradition Over the centuries, a number of Roman myths developed about Aeneas. According to Roman tradition, Aeneas fought with great courage in Troy until messages from Aphrodite and Hector convinced him to leave the city. Carrying his father on his back and holding his son by the hand, Aeneas led his followers out of burning Troy. During the confusion, Aeneas's wife Creusa became separated from the fleeing Trojans. Aeneas returned to search for Creusa but could not find her.

Aeneas and his followers found safety on Mount Ida, where they settled and began building ships. After several months, they set sail to the west. Dreams and omens (mystical signs of events to come) told Aeneas that he was destined to found a new kingdom in the land of his ancestors, the country now known as Italy.

Aeneas's Travels After surviving many dangers, including powerful storms and fierce monsters, Aeneas and his Trojan followers landed on the coast of North Africa. Along the way, his father Anchises died. At this point in Aeneas's tale, Roman storytellers mingled the history of the hero with earlier tales of a queen named **Dido** (pronounced DYE-doh), founder of the city of Carthage in North Africa.

According to Roman legend, Dido and Aeneas fell in love soon after the hero arrived in Carthage. Aeneas stayed with the queen until Mercury, the messenger of the gods, reminded him that his destiny lay in Italy. Aeneas sadly but obediently sailed away. When he looked back, he saw smoke and flames. Lovesick and abandoned, Dido had thrown herself onto a funeral pyre, a large pile of burning wood used in some cultures to cremate a dead body.

After stopping on the island of Sicily and leaving some of his followers to found a colony there, Aeneas sailed to Italy. Upon his arrival, he sought advice from the Sibyl (pronounced SIB-uhl), a powerful oracle, or person through which the gods communicated with humans. The Sibyl took him to the **underworld**, or land of the dead.

There Aeneas saw the ghost of Dido, but she turned away and would not speak to him. Then he saw the ghost of his father Anchises, who told him that he would found the greatest empire the world had ever known.

Founder of an Empire Encouraged by his father's prophecy, Aeneas went to Latium (pronounced LAY-shee-uhm) in central Italy. He became engaged to Lavinia, the daughter of the king of the Latins. Turnus, the leader of another tribe called the Rutuli, launched a war against the Trojan newcomers. Some of the Latins also fought the Trojans, but Aeneas, thrilled to have finally arrived at his destiny, refused to be defeated. First he killed Turnus and married Lavinia. Then he founded the city of Lavinium, where Latins and Trojans were united.

After Aeneas's death, his son Ascanius ruled Lavinium and founded a second city called Alba Longa, which became the capital of the Trojan-Latin people. These cities formed the basis of what came to be ancient Rome. Some legends claim that Aeneas founded the city of Rome itself. Others assign that honor to his descendant Romulus.

Roman historians later altered the story of Rome's origins to make Ascanius the son of Aeneas and Lavinia, thus a Latin by birth. Ascanius was also called Iulus, or Julius, and a clan of Romans called the Julians claimed to be his descendants. Julius Caesar and his nephew Augustus, who became the first Roman emperor, were members of that clan. In this way, the rulers of Rome traced their ancestry and their right to rule back to the demigod Aeneas.

Aeneas in Context

In the 700s BCE, the Greeks began establishing colonies in Italy and on the island of Sicily off the Italian coast. Legends often linked Greek heroes to these colonies, whose citizens liked to think of themselves as descendants of characters Homer had described in his works. By the 300s BCE, Rome was a rising power in the Mediterranean world. As the city grew larger and more powerful, it faced a dilemma. The Romans shared many myths and legends with the Greeks and had a lot of respect for Greece's ancient culture. At the same time, however, the Romans did not want to be overshadowed by Greek culture and tradition. They wanted their own connections to the ancient world of gods and heroes. Roman writers found a perfect link to the legendary past with Aeneas,

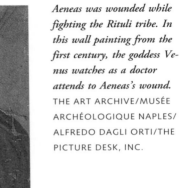

Aeneas was wounded while fighting the Rituli tribe. In this wall painting from the first century, the goddess Venus watches as a doctor attends to Aeneas's wound. THE ART ARCHIVE/MUSÉE ARCHÉOLOGIQUE NAPLES/ ALFREDO DAGLI ORTI/THE PICTURE DESK, INC.

who was supposed to have come to Italy around the time of the founding of Rome. Furthermore, because Aeneas was a Trojan, he could give the Romans what they wanted: an ancestry that was connected to the ancient heroes yet separated from the Greeks.

Key Themes and Symbols

Although Aeneas existed first as a character in **Greek mythology**, he later became an important part of the origin myth for Roman culture. Because of this, he is strongly identified as the ultimate mythological symbol of the Roman Empire. To the Romans, Aeneas represented heroism, as well as the drive to create a society that would be as good as or even better than that of the Greeks.

Aeneas in Art, Literature, and Everyday Life

Although many ancient authors wrote about Aeneas, the most complete and important version of his life and deeds is the ***Aeneid***, a long poem composed around 30 to 20 BCE by the Roman writer Virgil. Using a style similar to that of the Greek epics the *Iliad* and the ***Odyssey***, Virgil reshaped in Latin the legends and traditions about Aeneas to fit Rome's view of its own destiny. In the poem, Virgil tells the story of Aeneas's journey from Troy to Italy.

Like other figures from Greek and Roman mythology, Aeneas appears frequently in Western literature. In *The Divine Comedy*, written in the early 1300s CE by Italian poet Dante Alighieri, Aeneas is shown in Limbo, a realm of the **afterlife** where virtuous pagans (those who worship pre-Christian gods) dwell. In British mythology, Brutus, Britain's legendary first king, is considered the great-grandson of Aeneas. Generally, Aeneas represents duty and piety, but some authors have portrayed him less favorably. In his play *Cymbeline*, for example, William Shakespeare refers to the "false Aeneas" who abandoned Dido. Shakespeare also mentions Aeneas in his plays *Troilus and Cressida* and *Julius Caesar*.

Read, Write, Think, Discuss

Former British Prime Minister Winston Churchill said, "History is written by the victors." He meant that after a conflict is settled, the winners can retell it any way they like, and that retelling becomes accepted as correct. Imagine how the history of America would be told differently had the British defeated the American colonists during the American revolution. Now think of parts of the world where there is a struggle for control: Iraq, Kurdistan, Pakistan, Afghanistan, Darfur, and other areas. Using your library, the Internet, newspapers, and other sources, find out more about the factions at war in these areas. Pick one of these factions as a "winner" and write a version of the conflict from the winner's point of view.

SEE ALSO *Aeneid, The*; Aphrodite; Dido; Greek Mythology; *Iliad, The*; Roman Mythology; Romulus and Remus

Aeneid, The

Myth Overview

In approximately 30 BCE, the Roman poet Virgil began composing the *Aeneid* (pronounced uh-NEE-id), an epic, or long, grand-scale poem, that told the story of **Aeneas** and the founding and destiny of Rome. Using myth, history, and cultural pride, the *Aeneid* summed up everything the Romans valued most about their society. At the same time, it offered tales of adventure featuring gods and goddesses, **heroes** and ghosts, warriors and doomed lovers. Virgil died before finishing the work, but it established his reputation as the foremost poet of the Romans.

Creating a Roman Heritage The *Aeneid* tells the story of Aeneas (pronounced i-NEE-uhs), a hero of Troy, the city in Asia Minor that the Greeks destroyed during the Trojan War. According to legend, Aeneas survived the war and led a group of Trojans on a journey to the kingdom of Latium (pronounced LAY-shee-uhm) in central Italy, where Rome was eventually built.

The story of Aeneas was much older than Rome. The hero appears as a character in the ***Iliad***, an epic about the Trojan War by the Greek poet Homer. However, as Rome was emerging as the leading power in the Mediterranean world in the 200s BCE, the Romans became eager to claim Aeneas and the Trojans as their ancestors. Some Romans even visited Ilium, a Roman city in Asia Minor said to stand on the ancient site of Troy, Aeneas's home city.

Aeneas was an ideal figure to serve as the legendary founder of Rome. As the son of **Aphrodite** (called Venus in Roman mythology), the goddess of love, and Anchises (pronounced an-KY-seez), a member of the Trojan royal family, he had both divine and royal parents. In addition, the ancient tales portrayed Aeneas as dutiful, spiritual, brave, and honorable, which were virtues the Romans believed characterized their culture. Finally, Aeneas was part of the Greek heritage so admired by the Romans. As a Trojan rather than a Greek, however, he provided the Romans with a distinct identity that was not Greek but equally ancient and honorable.

A number of Roman writers contributed to the story of how Aeneas came to Italy so his descendants could build Rome. The person who assembled the parts of the legend into a great national epic, however, was

Nationality/Culture
Roman

Pronunciation
uh-NEE-id

Alternate Names
None

Appears In
Virgil's *Aeneid*

Publius Vergilius Maro, known as Virgil. His patron (someone who provides financial support for an artist) was Augustus, the first emperor of Rome. Augustus considered himself a direct descendant of Aeneas. Virgil's *Aeneid* glorified not just Rome but also Augustus, whose reign was portrayed as the fulfillment of the grand Roman destiny that the gods had predicted long ago.

Structure and Style Virgil modeled the *Aeneid* on the *Iliad* and the *Odyssey*, Homer's much-admired epics of ancient Greece. Like the Greek poems, the *Aeneid* features the Trojan War, a hero on a long and difficult journey, and exciting descriptions of hand-to-hand combat between brave warriors. It is also similar in form to the Greek epics: the twelve books of the *Aeneid* cover two major themes, the wanderings of Aeneas after the Trojan War, and the wars in Italy between the Trojans and the Latins.

The Story and Its Significance In Book 1 of the *Aeneid*, Aeneas and his followers arrive in Carthage in North Africa after escaping a storm sent by Juno (called **Hera** in Greek mythology), the queen of the gods. Early in the story, Virgil establishes the fact that Juno does her best to ruin Aeneas's plans because of her hatred for the Trojans, while Venus supports him. Jupiter (called **Zeus** in Greek mythology), the king of the gods, reveals that Aeneas will ultimately reach Italy and his descendants will found a great empire.

In Book 2, Aeneas tells **Dido** (pronounced DYE-doh), the queen of Carthage, how the Greeks won the Trojan War and how he escaped Troy. This story within a story continues in Book 3, as Aeneas describes to Dido the earlier attempts by the Trojan survivors to found a city. Book 4 reveals that Dido is in love with Aeneas, and the two become lovers; however, fate has other plans for the Trojan leader. Jupiter sends Mercury (called **Hermes** in Greek mythology), the messenger of the gods, to remind Aeneas that his destiny lies in Italy.

In Book 5 of the *Aeneid*, the Trojans reach Sicily, an island off the coast of Italy, and Aeneas organizes funeral games to honor the death of his father, Anchises. While the games are in progress, Juno attempts to destroy the Trojan fleet, but Jupiter saves most of the ships and the Trojans depart. In Book 6, the Trojans arrive at Cumae (pronounced KOO-may) in Italy, and Aeneas visits the shrine of the Cumaean Sibyl, a famous oracle, or person through which the gods communicated with humans. The oracle leads him on a visit to the **underworld**, where he

Epics and Nationalism

The *Aeneid* showed that an epic poem could express a people's values and glorify its history. After 1800, Europe saw a rise in nationalism (a strong loyalty and devotion to national identity combined with commitment to furthering a nation's interests), and European writers began producing national epics based on folktales, legends, and history. Many of these writers used the *Aeneid* and the ancient Greek epics of Homer as their models. Among the most famous national epics written at this time were the Finnish *Kalevala* (1835–1836), by Elias Lönnrot; the Estonian *Kalevipoeg* (1857–1861), by F. R. Kreutzwald; the German *Nibelungenlied* (circa 1200), by an anonymous poet; and the Latvian *Lāčplēsis* (1888), by Andrejs Pumpurs.

meets the ghost of his father. Another prophecy reveals to Aeneas that Rome will achieve greatness in the future.

Books 7 through 11 tell of the Trojans' arrival in Latium (pronounced LAY-shee-uhm), the kingdom of the Latins in western Italy. The newcomers are welcomed at first, but then war breaks out between the Trojans and the Latin tribes, sparked by the meddling of Juno. Venus helps Aeneas by giving him a new set of armor and weapons bearing images of Rome's future glory. Jupiter then forbids the gods to interfere further.

The final book of the *Aeneid* recounts the mighty battle between Aeneas and the Latin hero Turnus, chief opponent of the Trojans. Aeneas wins the fight and is free to marry Lavinia, daughter of the Latin king Latinus.

The *Aeneid* in Context

The *Aeneid* varies from Homer's epics in ways that reflect the different cultures of their respective authors. Literary scholars still do not know for sure that Homer existed. There may or may not have been an individual author who put the *Iliad* and the *Odyssey* into the versions in which they have been handed down. In any case, storytellers told and retold the Greek epics over a long period before they were written down. Many features of their style, such as the frequent repetition of phrases and images, reflect memorization methods used by oral storytellers. Virgil, by contrast, was an educated man writing a poem for readers, not listeners. He studied the traditional legends of Greece and Italy, determined his plot, and polished his language.

Virgil first wrote the entire *Aeneid* in prose, using normal sentence structure and format, and then turned it into verse a few lines at a time. As he lay dying, Virgil requested that the manuscript of his still-unfinished work be destroyed. Nevertheless, the emperor Augustus preserved the work and had it published soon after Virgil's death in 19 BCE. Augustus' decision was no doubt based on the unstable situation in late Republican Rome (91–30 BCE) and the need for a unifying myth that all Romans could rally behind. Rome had gone through a chaotic period during Virgil's life, including a series of civil wars, the assassination of Julius Caesar, and the fall of the Republic. Augustus, Julius Caesar's adopted great-nephew and successor, had to battle powerful rivals, including General Marc Anthony, for complete control of the newly created Roman Empire. After he solidified his power, he declared it his goal to purify Rome and restore its morality. The *Aeneid* helped proudly define Rome and unify the many groups within the empire who had squabbled for so long.

Key Themes and Symbols

Throughout the *Aeneid*, Virgil describes many prophecies, or predictions of the future. In all these prophecies, Rome becomes a great empire. The meaning of the prophecies is clear: Rome rules the world because it is fated to do so, a fact that has the support of the gods. At the end of the epic, Aeneas is able to marry Lavinia, a Latin princess. Their marriage symbolizes the union between the Latin and Trojan peoples, and their descendants represent the birth of the Roman Empire.

In Book 4, after Aeneas and his followers leave Carthage, Dido kills herself in despair. This episode shows Aeneas's willingness to **sacrifice** his own desires to obey the will of the gods. It also creates a legendary explanation for the very real hostility between Carthage and Rome.

The *Aeneid* in Art, Literature, and Everyday Life

Whatever Virgil may have thought about his work while he lay on his deathbed, others quickly recognized that the *Aeneid* was a masterpiece. Romans loved the poem. It gave them an impressive cultural history and justified the proud expectation that they were destined to rule the world. Yet even after the Roman Empire fell, people continued to read and admire the *Aeneid*.

During the Middle Ages, many Europeans believed that Virgil had been a magician and the *Aeneid* had magical properties. This could be because the story contained so many omens, or mystical signs of events to come. People would read passages from the work and search for hidden meanings or predictions about the future. So admired was Virgil that the Italian poet Dante Alighieri, who wrote during the late 1200s and early 1300s, made him a central character in his own religious epic, *The Divine Comedy*. In Dante's work, Virgil guides the narrator through **hell** and purgatory, but he is not able to enter **heaven** because he was not a Christian.

The *Aeneid* influenced English literature as well. Poets Edmund Spenser and John Milton wrote epics that reflect the work's influence. Poet John Dryden was one of many who translated the *Aeneid*, and his 1697 version is one of the best English translations. By contrast, the poets Samuel Taylor Coleridge, Percy Bysshe Shelley, and Lord Byron disliked Virgil's work, perhaps because it celebrates social order, religious duty, and national glory over the Romantic qualities that they favored: passion, rebellion, and self-determination.

The *Aeneid* has inspired musical composers as well as writers, and many operas have been based on Virgil's work. Among the best known are *Dido and Aeneas* (1690), by English composer Henry Purcell, and *The Trojans* (1858), by the French composer Hector Berlioz.

Read, Write, Think, Discuss

It is widely accepted that Virgil wrote the *Aeneid* in an attempt to bring glory to the Roman culture in which he lived. Compare Aeneas to more recent heroes, such as Superman or Captain America, who represent and fight for ideals important to modern Americans. How are they similar? Are there ways in which Aeneas is different from these modern comic book heroes?

SEE ALSO Aeneas; Aphrodite; *Iliad, The*

African Mythology

African Mythology in Context

A vast continent, Africa is home to many cultures and a thousand or more languages. Although no single set of myths and legends unites this diverse population, different cultural groups and regions share some common mythological elements. Like myths from other parts of the world, those of Africa reflect its people's beliefs and values. But while the mythologies of many other cultures no longer play an active role in religious beliefs, African myths and legends function as a meaningful part of everyday life. Some African myths deal with universal themes, such as the origin of the world and the fate of the individual after death. Many more spring from the continent's own environments and history.

Roots of African Myths and Legends The Sahara, a vast desert dividing the continent into two main regions, runs from east to west across the widest part of northern Africa. North Africa consists of the Mediterranean coast from Morocco to Egypt and includes the valley of the Nile River as far south as Ethiopia. With strong ties to the Mediterranean and Arab worlds, North Africans felt the influence of Christianity by the 300s CE. In the 700s, much of the area came under the influence of Islam.

Before the modern era, Africans south of the Sahara had relatively little contact with the rest of the world. Islam spread south past the Sahara very slowly, especially compared with its sweep across North Africa. Christian missionaries were not very active there until the 1800s. Since then, the spread of Islam and Christianity has overshadowed many indigenous (or native) religions, myths, and legends of sub-Saharan Africa. Despite this fact, the traditional beliefs have not completely disappeared. In some places they have blended with new religions from other cultures, so that an African Muslim might combine Islam with the traditional practice of ancestor worship.

Sub-Saharan myths and legends developed over thousands of years. Among the influences on their development were the mass movements of people that took place from time to time. About seven thousand years ago, the ancestors of the Khoisan people, an indigenous African group, began moving from the Sahara toward southern Africa. Five thousand years later, people who spoke Bantu languages began spreading out from Cameroon, on Africa's west coast, until they eventually inhabited much of sub-Saharan Africa. Such migrations caused myths and legends to spread from group to group and led to a mixing of cultural beliefs. The migrations also gave rise to new stories about events in the history of those peoples. For instance, as Bantu groups settled in new homelands, they developed legends to explain the origins of their ruling families and the structure of their societies.

African cultural groups did not use written language until modern times. Instead, they possessed rich and complex oral traditions, passing myths, legends, and histories from generation to generation verbally. In some cultures, professional storytellers, called griots (pronounced GREE-oo), preserved the oral tradition. Written accounts of African mythology began to appear in the early 1800s with the arrival of European explorers and colonizers, and present-day scholars work to record the continent's myths and legends before they are lost to time and cultural change.

Core Deities and Characters

African mythologies include supernatural beings who influence human life. Some of these beings are powerful deities or gods. Others are lesser spirits, such as the spirits of ancestors.

Deities Most African traditional religions have multiple gods, often grouped together in family relationships. Nearly every culture recognizes a supreme god, an all-powerful creator who is usually associated with the sky. Various West African peoples refer to the highest god as Amma or **Olorun**, while some East Africans use the name Mulungu. Africans who have adopted Christianity or Islam sometimes blend the supreme deity of those faiths with the supreme deity of traditional African religion and mythology.

In most African religions, the supreme god is a distant being no longer involved in day-to-day human life. People rarely call on this deity. Instead, they address lesser gods, many of whom have distinct functions. The Yoruba people of Nigeria, for example, worship a storm god, Shango, who controls thunder and lightning.

The number of gods and goddesses varies from culture to culture. The Buganda people of east-central Africa have twenty or more deities. Many populations regard the earth, **sun**, and moon as gods. In the Congo River region, the most densely wooded part of Africa, the forest itself is a deity, or else a mysterious other world where spirits dwell.

Spirits African mythology is filled with spirits, invisible beings with powers for good or evil. Spirits are less grand, less powerful, and less like humans than the gods, who often have weaknesses and emotions. Many spirits are associated with geographical features, such as mountains, rivers, wells, trees, and springs. Nations, peoples, and even small communities may honor local spirits unknown beyond their borders.

All humans, animals, and plants have spirits, as do elements, such as water and **fire**. Some spirits are helpful, others harmful. People may worship spirits and may also try to control them through magical means, usually with the aid of a skilled practitioner or healer, often known as a shaman, who leads them in rituals. People thought to have evil spirits are considered dangerous witches.

Ancestors Many Africans believe that human spirits exist after death. According to some groups, these spirits live underground in a world much like that of the living, but upside down. The spirits sleep during the day and come out at night. Other groups place the realm of the dead in the sky. The Bushmen of southern Africa say that the dead become stars.

Still other African groups believe that the spirits of dead ancestors remain near their living descendants to help and protect them as long as these living relatives perform certain ceremonies and pay their ancestors due respect. Believing that the spirits of chieftains and other important people offer strong protection, the Zulu of South Africa hold special ceremonies to bring them into the community. In some cultures, it is said that the soul of a dead grandfather, father, or uncle can be reborn in a new baby boy. Another common belief is that dead souls, particularly those of old men, may return as snakes, which many Africans regard with respect.

Ancestor cults—or groups that worship dead relatives—play a leading role in the mythologies of some peoples, especially in East and South Africa. The honored dead—whether members of the immediate family, the larger clan or kinship group, the community, or the entire culture—become objects of worship and subjects of tales and legends. An example occurs among the Songhai people, who live along the Niger River. They honor Zoa, a wise and protective ancestor who long ago made his son chieftain.

Many groups trace their origins, or the origins of all humans, to first ancestors. The Baganda, the people of Buganda in present-day Uganda, say that the first ancestor was Kintu, who came from the land of the gods and married Nambi, daughter of the king of **heaven**. The Dinka of the Sudan speak of Garang and Abuk, the first man and woman, whom God created as tiny clay figures in a pot.

Rulers and Heroes Ancestral kings and **heroes** may be transformed into minor deities for communities or entire nations. The line between legend and history is often blurred. Some mythic ancestors began as real-life personages whose deeds were exaggerated over time, while others are purely fictional. The Yoruba storm god Shango, for example, may originally have been a living mighty warrior-king.

The Shilluk, who live along the Nile in the Sudan, trace their ancestry to Nyikang, their first king. Later kings were thought to have been Nyikang reborn into new bodies, and the well-being of the nation depended on their health and vigor. The first king of the Zulu was supposed to have been a son of the supreme god. Many African peoples traditionally regarded their rulers as divine or semi-divine.

Other legends involve cultural heroes who did great things or lived their lives according to important values. The Soninke people of Ghana in West Africa have a song cycle—a group of songs performed in a particular order that relate to an underlying theme—called *Dausi*. In part of it, *Gassire's Lute*, a hero must choose between his own desires and his duty to society.

The Mandingo people built a large empire in Mali. Their griots recited tales of kings and heroes. *Sunjata*, a story of magic, warfare, kingship, and fate, is known across large portions of West Africa.

Major Myths

The myths of people living along the Nile and on the fringes of the Sahara, as well as the Bantu around the Niger and Congo Rivers, are more generally concerned with the origins of social institutions, such as clans and kingships, than with cosmic themes, such as the creation of the world. In contrast, the non-Bantu groups of the Niger River area, especially the Dogon, Yoruba, and Bambara, have complex and lengthy tales about the origins of things found in the natural world. Fables, folklore, and legends about **tricksters** and animals are found in nearly all African cultures.

How Things Came To Be Many myths explain how the world came into existence. The Dogon say that twin pairs of creator spirits or gods called Nummo hatched from a cosmic egg. Other groups also speak of the universe beginning with an egg. People in both southern and northern Africa believe that the world was formed from the body of an enormous snake, sometimes said to span the sky as a rainbow.

The Fon people of Benin tell of Gu, the oldest son of the creator **twins** Mawu (moon) and Lisa (sun). Gu came to earth in the form of an iron sword and then became a blacksmith. His task was to prepare the world for

Gods and Tricksters Cross the Sea

Between the 1500s and the 1800s, many thousands of Africans were brought to the Americas as slaves. Their myths and legends helped shape the black cultures that developed in the Caribbean islands and the United States. The Caribbean religion known as vodún or voodoo, for example, involves the worship of the *vodu*, meaning "spirit" in the West African language Fon. Enslaved blacks also told traditional stories about the spider Anansi, who was sometimes also depicted as a trickster hare. Anansi came to be called Anancy, and the hare became Brer (Brother) Rabbit, the character who appears in the Uncle Remus animal fables that were collected by Joel Chandler Harris in the late 1800s.

people. He taught humans how to make tools, which in turn enabled them to grow food and build shelters. The San Bushmen of the south say that creation was the work of a spirit named Dxui, who was alternately a man and many other things, such as a flower, a bird, or a lizard.

Myths from across Africa also tell how death came into the world. Some relate that the supreme god meant for humans to be immortal, meaning they would live forever; however, through an unlucky mistake, they received death instead of eternal life. One story tells of a god who told a cautious chameleon to carry the news of eternal life to earth. In that story, a faster lizard with news of death arrives first. The Mende people of Sierra Leone say that a toad with the message "Death has come" overtakes a dog with the message "Life has come" because the dog stops to eat along the way.

Other myths explain that death came into the world because people or animals angered the gods. The Nuer people of the Sudan blame death on a hyena who cut the rope that connected heaven and earth. Their neighbors, the Dinka, say that a greedy woman, not satisfied with the grain the high god gave her, planted more grain. She hit the god in the eye with her hoe, and he cut the connecting rope. A tale told by the Luhya people of present-day Kenya relates that a chameleon cursed people with death because a man broke the laws of hospitality by refusing to share his food with the chameleon.

Twins Many African peoples regard twins as special, almost sacred, beings. Twins represent the duality—the tension or balance between paired or opposing forces—that is basic to life. Some groups, such as the non-Bantu peoples of the Niger and Congo regions, believe that twins of opposite sexes are symbols of this duality.

Twins appear in many African myths and legends. In some stories, they are brother and sister who unite in marriage. In others, they seem to be two sides of a single being. The supreme god of the Fon people of West Africa is Mawu-Lisa, usually described as brother and sister twins who became the parents of all the other gods, also born as twins.

Trickster and Animal Fables Many African myths feature a trickster. The trickster may be a god, an animal, or a human being. His pranks and mischief cause trouble among gods, among humans, or between gods and humans.

West Africans tell many tales of a wandering trickster spirit known as Eshu among the Yoruba and Legba among the Fon. This trickster is associated with change and with quarrels. In some accounts, he is the messenger between the human world and the supreme god.

Animal tricksters are often small, helpless creatures who manage to outwit bigger and fiercer animals. **Anansi**, the spider trickster of the Ashanti people, is known throughout West and Central Africa. Tortoises and hares also appear as tricksters. In one such tale, the hare tricks a hippopotamus and an elephant into clearing a field for him.

Other stories about animals show them helping humans. The San Bushmen say that a sacred praying mantis gave them words and fire, and the Bambara people of Mali say that an antelope taught them how to farm. A popular form of entertainment involves sharing animal fables, stories about talking animals with human characteristics. Many of these fables offer imaginative explanations for features of the natural world, such as why bats hang with their heads downward or why leopards have spots.

Key Themes and Symbols

One of the more common themes throughout African mythology is the focus on ancestors. There is a reciprocal relationship between the dead ancestors and the living community. As long as the community continues to revere and respect the dead ancestor, the ancestor will protect the community. The rituals of ancestor worship assured that cultures without a written language or texts could remember their history through their ancestors and pass down that history from generation to generation.

Another theme in African mythology is the presence of animals who interact with humans. These animals may be responsible for creating the

A shrine of Shango, the Yoruba god of thunder, furnished with statues of female devotees. Yoruba, Nigeria. WERNER FORMAN/ ART RESOURCE, NY.

world, such as in the myth of the rainbow snake. They may also be the teachers who helped humans create societies and cultures. The praying mantis of the San people, for example, taught them how to use words and fire; and the Bambara credit the antelope with teaching them how to farm.

The references in African mythology to animals as co-creators of human societies reinforce the view of humans and nature as being interconnected.

African Mythology in Art, Literature, and Everyday Life

Although the myths of various African cultures have existed primarily in oral form, there are some notable exceptions. Joel Chandler Harris's *Uncle Remus* books collect many of the modified West African tales that were shared among slaves in the early United States. Made popular in the late 1880s when they were first published, the books have been criticized in more recent years for being patronizing and racist. In 1946, the Walt Disney Company created an animated film consisting of several of the tales, titled *Song of the South*.

Children's author Gerald McDermott has also created books based on various African mythological tales, including *Anansi the Spider: A Tale from the Ashanti* (1972) and *Zomo the Rabbit: A Trickster Tale from West Africa* (1992). African mythology also plays a central role in the contemporary fantasy novel *Anansi Boys* (2005) by Neil Gaiman.

Read, Write, Think, Discuss

African mythology is made up of many different stories taken from many different tribes and cultures across the continent. Using your library, the Internet, or other available resources, research one of the cultures or tribes mentioned above, such as the Yoruba, the San, or the Baganda. Where do they live? What are some other important aspects of their society? Try to locate at least one myth from this culture that has not already been mentioned.

SEE ALSO Anansi; Animals in Mythology; Brer Rabbit; Ile-Ife; Leza; Mwindo; Olorun; Sunjata; Tricksters

Afterlife

Theme Overview

Cultures the world over recognize that every life will end in death. However, many claim that some invisible but vital part of the human being, such as the spirit or soul, continues to exist after death. This is known as the afterlife, a state of being that people enter when they die, or a place to which they or their souls go. In some traditions, the individual possesses more than one soul, and each of these may have a separate fate.

Major Myths

Some cultures have associated the afterlife with a geographic location. The notion of the existence of an **underworld** beneath the world of the living is common. The Babylonians, Assyrians, and other peoples of ancient Mesopotamia, for example, thought the dead lived on in a dusty, bleak underworld called the Dark Earth. Any pit, cave, or pond could be an entrance to that place. People on the islands of Melanesia in the southeastern Pacific Ocean imagine an underground world that is the mirror image of the upper world. Stories from the island of New Guinea, north of Australia, describe an underworld that lies beneath the ocean. Divers have claimed to see the souls of the dead working in undersea gardens. In Navajo mythology, the dead descend into a watery underworld. According to the Ibo of Nigeria, the underworld is ruled by the goddess Ala, who receives the dead into her womb.

Other cultures have placed the afterlife in the sky or among the stars. The Pueblo Indians of the American Southwest believe that the dead become rain clouds. Some Native Americans of the Southeast say that the souls of the dead dwell either in the heavens or in the west.

The west, where the **sun** sets each day, has often been associated with the afterlife of the spirits. Polynesian islanders, in the central and southern Pacific Ocean, locate their ancestral island in the west and believe that spirits of the dead can return there. The Celtic people from western Europe pictured an other world that was sometimes underground or under the sea, and sometimes an island in the west.

In most accounts, the Celtic other world was a magical place filled with enjoyable activities, such as feasting and, for heroic warriors, fighting. Some descriptions, though, indicate that the land of the dead had a grim and dangerous side. Annwn (pronounced AN-oon), the realm of the dead in Welsh mythology, could be fearsome. Less frightening was **Valhalla** (pronounced val-HAL-uh) of **Norse mythology**, a vast palace where warriors slain in battle spent the afterlife feasting, singing, and indulging in playful combat. Their afterlife was not eternal, however. One day Valhalla and the world would be swept away in the gods' last battle. In addition, not all warriors went to Valhalla. **Freyja** (pronounced FRAY-uh), goddess of love and death, took half of them to her own palace in the afterworld.

In contrast to vivid, lively, and joyous visions of the world beyond, the afterlife pictured by the peoples of the ancient Near East was dim and shadowy. The early Jews called their dismal, ghostly underworld Sheol (pronounced SHEE-ohl). The spirits who dwelled in the Assyro-Babylonian underworld felt neither pain nor pleasure but lived a pale, washed-out version of life on earth, complete with a royal court ruled by Nergal and Ereshkigal, the king and queen of the dead. The Babylonian heroic poem, the *Epic of Gilgamesh*, contains a description of the afterlife in which the hero's dead friend Enkidu returns as a spirit to describe his existence in the "house of dust."

Different Fates Peoples of the ancient Near East, such as the Mesopotamians and the early Jews, believed that the afterlife was the same for everyone. Other cultures, however, have expected the dead to be divided into different afterworlds. The Polynesians believe that the souls of common people, victims of black magic, and sinners are destroyed by **fire**. The souls of the upper classes, by contrast, journey to a spirit world where they live among their ancestors. Some ancient Chinese people believed that the afterlife was different for good and bad people: the souls of good people rose to the court of Tien (pronounced Tyen), or **heaven**, while the souls of bad people descended into one of the eighteen levels of **hell**, depending on their crimes in the world.

The Maya people of Central America believed that the souls of the dead went to an underworld known as Xibalba (pronounced shi-BAHL-buh). To escape and go to heaven, the souls had to trick the underworld gods. Among the Aztecs of Mexico, slain warriors, merchants killed during a journey, and women who died in childbirth joined the sun in the heavens. The ordinary dead spent four years traveling through the nine layers of an underworld called Mictlan (pronounced MEEKT-lahn), only to vanish when they reached the ninth level. The Aztecs believed that the rain god **Tlaloc** (pronounced TLAH-lok) was responsible for the deaths of people who died by drowning or of certain diseases such as leprosy. Tlaloc then sent these people to a happy afterlife that ordinary Aztecs did not share. Wall paintings in the ancient Mexican city of Teotihuacán (pronounced tay-uh-tee-wah-KAN) show the garden paradise that welcomed the souls of Tlaloc's dead.

In Norse mythology, warriors went to heavenly palaces, while other individuals ended up in a cold underworld called Niflheim (pronounced NIV-uhl-heym), or **Hel**. Among the Inuit (pronounced IN-yoo-it), or Eskimo, of Greenland, a happy land in the sky is the reward for the souls of people who have been generous or have suffered misfortunes in life; others go to an underworld ruled by the goddess **Sedna**. The Pima and Papago peoples of the American Southwest say that the spirits of the departed travel to a place in the east where they will be free from hunger and thirst.

Some cultures hold the view that the souls of the dead face judgment: the good are rewarded in the afterlife, while the evil are punished. The ancient Egyptians, for example, believed that a soul had to convince the gods that he or she had committed no sins in life. The dead person's heart was placed on one side of a set of scales with a feather from the headdress of Ma'at (pronounced MUH-aht), the goddess of judgment, on the other. If the two balanced, the soul was declared sinless. A monster devoured those who failed the test.

The Zoroastrians of ancient Persia believed that the afterlife held a reward for the virtuous, or those of moral excellence. Those who lived a just earthly life experienced a form of pure light that signified the presence of **Ahura Mazda**, their only god, who stands for goodness, justice, and order. The ancient Greeks imagined the afterlife as a shadowy realm, called **Hades** (pronounced HAY-deez) after its ruling deity. They also spoke of a deeper pit of hell, Tartarus, to which those who had acted wrongly were sent to receive punishment. In the Shinto mythology of Japan, the dead go to a land of darkness known as Yomi, where they may be punished for their misdeeds.

After about 200 BCE, the Jewish concept of Sheol gave way to a vision of judgment after death. The good entered the presence of God, while the wicked roasted in a hell called Gehenna (pronounced geh-HEN-na). This influenced the Christian and Islamic ideas about hell as a state or place of punishment for evil. Heaven, in contrast, is the union of virtuous souls with God. According to the Roman Catholic Church, there is a state of being between heaven and hell called purgatory, in which tarnished souls are purified on the way to heaven.

The Journey to the Afterlife Many cultures have regarded death as the beginning of the soul's journey to the afterworld. The ancient Greeks pictured sea horses and dolphins carrying virtuous souls to the Elysian (pronounced il-EE-shun) Fields, also known as the Islands of the Blessed. Less noble Greeks undertook a darker journey, asking a boatman named Charon (pronounced KAIR-uhn) to ferry them across the river Acheron (pronounced ACK-er-on), which marked the boundary between the world and Hades.

Many Pacific islanders viewed the journey as a leap. Every island had a *reinga*, or leaping place, from which the soul was thought to depart. For the Maori of New Zealand, that place is the northernmost point of North Island, known as Cape Reinga. A sacred tree was often associated with the reinga. The Hawaiians believed that the souls of children lingered near the tree to give directions to the newly dead. Other Pacific peoples thought souls swam to the afterlife, and those weighted with sin would sink.

In some cultures, bridges linked the living world and the afterworld, and the crossing was not always easy. The Norse bridge shook if someone not yet dead tried to cross it before his or her time. The Zoroastrians had to cross a bridge the width of a hair. The just survived the crossing; the unjust fell into hell. Both the rainbow and the Milky Way were thought by various peoples to represent the bridge to the land of the gods or spirits.

The Fiji islanders of the south Pacific spoke of a Spirit Path with many dangers, a journey so difficult that the only ones who could complete it were warriors who had died violent deaths. A Native American myth of the far north says that the dead person's shadow must walk a trail the person made during life. Along the way, the person's ghost tries to keep the shadow from reaching the heavenly afterlife.

The living sometimes attempted the journey to the afterworld in search of the secrets, wisdom, powers, or treasures associated with the realm of spirits and of the dead. Welsh **heroes** entered the realm of Annwn to steal a magic cauldron, or kettle. Greek legends tell of the journeys of **Orpheus** and **Odysseus** to the land of the dead. The Navajo believe that searching for the realm of the dead can bring death to the living.

Return of the Dead In his play *Hamlet*, William Shakespeare called death "The undiscovered country from whose bourn [boundary]/No traveler returns." Yet myths and legends from around the world say the dead do interact with the world of the living in one way or another.

In some cultures, the dead are thought to linger near the living as shades, or spirits. Southeastern Native Americans believe that newly dead souls remain near their villages hoping to persuade others to join them.

In some African myths, the souls of the dead stay close to living relatives in order to help and advise them. To consult with their dead ancestors, Mayan rulers performed a bloodletting ritual known as the Vision Serpent ceremony. During the ceremony, participants experienced visions in which they communicated with the dead.

The belief that the spirits of the dead can do good or ill in the world of the living lies behind some forms of ancestor worship. Ghosts of the dead, whether malicious, helpful, or merely sad, appear in the myths and folktales of many cultures. The Chinese perform ceremonies to honor the spirits of their ancestors and ensure that they will have good feelings toward their descendants. Some Native Americans honor the ghosts of their dead with annual feasts. The Navajo, however, avoid dwelling on death and never mention the dead in their rituals.

The dead sometimes return in another way as well: the soul may be reincarnated, meaning reborn in another body. The notion of multiple rebirths through a series of lifetimes is basic to the Hindu and Buddhist traditions. Those who act wrongly in life may be reborn as less fortunate people or as animals or insects. Cultures in some areas of Africa also believe that souls are reborn, sometimes after a period spent in the underworld, or land of the dead.

Preparation for the Afterlife In many cultures, rituals associated with death were meant to help the deceased in his or her journey to the afterlife. The Greeks, for example, provided the dead with coins to pay the ferryman Charon. Although the Romans were less certain about the afterlife than the Greeks, they often followed the same custom and sometimes added treats for the dead person to offer to **Cerberus** (pronounced SUR-ber-uhs), the three-headed dog that guarded the entrance to the underworld. The Tibetan *Book of the Dead* gives instructions for the soul to follow on its journey between death and rebirth.

The ancient Egyptians believed that the body had to be preserved after death in order for the spirit to survive, so they went to great lengths to prepare for the afterlife. They built tombs to protect their dead. The most elaborate are the great monuments known as the pyramids. Within the tombs, they placed grave goods, such as food, furniture, and even servants, for the dead person to use in the next life. The Egyptians also developed an elaborate form of mummification, or drying and preserving a body to keep it from decomposing after death. The full process could take as long as two hundred days and was available only to the upper classes.

The Egyptians provided their dead with written instructions, including advice on how to survive the hazardous journey after death and guidebooks to the afterworld. The afterlife took many forms but was often pictured as a comfortable existence in a luxuriant realm of rivers, fields, and islands, although the royal dead were said to join the god **Osiris** (pronounced oh-SYE-ris) in the heavens. Texts inscribed on the walls of royal tombs included prayers, hymns, and magical spells to protect the dead from the dangers of the soul's journey. They were included in one of the most famous collections of ancient Egyptian writings, the *Book of the Dead*, copies of which were often buried with the dead.

The Sumerians of Mesopotamia usually made no attempt to preserve the bodies of their dead or to bury them elaborately. One striking exception is a set of royal graves found in the ruins of the ancient city of Ur, located in present-day Iraq. The graves contained not only rare and precious goods but also the bodies of servants, dancing girls, charioteers, and animals, all slain to serve the dead in the afterlife. The Germanic peoples also buried grave goods with their chieftains. An early medieval burial mound at Sutton Hoo in eastern England contained an entire ship along with a quantity of gold and silver items.

The grave goods of male Bushmen of Africa consist of the dead man's weapons. People preparing the body for burial coat it with fat and red powder and bend it into a fetal position, also known as a curled sleeping position. Then they place it in a shallow grave facing in the direction of the rising sun. Other South African tribes follow a different practice. They break the bones of dead people before burial to prevent their ghosts from wandering.

Afterlife in Context

Religions throughout the ages have included a belief in an afterlife. In some cultures, the afterlife is regarded as a place of pleasure and joy. In others, it is a gloomy shadow of earthly existence, a slow fading away, or a remote and unknowable realm. Expectations about the organization of the afterlife also differ. In some societies, everyone is thought to meet the same fate. In others, people are believed to take different paths, depending on how they conducted their earthly lives. Sometimes a judgment by a deity determines the individual's final destiny, or what will happen to them.

These statues depict the spirits of Aztec women who died in childbirth. The Aztecs believed that the spirits of these women joined the sun in the heavens. THE ART ARCHIVE/NATIONAL ANTHROPOLOGICAL MUSEUM MEXICO/GIANNI DAGLI ORTI/THE PICTURE DESK, INC.

Varying visions of the afterlife reveal much about each culture's hopes and fears for the afterlife, and often contain lessons about how people should live. Generally, religions have rules, laws, commandments, or philosophies that ordinary people must follow in order to obtain a good afterlife. Hindus and Buddhists, for example, believe in rebirth and follow the law of karma. Karma, which in the original Sanskrit language means "actions," refers to the good and bad acts an individual performs during his or her many lives, and the effects, or consequences, of those acts for future lives. Karma does not depend on the judgment of a deity, but is a rational law of nature that simply accepts that humans are responsible for their behavior and will reap the consequences of their actions in their afterlives. The law of karma provides a positive incentive for individuals to do good acts, since they can shorten the number of rebirths they must endure and more quickly achieve *nirvana*, or liberation from rebirth and unity with the divine.

In contrast, Christianity presents a linear notion of life and death, which occur only once for each human. In this view, humans have only one chance, or lifetime, to either be rewarded or punished, and Christians must abide by the Ten Commandments in order to achieve a good afterlife. Upon death, individuals will be judged by a deity and assigned either to heaven, hell, or purgatory. Christianity emphasizes punishment and judgment, and the fear of hell is a strong motivator for many to avoid sin and its consequences.

The Afterlife in Art, Literature, and Everyday Life

The idea of the afterlife is a common subject in art and literature, even in modern times. Literary views of the afterlife are not limited to religious texts. Dante's epic about Catholic afterlife, *The Divine Comedy* (c. 1320), for example, is one of the most well-known pieces of literature of all time. In it, the author offers views of three different destinations in the afterlife: purgatory, heaven, and hell. More recently, the Alice Sebold novel *The Lovely Bones* (2002) offers a description of the heavenly world the main character occupies after she is murdered.

Painted depictions of the afterlife were common throughout Europe during the Middle Ages and the Renaissance. One of the most famous paintings of the afterlife is *The Garden of Earthly Delights* by Hieronymus Bosch (c. 1504). The painting, which is made up of three panels, shows a vision of hell in its third panel.

The subject of the afterlife is a popular theme in movies and television shows as well. Movies, such as *Defending Your Life* (1991) and *What Dreams May Come* (1998), present unique visions of the afterlife, while the television show *Dead Like Me* (2003) centers on a group of undead "reapers" who have been chosen to escort the souls of the soon-to-be-dead to the next world.

Read, Write, Think, Discuss

Many people who have had near-death experiences—injuries or traumas that cause their bodies to "die" for a short time—claim to have seen "the afterlife." Doctors try to explain these experiences as delusions caused by various chemicals in the brain. Using your library, the Internet, or other resources, find out more about what people who have had near-death experiences report seeing and feeling, and find out more about how these sensations are explained by doctors. Then write your conclusions: are these people glimpsing the afterlife or not?

SEE ALSO Cerberus; Gilgamesh; Hades; Heaven; Hel; Hell; Orpheus; Osiris; Reincarnation; Underworld; Valhalla; Valkyries

Agamemnon

Character Overview

According to **Greek mythology**, Agamemnon (pronounced ag-uh-MEM-non) was the king of Mycenae (pronounced mye-SEE-nee), a kingdom of ancient Greece. The leader of the Greeks in the Trojan War, he is one of the central figures in the *Iliad*, Homer's epic poem about the war. Greek writers generally portray Agamemnon as courageous but also as arrogant and overly proud, flaws that bring him misfortune and eventually lead to his death. The story of Agamemnon is often seen as a warning about the dangers of hubris, or too much self-confidence.

Agamemnon was one of two sons of Atreus (pronounced AY-tree-uhs), the king of Mycenae. While Agamemnon was still a youth, Atreus was murdered by his nephew Aegisthus (pronounced ee-JUS-thus). Agamemnon and his brother Menelaus (pronounced men-uh-LAY-uhs) fled to Sparta where King Tyndareus (pronounced tin-DAIR-ee-uhs) granted them refuge and protection. The king gave his daughters to the brothers as wives. One daughter, Clytemnestra (pronounced klye-tem-NES-truh), was already married, but Agamemnon killed her husband Tantalus and then married her. Menelaus took her beautiful sister **Helen** as his bride.

Agamemnon later returned to Mycenae, killed his uncle, and reclaimed his father's throne. He and Clytemnestra had four daughters, Chrysothemis (pronounced kry-so-THEEM-uhs), **Electra**, Iphianissa (pronounced if-ee-uh-NISS-uh), and Iphigenia (pronounced if-uh-juh-

Nationality/Culture
Greek/Roman

Pronunciation
ag-uh-MEM-non

Alternate Names
None

Appears In
Ovid's *Metamorphoses*, Hyginus's *Fabulae*

Lineage
Son of Atreus and Aerope, King and Queen of Mycenae

NYE-uh), and a son, Orestes (pronounced ohr-ES-teez). Meanwhile, Menelaus became king of Sparta after the death of Tyndareus.

Some time later, Paris, the second son of King Priam of Troy, visited Menelaus in Sparta. The goddess **Aphrodite** had promised Paris earlier that he would have the love of Helen, the most beautiful woman in the world. When Paris returned to Troy, he took Helen with him. At the time of Menelaus's marriage to Helen, all the rulers of the Greek city-states had promised to come to her defense if necessary. Menelaus reminded them of their promise, and they agreed to go to war against Troy to bring Helen back. Agamemnon was chosen to lead the Greeks in battle.

Agamemnon prepared a fleet of ships to carry the Greeks to Troy. Just before the ships were ready to sail, however, he insulted the goddess **Artemis** (pronounced AHR-tuh-miss) by boasting that he was a better hunter than she and by killing a sacred stag. As punishment, Artemis caused the winds to die down so that the Greek fleet could not sail.

A seer, or person who can see the future, told Agamemnon that he could please Artemis and gain favorable winds by sacrificing his daughter Iphigenia to the goddess. The king tricked Clytemnestra into sending Iphigenia to him by saying that she was to marry the great warrior **Achilles**. When his daughter arrived, Agamemnon killed her. Although the **sacrifice** pleased Artemis, who allowed the Greek ships to sail, his actions would later result in terrible consequences for Agamemnon.

The Trojan War The Greeks fought the people of Troy for nine years and seized many of their cities; however, they failed to capture the city of Troy. This is the point at which the *Iliad* begins, and Agamemnon's arrogance and pride really come into play.

After winning a battle against the Trojans, Agamemnon was given a female prisoner named Chryseis (pronounced kry-SAY-is) as part of his reward for victory. She is the daughter of Chryses (pronounced KRY-sez), a priest of the god **Apollo**. Chryses begged for the return of his daughter, but Agamemnon refused. Angered, Apollo sent a plague to devastate the Greek forces.

The hero Achilles (pronounced uh-KILL-eez) demanded that Chryseis be returned to her father. Agamemnon still refused. He finally agreed on the condition that he be given Briseis (pronounced bry-SAY-is), a Trojan captive who was part of the reward given to Achilles. Achilles became so angry that he laid down his arms and refused to fight any

The priest Chryses presented gifts to Agamemnon in an attempt to ransom his daughter Chryseis, who was part of the spoils of war given to Agamemnon. GILLES MERMET/ART RESOURCE, NY.

longer. This proved to be a costly mistake, because without Achilles the Greeks began to lose ground.

Achilles returned to the battle only after learning of the death of his close friend Patroclus (pronounced pa-TROH-kluhs). When he rejoined the Greek forces, the tide of battle turned. The Greeks drove off the Trojans, killed the great Trojan warrior Prince **Hector**, and went on to defeat the people of Troy and destroy their city. After the war, Agamemnon took the Trojan princess **Cassandra** back home as a prize.

The Death of Agamemnon While Agamemnon was away fighting the Trojans, his wife Clytemnestra took his nephew Aegisthus as her lover. As Agamemnon sailed home from Troy, Clytemnestra was plotting to kill him in revenge for his sacrifice of their daughter Iphigenia. Cassandra, who had the power to foretell the future, warned Agamemnon that his wife would kill him. However, the gods had put a curse on Cassandra: although she would make accurate predictions, no one would believe them. True to the curse, Agamemnon ignored Cassandra's warning.

When Agamemnon returned home, Clytemnestra welcomed him by preparing a bath so that he might purify himself. As the king stepped out of the bath, Clytemnestra wrapped him in a garment that bound his arms so he could not move. Aegisthus then stabbed Agamemnon to death while Clytemnestra killed Cassandra. Another version of the story says that Clytemnestra herself slew Agamemnon with an ax. Agamemnon's son Orestes eventually avenged his father's murder by killing both Clytemnestra and Aegisthus with the help of his sister Electra.

Agamemnon in Context

Agamemnon was the leader of the Greek armies during the Trojan War, a nine-year battle between the Greeks and the Trojans. Although most ancient Greeks believed the Trojan War to be a historical fact, there is little remaining evidence that the war actually happened. By the 1800s CE, many scholars were convinced that the war was not a real event, and that Troy itself was probably not even a real place. However, more recent archeological finds suggest that Troy was indeed a real city, located in present-day Turkey.

The ancient Greeks, like the people of most ancient cultures in which warfare was common, valued strength and bravery, and Agamemnon had both. His mission to Troy was successful. But he does not fare as well as the clever **Odysseus** (another key Greek leader during the war) who knew better when to fight, when to persuade, and when to lie low. Agamemnon was overly proud and blindly ambitious—both qualities that lead him to destruction. Ancient Greece was made up of independent city-states that often clashed. It is clear that, to the Greeks, an effective leader must be more than a brave and capable fighter—he must be diplomatic and clever, too. Agamemnon was not.

Key Themes and Symbols

One of the basic themes of Greek mythology is that all humans have a fate that cannot be escaped and limits they should not try to exceed. The Greeks believed that individuals must face their fate with pride and dignity, gaining as much fame as possible. Agamemnon believed he could change fate by his own actions, and was therefore guilty of hubris. People guilty of hubris would eventually be punished by Nemesis, the goddess of vengeance. Agamemnon's tale also warns of the danger of pride. In ancient Greek mythology, most humans who boast that their beauty or skills surpass those of the gods are punished severely.

Agamemnon in Art, Literature, and Everyday Life

Agamemnon is a favorite character in many works of literature besides the *Iliad.* The ancient Greek playwrights Aeschylus (pronounced ES-kuh-lus), Euripides (pronounced yoo-RIP-i-deez), and Sophocles (pronounced SOF-uh-kleez) wrote a number of plays based on the life of Agamemnon. He was also a popular subject of ancient Roman authors such as Ovid and Seneca. Later writers, including William Shakespeare and French playwright Jean Racine, included Agamemnon as a character in their works. In modern times, Agamemnon has served as a model for characters in works by poet T. S. Eliot and playwright Eugene O'Neill. Agamemnon has also been portrayed in films, usually those that relate the events of the Trojan War. Actor Sean Connery appeared as Agamemnon in the 1981 time-travel comedy *Time Bandits*, directed by Terry Gilliam.

Read, Write, Think, Discuss

How does Agamemnon's sacrifice of his daughter Iphigenia change the course of both the Trojan War and his own life? What choice would you have made if you were in his position? Why?

SEE ALSO Achilles; Aphrodite; Apollo; Cassandra; Electra; Greek Mythology; Hector; Helen of Troy; *Iliad, The*

Ahriman

Character Overview

Ahriman (pronounced AH-ri-muhn), also known as Angra Mainyu (pronounced ANG-ruh MAYN-yoo), was the spirit of evil and

---

Nationality/Culture
Persian/Zoroastrian

Pronunciation
AH-ri-muhn

Alternate Names
Druj, Angra Mainyu

Appears In
The Gathas, the Avesta, the Book of Arda Viraf, the Bundahishn

Lineage
None

darkness in **Persian mythology** and in Zoroastrianism, a religion that attracted a large following in Persia around 600 BCE. Often called Druj ("the Lie"), Ahriman was the force behind anger, greed, envy, and other negative and harmful emotions. He also brought chaos, or the breakdown of order and structure, into the world. In Zoroastrianism, Ahriman is contrasted with **Ahura Mazda**, the supreme creator of order and goodness. In the Islamic religion, Ahriman is identified with Iblis, the devil.

Major Myths

The Zoroastrian history of the world was seen as a struggle between these two forces. Ahura Mazda had the backing of the *yazatas* (angels), while

Ahriman created a host of demons called *daevas* to spread his evil influence by appealing to the envy, greed, and desire for power felt by human beings.

In the beliefs of early Zoroastrianism, good and evil fought for control of the world—Ahura Mazda from the heavens and Ahriman from the **underworld**, or land of the dead. The two forces were evenly matched, and constantly struggled back and forth. Ahura Mazda represented **fire**, sunlight, and life. Ahriman was the lord of darkness and death. Zoroastrians later came to view Ahura Mazda as the supreme ruler who would one day achieve final victory over Ahriman.

Ahriman in Context

Zoroastrianism views Ahriman and Ahura Mazda as locked in an enduring conflict. This opposition of good and evil is called dualism, and Zoroastrianism was only one among several Persian religions, including Zurvanism (the religion of the Magi) and Manichaeism, that adhered to this philosophy.

The idea of a dark, evil force pitted against a good, creative force is central to the major monotheistic religions (religions with one god) of the world—Judaism, Christianity, and Islam. Where Zoroastrianism differs from these faiths is in the relative power of the good and evil forces. In the major monotheistic faiths, the supreme god is all-powerful, whereas in the Zoroastrian faith, the powers of good and evil are more evenly balanced, although Zoroastrians believe that the forces of good will eventually triumph.

An important aspect of the good-versus-evil struggle in Zoroastrianism is the notion of free will, or moral choice. Zoroaster believed that in the conflict between good and evil, good will ultimately triumph by choice: everything that Ahura Mazda created, including humanity, is good, so in the end, humans will choose good over evil.

Key Themes and Symbols

Ahriman was seen as the force responsible for greed and the desire for money or other material things. Ahriman also represented darkness and death, as well as chaos. In modern terms, Ahriman was a symbol of the evil that continually battled against the goodness of Ahura Mazda.

But Ahriman does not have an absolute grasp on humanity; the themes of goodness and free will run throughout Zoroastrianism. Humans are

Heresies

Religious scholars have long sought a satisfactory answer to the still-unanswered question: If God is all-powerful, why is there a devil? That is, how can the devil be a serious threat if God is so much stronger? This particular area of confusion has given rise over the centuries to various ideas called "heresies" (ideas that are different from accepted teachings) by the Christian church. The Manichaeans of the third century, and the Cathars and the Albigensians of the twelfth and thirteenth centuries, all differed from Christian teaching by adopting a view of the universe in which good and evil were equally powerful.

good because they were created by Ahura Mazda, who created only good, and they will use their free will to choose good over evil. Humans demonstrate their free will by actively upholding the order of Ahura Mazda's creation: following laws, performing good acts, and rejecting evil. By choosing good, humans will eventually eliminate evil from existence.

Ahriman in Art, Literature, and Everyday Life

Although similar to **Satan**, Mammon, and many other evil characters found in mythologies and religious teachings around the world, Ahriman is not very well known to those who are unfamiliar with Zoroastrianism. Ahriman has appeared several times in the *Final Fantasy* video game series as an enemy to be fought by the player; he has appeared under the names Ahriman and Angra Mainyu, and is usually depicted as a winged monster with a single eye. Ahriman has also appeared as a demon in the DC Comics series *Wonder Woman*.

Read, Write, Think, Discuss

The idea of two opposing forces at war in the universe, such as Ahriman and Ahura Mazda, is common in literature and film. Can you think of any books or movies that are based on this idea? Write down at least two examples, and explain how they handle this theme.

SEE ALSO Ahura Mazda; Angels; Devils and Demons; Persian Mythology

Ahura Mazda

Nationality/Culture
Persian/Zoroastrian

Pronunciation
ah-HOO-ruh MAHZ-duh

Alternate Names
Ohrmazd, Spenta Mainyu

Appears In
The Avesta, the Gathas, the Book of Arda Viraf, the Bundahishn

Lineage
None: in Zoroastrianism, Ahura Mazda is an uncreated God and Creator of good

Character Overview

Ahura Mazda (pronounced ah-HOO-ruh MAHZ-duh), whose name means "wise lord," was the most important god in ancient **Persian mythology**. When the religion known as Zoroastrianism became widespread in Persia around 600 BCE, Ahura Mazda became its supreme deity or god. The Persians considered him to be the creator of earth, the heavens, and humankind, as well as the source of all goodness and happiness on earth. He was known to later Zoroastrians as Ohrmazd (pronounced OR-muzd).

Major Myths

Ahura Mazda created six divine beings, or **angels**, to help him spread goodness and rule the universe. One of the most important angels was Asha Vahishta ("Excellent Order" or "Truth"), who was associated with justice. Another key angel was Vohu Manah ("Good Mind"), who symbolized love and sacred wisdom and welcomed souls to paradise.

One now-extinct branch of Zoroastrianism, known as Zurvanism, viewed Ahura Mazda and the evil spirit **Ahriman** (pronounced AH-ri-muhn; also known as Angra Mainyu) as two opposite-but-equal twin spirits—good and evil—battling for control of the world. The founder of Zoroastrianism, however, viewed Ahura Mazda as the transcendental deity, the "uncreated God and Creator of good" who represented creation, truth, and order. Zoroastrians thus considered Ahura Mazda to be the more powerful force who would ultimately triumph over the evil Ahriman.

Ahura Mazda in Context

Ahura Mazda is an important figure in Zoroastrianism, a religious movement based on the philosophies of a prophet and poet named Zoroaster, who lived in Iran around 1000 BCE. Zoroastrians believe that the world was created and is ruled by a single god, Ahura Mazda, and that humans are forever being tested by the temptations of evil. Since Ahura Mazda is considered the supreme god of the Zoroastrians, he is

A relief sculpture depicting Ahura Mazda, the chief Zoroastrian deity, giving the royal crown to Ardashir I.
SEF/ART RESOURCE, NY.

often compared to the main gods from other religions: ancient Greeks, for example, believed that "Ahura Mazda" was simply another name for **Zeus**. Unlike the ancient Greeks and Romans, however, Zoroastrians believed in free will. They did not think that fate or the meddling of gods determined a person's destiny. This idea of individual free will also relates to the Zoroastrian view that good will conquer evil; because Ahura Mazda created everything good—including humanity—humans will ultimately choose good over evil through their free will.

Key Themes and Symbols

Ahura Mazda was associated with light and **fire**, the emblems of truth, goodness, and wisdom. Zoroastrians would often pray using a flame or other source of light as the point of focus for their prayers, much like Christian churches use a crucifix as a focal point for worshippers. The symbol most commonly associated with Zoroastrianism is an image of

Ahura Mazda shown as a figure with eagle-like wings and tail. Ahura Mazda appears in Persian art and texts as a bearded man wearing a robe covered with stars. Dwelling high in **heaven**, he had the **sun** for an eye.

Ahura Mazda in Art, Literature, and Everyday Life

Many stone reliefs and statues of Ahura Mazda have been found at ancient Persian sites. However, as the religion became less popular over the centuries, depictions of Ahura Mazda also became less abundant. As with many mythological figures, Ahura Mazda has been given new life in modern times as a character in comic books. Notable appearances include the long-running DC Comics series *Wonder Woman*, and the comic book series *Dawn: Lucifer's Halo* by Joseph Michael Linsner (1997).

Read, Write, Think, Discuss

The ancient land known as Persia now falls mostly in the country of Iran. Using your library, the Internet, or other available resources, locate a map that shows the extent the ancient Persian Empire. What other present-day countries did the Persian Empire include?

SEE ALSO Ahriman; Angels; Persian Mythology

Aladdin

Character Overview

Nationality/Culture
Arabic

Pronunciation
uh-LAD-in

Alternate Names
None

Appears In
The Book of One Thousand and One Nights

Lineage
Son of a poor tailor

Aladdin (pronounced uh-LAD-in) appears in the collection of stories known as *The Book of One Thousand and One Nights* (or the *Arabian Nights*). Legends from Europe to China often contained characters like Aladdin, that is, ordinary people who came into possession of magical devices and used them to gain wealth and power. Aladdin's magical tools were a ring and a lamp that controlled supernatural beings known as **genies**.

Aladdin was the lazy, irresponsible son of a poor tailor. A sorcerer, or wizard, tricked him into entering a treasure-filled cave to seize a magical lamp. Before Aladdin went inside the cave, the sorcerer gave him a ring that would protect him against evil. Aladdin found the lamp, but he refused to give it to the sorcerer until he was outside the cave. The sorcerer blocked the entry to the cave, imprisoning Aladdin within.

Through a series of accidents, Aladdin discovered that rubbing the ring brought forth powerful genies, or magic spirits who take human form and serve the person who calls them. The genies released him from the cave. He also discovered he could summon them by rubbing the lamp. The genies offered to fulfill Aladdin's every wish. He asked for, and received a magnificent palace and the permission to marry the sultan's, or king's, daughter.

The sorcerer, meanwhile, was determined to gain control of the magic lamp. He tricked Aladdin's wife into exchanging the lamp for a new one, and then commanded the genie of the lamp to move Aladdin's palace to Africa. In time, Aladdin and his wife defeated the sorcerer and recovered the lamp. Then they had to prevent the sorcerer's wicked younger brother from seizing it. After various adventures, the couple returned home where Aladdin became sultan and lived a long and happy life.

Aladdin in Context

Although Aladdin's tale comes from Arabic culture, the story actually takes place in a mythical city in China. China was considered an exotic and mysterious place where unusual things could happen. People in ancient cultures often believed that such faraway lands were home to magical creatures and treasures, such as the special lamp that Aladdin finds.

The story of Aladdin has an interesting history. Recent scholarship has shown that Aladdin was not actually one of the original characters in *The Book of One Thousand and One Nights.* The original tales were versions of Arabic, Persian, and Indian stories that had changed over time and had been adapted by different storytellers for different audiences. The oldest mention of the text containing the tales dates to about the ninth century. The earliest existing manuscript, a Syrian version, dates to the fourteenth century—and contains no mention of Aladdin. By the sixteenth century, Egyptian versions of the text do contain an Aladdin story, but its origin is uncertain. The Western world was introduced to the tales in an early eighteenth-century French translation by Antoine Galland, who used the Syrian version as his source. Nineteenth-century editions combined stories from both the Syrian and Egyptian versions and included the Aladdin story. The

A scene from the Disney animated film **Aladdin** *(1992). This movie adapted the ancient Persian folktale for today's children.* THE KOBAL COLLECTION.

folklore and fairy tales of Europe were enjoying increased popularity at the time (the Mother Goose stories and fairy tales of the Grimm brothers appeared in the nineteenth century), so Aladdin and the other tales in *The Book of One Thousand and One Nights* were greeted enthusiastically and remain popular to this day.

Key Themes and Symbols

The interactions between Aladdin and the sorcerer are very much like other trickster tales found in cultures around the world. The sorcerer is a trickster character, willing to deceive Aladdin and trap him in a cave in order to get the magical lamp. Aladdin himself is a trickster, however, and cleverer than the sorcerer realizes. Aladdin also represents the power of a person to determine his future through his own actions, a stark contrast to many mythical tales about the gods foretelling a person's future path in life.

Aladdin in Art, Literature, and Everyday Life

The story of Aladdin has proven to be one of the most popular Arabic tales ever told. In addition to appearing in translated form around the world as part of *The Book of One Thousand and One Nights*, the tale is often told on its own in children's books or in staged productions. The story of Aladdin has been filmed on numerous occasions, with the 1992 Disney animated production *Aladdin* being the most well-known movie version of the tale.

Read, Write, Think, Discuss

An ancient proverb warns: "Be careful what you wish for—you might get it." Using your library, the Internet, or other available resources, research fairy tales and myths that show the negative consequences of a wish fulfilled. Compare these mythical situations to your own life: have you ever been "burned" by getting exactly what you wished for?

SEE ALSO Genies; Persian Mythology

Amaterasu

Character Overview

Amaterasu (pronounced ah-mah-te-RAH-soo), goddess of the **sun** and of fertility, is one of the most important figures in **Japanese mythology** and in the Shinto religion. Her name literally means "shining in **heaven**." According to legend, she is the first ancestor of the imperial, or royal, family of Japan.

Major Myths

Daughter of the creator god Izanagi (pronounced ee-zah-NAH-gee), Amaterasu taught humans to plant rice and weave cloth. In one story, her brother, Susano-ô, angered the goddess by interfering with her activities. He destroyed rice fields, spread filth in her sacred buildings, and dropped a skinned horse through the roof of the weavers' hall. Furious at Susano-ô's actions, Amaterasu went into a cave and locked the

Nationality/Culture
Japanese/Shinto

Pronunciation
ah-mah-te-RAH-soo

Alternate Names
None

Appears In
The *Kojiki*, the *Nihon Shoki*

Lineage
Daughter of Izanagi

entrance. Her withdrawal plunged the earth into darkness and prevented the rice from growing.

To lure the sun goddess out, the other gods gathered outside the cave with various sacred objects, including a mirror and some jewels. A young goddess began dancing, causing the others to burst into laughter. Wondering how they could make merry in her absence, Amaterasu peeked out to see what was amusing them. Those outside the cave told Amaterasu of another goddess more brilliant than she. Curious, Amaterasu looked and saw her reflection in the mirror. The image of her own brilliance so astonished her that she stepped out of the cave. One of the gods hung a rope across the cave door to prevent her from returning to it and depriving the world of her light.

Amaterasu in Context

Amaterasu is a central figure in the Shinto religion, which was once the official religion of Japan. Although no firm dates have been established, it is possible that Shinto was developing in Japan at around the same time the ancient Romans developed their own mythology, circa 300 BCE. The first written accounts that document details of Shinto are the *Kojiki* and the *Nihon Shoki*, both written in the early 700s CE.

Many followers of Shinto considered Amaterasu to be the most important god of all, since the sun was critical to the growth of crops such as rice. The story of Amaterasu's retreat into the cave—followed by her return to bring light to the world—mirrors the cycle of the agricultural season, in which crops cannot grow during the winter, but return during the summer months.

Japan's earliest emperors were believed to be descended directly from Amaterasu, which supposedly supported their right to rule. The mirror that drew Amaterasu out of the cave is supposedly housed in her shrine at Ise, and is considered one of Japan's three imperial (royal) treasures—along with jewels and a sword—that are symbols of this right to rule. The presence of hundreds of bronze mirrors in tombs across Japan indicate their religious importance to the Japanese people; early peoples believed that the mirror reflected the spirit of the person who looked into it.

Key Themes and Symbols

As a sun goddess, Amaterasu is closely associated with light and the sun. She is almost always pictured giving off rays of light. Amaterasu is also closely associated with love and compassion. Another important symbol associated with Amaterasu, taken from the myth, is the mirror, which represents wisdom.

Amaterasu in Art, Literature, and Everyday Life

As one of the central figures in the Shinto religion, Amaterasu was a popular subject in Japanese art through the first half of the twentieth century. After World War II, Shinto was no longer the official state religion, and Shinto influences were not as strong in Japanese art and literature after that time. Amaterasu sometimes appears in Japanese animated films and comics and served as the main character for the 2006 video game *Okami* by Capcom. In the game, the player controls Amaterasu, embodied as a white wolf carrying a mirror on its back, in an effort to bring light and color back to the world.

Read, Write, Think, Discuss

The term "sun worshipper" today usually refers to someone who enjoys tanning or spending time outdoors in sunny areas such as the beach. Overwhelming medical evidence shows that such behavior puts a person at a much greater risk of developing skin cancer. Skin cancer is currently the most commonly diagnosed form of cancer, with about one million cases reported each year in the United States.

If ancient cultures had the same medical information we do today, do you think sun gods such as Amaterasu would remain as important and well-regarded in their belief systems? Why or why not?

SEE ALSO Izanagi and Izanami; Japanese Mythology

Amazons

Character Overview

In **Greek mythology**, the Amazons (pronounced AM-uh-zonz) were a nation of fierce female warriors, descendants of **Ares** (pronounced AIR-eez), the god of war. The legendary Amazons lived in an all-female

Nationality/Culture
Greek/Roman

Pronunciation
AM-uh-zonz

Alternate Names
Antianeira, Androktones

Appears In
The *Iliad*, the *Odyssey*

Lineage
Descendants of Ares

society in southern Russia or northern Asia Minor. Occasionally, the women had children with men from surrounding tribes. The Amazons kept and raised only the girls, killing or making slaves of the male children or sending them to live with their fathers.

Scholars disagree on the meaning of the name Amazon. Some say it means "breastless." This comes from the Greek belief that the Amazons cut off the right breast of each girl so she could handle a bow and arrow more easily. Other scholars believe that the name may mean "without grain" (or bread) and may have come from the Greek word for barley, *maza*. They reason that the Amazons, as hunters, ate only meat and did not make bread. The word "Amazon" may also come from the name of an Iranian ethnic group meaning "warriors."

The Amazons appeared frequently in Greek myth and legend. One of the twelve labors of **Heracles** (known as Hercules to the Romans) was to capture the belt of the Amazon queen Hippolyta (pronounced hi-PAHL-i-tuh). When Heracles reached the land of the Amazons, Hippolyta received him warmly and agreed to give him her belt. But **Hera** (pronounced HAIR-uh), queen of the gods, convinced the rest of the Amazons that Heracles was kidnapping Hippolyta, so they attacked him. Believing the queen had tricked him, Heracles killed her before sailing back to Greece with the belt. In another Greek tale, the hero **Theseus** (pronounced THEE-see-uhs) attacked the Amazons and carried off their queen. The Amazons responded by going to war against Athens, but Theseus defeated them after a terrific struggle.

During the Trojan War, the Amazon queen Penthesilea brought extra troops to help the Trojans after the warrior **Hector** was killed. For this, the Greek hero **Achilles** killed her. Afterward, it is said that he fell in love with her corpse and regretted taking her life. The Amazons also appear in works by the Greek writers Herodotus and Apollodorus.

The legend of the Amazons lived on long after the time of the ancient Greeks and Romans. In the 1500s, the Spanish explorer Francisco de Orellana claimed to have met a tribe of female warriors while exploring the Marañon River in South America. He supposedly renamed the river the Amazon in their honor.

Amazons in Context

The legend of the Amazons may have come from the possibility that women in some ancient societies took part in battle. In many cases, these

were matriarchal societies, in which a family's name, property, and wealth were passed down through the mother's side of the family. The Greeks had a patriarchal society, in which a family's name, property, and wealth were passed down through the father's side of the family. To the

The Slavic Amazons

Powerful female warriors also appeared in the folktales of Slavic peoples from southeastern Europe. Led by the warrior Vlasta, these women lived in a castle by the Vltava River, in the modern Czech Republic. They were aggressive not only in their battles with men, but also in their pursuit of them. In one story, the female warrior Šàrka fought the Slavic hero Dobrynia. She grabbed him by his hair, pulled him off his horse, and put him in her pocket. She released him only after he promised to marry her. In most of the stories, the female warriors ended up either dead or married to a hero.

Greeks, matriarchal practices seemed unnatural and barbaric. As a result, they created stories about fierce, man-hating women. In many Greek tales, the Amazons are defeated and killed by male warriors as punishment for taking a role considered wrong for females.

Key Themes and Symbols

Amazons represent strength and skill with weapons normally associated with men. They are often portrayed in a manner similar to that of the goddess **Athena**, with a crescent shield and helmet. The Amazons are usually pictured fighting on horseback with spears, bows and arrows, and axes. Some scholars have argued that the myth of the Amazons symbolizes the unknown dangers Greeks faced when venturing out to the coasts of Asia Minor and elsewhere along the Black Sea, which was inhabited by people the Greeks generally considered savage.

Amazons in Art, Literature, and Everyday Life

Amazons were a popular subject in ancient Greek art, appearing frequently on vases and in relief sculptures on buildings like the Parthenon. More recently, the DC Comics superheroine Wonder Woman (created in 1941) is based on the Amazon myth. In the comic, Wonder Woman is said to be the daughter of Hippolyta, queen of the Amazons.

The term "Amazon" has developed a more general meaning over the centuries. Tall, strong, or aggressive women are often referred to as

Amazons, even in modern times. The term is also used to refer to Amazon.com, one of the world's largest Internet-based stores, though its founder, Jeff Bezos, took the name from the South American river, not the mythical tribe of female warriors.

Read, Write, Think, Discuss

Although the ancient Greeks wrote of these unusual female warriors over two thousand years ago, the idea of women fighting in wars is still a controversial one. Using your library, the Internet, and other resources, research the topic of women soldiers in combat. What are the arguments in favor of women fighting alongside men? What are the arguments against it? What is your opinion on the issue?

SEE ALSO Achilles; *Aeneid, The*; Hera; Heracles; *Iliad, The*; Theseus

Amun

Character Overview

At first, Amun (pronounced AH-muhn) was only one of many deities (or gods) worshipped by the Egyptians. As he became more important, he was combined with the **sun** god **Ra** to form a new deity called Amun-Ra. Egyptians honored Amun-Ra as king of the gods and creator of the universe. They also believed him to be the father of the pharaohs, or kings of ancient Egypt, and believed he would help these rulers triumph in battle. The worship of Amun-Ra remained strong throughout Egypt until almost the time of the birth of Jesus. The ancient Greeks associated Amun-Ra with **Zeus**, their own supreme god.

Nationality/Culture
Egyptian

Pronunciation
AH-muhn

Alternate Names
Amon, Amun-Ra

Appears In
Egyptian creation myths

Lineage
Father of the Pharaohs

Major Myths

According to an Egyptian creation myth, Amun is one of sixteen gods that, when paired off within the group, represent some different aspect of the pre-created world. The pairing of Amun and Amaunet represents "concealment." In at least one tradition, Amun actually fathered

Changing Identities of Egyptian Gods

The ancient Egyptians often combined different gods into a single deity, a process that scholars call "syncretism." There are many reasons why the Egyptians practiced syncretism. In some cases it was a political decision meant to encourage loyalty and maintain peace—as during the reign of the Ptolemies (a Greek dynasty that ruled Egypt for three hundred years), when the Greek deities Zeus and Helios were linked with the Egyptian deities Osiris and Apis to form the Greco-Egyptian deity Serapis. In other cases, there is not any clear reason why gods were linked. In general, however, these linkages did not prevent Egyptians from continuing to worship the gods individually. The identities of Egyptian gods were not fixed or stagnant, but changed to accommodate political and social changes, so the Egyptians could worship both Serapis and Osiris at the same time.

this group of gods, and Amun's importance can be seen in that he himself had no father. In other words, he did not need another god to create him.

Reliefs from New Kingdom temples describe a myth in which Amun falls in love with the queen of Egypt. He visits her in the form of her husband, the king, and fathers a child. When the child is born, Amun declares the child to be his and presents his son to the other gods as the future king.

Amun in Context

For much of the history of ancient Egypt, Amun was honored as the supreme god in the Egyptian pantheon, the entire collection of gods and goddesses recognized by a group of people. But political changes in Egypt affected his popularity at different times. He was originally a local deity in Hermopolis, a city in southern Egypt, and had power over the air or wind. By 2000 BCE, Amun's popularity had spread to the capital of Thebes, and rulers—perhaps in an effort to increase their own popularity amongst the people—began to honor him as the national god of Egypt. However, after invaders known as the Hyksos (pronounced HICK-sus) conquered northern Egypt in the 1700s BCE, only people in the south continued to worship Amun. When the Egyptians drove out the Hyksos in the 1500s BCE, Amun's influence expanded rapidly, as did the size and splendor of his temples. Two of the largest temples of ancient Egypt, located at Luxor and Karnak, were devoted to the worship of Amun, and his followers controlled great wealth.

Key Themes and Symbols

Amun usually appears in Egyptian art as a bearded man wearing a headdress of two ostrich feathers, a broad necklace, and a close-fitting garment. His skin is typically blue, perhaps to show his connection to the wind and the air. In one hand, he has an ankh (pronounced AHNK), the Egyptian symbol of life, and in the other, he holds a scepter, a symbol of authority. He is often portrayed sitting on a throne like a pharaoh. As Amun-Ra, the god is sometimes shown with the head of a hawk topped by a golden disk representing the sun, which is encircled by a serpent. He is also associated with the ram and the goose.

The Egyptian god Amun, holding the ankh, the symbol of life, in his right hand, and a sceptor, the symbol of authority, in his left hand. © MARY EVANS PICTURE LIBRARY/THE IMAGE WORKS.

Amun in Art, Literature, and Everyday Life

Amun was one of the most popular subjects of ancient Egyptian art. His image appears on ancient monuments throughout Egypt and remains a popular symbol of ancient Egyptian beliefs. It has been suggested that the Judeo-Christian use of the word "amen" at the end of a prayer is derived from the name Amun, though many scholars dispute this claim.

Read, Write, Think, Discuss

What does the history of Amun indicate about ancient Egyptian religious beliefs? Do they seem to remain fixed and unchanging, or do they seem to change and evolve over time? Do you think this is also true for other religions?

SEE ALSO Egyptian Mythology; Ra; Zeus

Anansi

Nationality/Culture
West African

Pronunciation
uh-NAHN-see

Alternate Names
None

Appears In
West African trickster tales

Lineage
Son of Nyame and
Asase Ya

Character Overview

Anansi (pronounced uh-NAHN-see), the spider, is one of the most popular animal **tricksters** from West **African mythology**. Tricksters are mischievous figures who often oppose the will of the gods, which results in some kind of misfortune for humans. Like many trickster figures, the sly Anansi can change his appearance to look like a human, a rabbit, a fox, or other animals.

West Africans originally thought Anansi to be the creator of the world. He often acted as a go-between for humans in their dealings with the sky god Nyame (pronounced N-ya-mae), and supposedly persuaded Nyame to create both night and rain. In most stories, however, Anansi is a crafty and cunning trickster who makes life more enjoyable for himself, or more difficult for others, by fooling humans, other animals, and even the gods themselves. By using his cleverness and what he knew of his victims' ways of thinking, Anansi was able to trick them to achieve his aims.

In one well-known tale, Anansi asks God for an ear of **corn** and promises to repay it with one hundred servants. He takes the corn to a village and tells the people that it is sacred. During the night, Anansi feeds the corn to the chickens. The next morning, he accuses the villagers of stealing the corn and they give him a bushel of it to make up for the lost ear.

Anansi then meets a man on the road and exchanges the corn for a chicken. He visits another village and tells the people that the chicken is sacred. That night he kills the chicken. The next morning the frightened villagers give him ten sheep to replace it. Anansi later exchanges the sheep for a corpse, which he takes to a third village and tells the people that it is the sleeping son of God. When the villagers cannot wake the corpse the next morning, Anansi says they have killed God's son. The terrified villagers offer him one hundred of their finest young men. Anansi takes them to God to fulfill his part of the bargain.

Anansi in Context

The character of Anansi is believed to have come from the Ashanti tribe, located in the West African country of Ghana. The character became quite popular among other nearby tribes, including the Akyem and Nzema. As members of these tribes were taken west during the slave trade, the stories of Anansi were brought to the West Indies, South America, and North America. In some parts of North America, Anansi became known as Aunt Nancy or Miss Nancy in African American folklore.

The traditional role of the trickster in many cultures is to survive challenges and dangers by using cleverness or deceit. The trickster is not usually a physically strong or intelligent individual, so he is not the heroic figure of myth and legend. But tricksters often get what they want and survive in a dangerous world by using their wits—making them especially popular among weaker segments of society. The popularity of Anansi's stories among African American slaves might be due in part to his role as a survivor.

Key Themes and Symbols

Though the trickster can take the form of many different humans and animals, Anansi is most often depicted as a spider. The spider is an apt form for a trickster god because spiders spin webs to catch the careless— just as Anansi spins webs of deceit to achieve his goals. He is symbolic of the trickster character commonly found in mythologies around the world in that he is usually selfish, clever, and willing to cause mischief for his own amusement or benefit. He is also more understanding of the human condition than other deities.

Anansi in Art, Literature, and Everyday Life

Anansi is one of the most popular characters from African mythology and is often featured in folk tales and children's stories. Anansi also plays a central role in the Neil Gaiman fantasy novel *Anansi Boys* (2005), a contemporary story about a man who discovers that his dead father was Anansi and that his brother has inherited their father's special powers.

Read, Write, Think, Discuss

Trickster characters are common in television shows. They are usually portrayed as schemers whose grand plans always seem to land them in trouble. Lucy Ricardo from the television show *I Love Lucy* fits the description of a trickster in many ways. Can you think of a television show or movie you enjoy that contains a trickster character? What qualities or behaviors make you think that the character is a trickster?

SEE ALSO African Mythology; Tricksters

Androcles

Nationality/Culture
Roman

Pronunciation
AN-druh-kleez

Alternate Names
Androclus

Appears In
Noctes Atticae

Lineage
Unknown

Character Overview

According to legend, Androcles (pronounced AN-druh-kleez) was a Roman slave who lived in Africa in the first century CE. After escaping from his cruel master, the former slave Androcles hid in a cave. While there, a lion with a thorn stuck in its paw entered the cave. The lion showed its swollen paw to Androcles, who carefully removed the thorn and befriended the animal.

Some years later, Androcles was captured and thrown into an arena to be killed by lions. One of the lions, however, was the same animal that Androcles had helped in the cave. The lion recognized Androcles and refused to hurt him. The animal even protected Androcles from the other wild beasts. When the spectators in the arena saw what was happening, they demanded that Androcles be set free.

Androcles in Context

In ancient Rome, slaves were common and were considered to be the lowest class of citizen in the empire. Slaves were often forced to participate in public "games" where they were made to battle each other to the death, or try to protect themselves against fierce beasts such as lions and bears. These displays were usually held in the Coliseum, a great stadium built in the first century CE, or along the outdoor racing track known as the Circus Maximus. The story of Androcles is unique in Roman culture because it humanizes slaves and offers a sympathetic view of their situation.

Key Themes and Symbols

One of the main themes of the story of Androcles is the power of friendship and charity. Because Androcles helps the lion, a creature that many would be too scared to help, his life is spared as a reward for his charitable act. In later centuries, some authors created new versions of the story of Androcles in which the slave was instead a Christian who was being punished by Romans for his religious beliefs. The story was seen as a lesson on charity and loyalty, important themes in Christian teachings.

Former slave Androcles was saved from his death sentence in a Roman arena when the lion that was supposed to kill him turned out to be an animal he had helped many years before. The lion's gentle reaction to Androcles swayed the crowd to Androcles' side, and they demanded his release. © PRIVATE COLLECTION/© LOOK AND LEARN/THE BRIDGEMAN ART LIBRARY.

Androcles in Art, Literature, and Everyday Life

The legend of Androcles appeared in *Noctes Atticae* (Attica Nights), a story written by Roman author Aulus Gellius around 150 CE. According to Gellius, the original version came from the author Apion, though the text has been lost. The story of Androcles has also appeared in many collections of fables attributed to Aesop. Much later, the legend became the inspiration for the play *Androcles and the Lion*, written in 1912 by Irish author George Bernard Shaw.

Read, Write, Think, Discuss

Scholars have noted that the story of Androcles is about two creatures, a human and a lion, each overcoming their basic instincts or fears for the sake of the other. How is that shown in the tale? Do you think that this is a good description of friendship in general? Why or why not?

SEE ALSO Animals in Mythology

Andromeda

Nationality/Culture
Greek/Roman

Pronunciation
an-DROM-i-duh

Alternate Names
None

Appears In
Ovid's *Metamorphoses*,
Hyginus's *Fabulae*

Lineage
Daughter of Cepheus and
Cassiopea, King and
Queen of Joppa

Character Overview

In **Greek mythology**, Andromeda (pronounced an-DROM-i-duh) was the beautiful daughter of King Cepheus (pronounced SEE-fee-us) and Queen Cassiopea (pronounced kas-ee-oh-PEE-uh) of Joppa in the ancient kingdom of Ethiopia. Cassiopea once boasted that Andromeda was more beautiful than the Nereids (pronounced NEER-ee-idz), a group of sea **nymphs**, or female nature deities. Offended by this boast, the Nereids complained to the sea god **Poseidon** (pronounced poh-SYE-dun), who punished Joppa by sending a flood and a sea monster to ravage the coastal kingdom.

An oracle (a person through which gods communicated with humans) told Cepheus that the only way to save his kingdom was to chain Andromeda to a rock at the foot of a cliff and let the sea monster eat her. Cepheus did so, and Andromeda awaited her fate. While passing by, the hero **Perseus** (pronounced PUR-see-uhs) saw the chained Andromeda and fell in love with her. He asked Cepheus for her hand in marriage, and Cepheus agreed as long as Perseus would slay the sea monster.

As it happened, Perseus had just killed a beastly Gorgon named **Medusa**, one of three snake-haired sisters whose appearance can turn anyone who looks at her to stone. He had her head in a bag. He showed the head to the sea monster, which immediately turned to stone. Unknown to Perseus, Cepheus had already promised Andromeda to her uncle Phineus (pronounced FIN-ee-uhs). At the marriage feast for Perseus and Andromeda, Phineus showed up with a group of armed men and demanded that Andromeda be given to him. However, Perseus once again used the head of Medusa and turned Phineus and his men to stone.

Perseus and Andromeda had seven children and remained together for the rest of their lives. According to the Greek historian Herodotus (pronounced heh-ROD-uh-tuhs), the kings of Persia were descended from the couple's first son, Perses (pronounced PUHR-sees). When Andromeda and Perseus died, the goddess **Athena** placed them in the sky as constellations, along with Andromeda's parents and the sea monster.

Andromeda in Context

The story of Andromeda includes the practice of human **sacrifice**, or the taking of a person's life in order to please the gods. This same practice is mentioned in myths of the Trojan War, where **Agamemnon** (pronounced ag-uh-MEM-non) must kill his daughter Iphigenia (pronounced if-uh-juh-NYE-uh) in order to gain easy passage to Troy for his army. Despite being mentioned in Greek myths, there is no archeological evidence that ancient Greeks actually performed human sacrifices. Ancient Romans engaged in human sacrifice, mostly involving ritual gladiatorial combat or the offering of criminals or captured prisoners of war to the gods. By the late Republic, the practice was replaced by animal sacrifice or became merely symbolic, and it was banned by decree in 97 BCE.

Key Themes and Symbols

The story of Andromeda focuses on sacrifice and the dangers of boastfulness. Poseidon punishes all of Joppa when Cassiopea boasts about her daughter's beauty. Cepheus and Cassiopea are told that the only way to satisfy Poseidon is by sacrificing their daughter to a sea monster. Andromeda herself represents innocence; she does nothing that would justify an awful fate. Perseus, then, acts as a force of justice, rescuing Andromeda from her unfair fate.

Andromeda in Art, Literature, and Everyday Life

The story of Andromeda was popular among the ancient Greeks. The playwrights Sophocles (pronounced SOF-uh-kleez) and Euripides (pronounced yoo-RIP-i-deez) both wrote plays recounting her tale. In the nineteenth century, Andromeda was the subject of poems by both Gerard Manley Hopkins and Charles Kingsley.

The story of Andromeda and Perseus was a key element of the 1981 fantasy film *Clash of the Titans,* though the sea monster is referred to as the Kraken, a creature taken from Scandinavian myth. Andromeda is also the name given to a constellation, or group of stars, found in the northern portion of the night sky. Her V-shaped constellation is notable for containing a cloudy group of stars known as M31, or the Andromeda Galaxy.

Read, Write, Think, Discuss

Andromeda is nearly sacrificed by her father in an effort to save his kingdom. With her single death, he hopes to ensure the safety of many other people. Is it right for an innocent person to die if it will result in saving the lives of many others? Why or why not?

SEE ALSO Athena; Gorgons; Greek Mythology; Medusa; Nymphs; Perseus; Poseidon; Zeus

Angels

Nationality/Culture
Various

Alternate Names
Cherubim, Seraphim, Malaaikah

Appears In
The Holy Bible, the Qur'an

Lineage
None

Character Overview

In many of the world's religions, angels are spiritual beings who act as intermediaries, or mediators, between God and humans. As messengers of God, angels may serve any number of purposes. Their role may be to teach, command, or inform individuals of their destiny, or future path in life. Angels may also act to protect or help people.

The word "angel" comes from the Greek word *angelos,* meaning "messenger." In Western religions, the word specifically describes a benevolent, or kind and helpful, being. However, in most other religions, the line separating "good" angels from "bad" angels is not always clear. An angel may act benevolently in one situation but with evil intent in another.

The Nature of Angels The world's religions hold different views about the nature of angels. Some regard angels as divine beings who deserve to be worshiped rather than just treated as messengers of God. Disagreement also exists about the bodies of angels. Some think that angels have physical bodies. Others insist that angels only appear to have such bodies. Still others believe that angels are purely spiritual beings who have the ability to assume material (touchable) bodies.

Zoroastrianism and Judaism The view of angels in Judaism was influenced by Zoroastrianism, a faith founded by the ancient Persian prophet Zoroaster. Zoroastrian mythology describes a fight between **Ahura Mazda** (pronounced ah-HOO-ruh MAHZ-duh) and **Ahriman** (pronounced AH-ri-muhn), which are forces of good and evil with armies of angels and devils. Like Ahura Mazda, the Old Testament

god Yahweh (pronounced YAH-way) has an army of angels. These warrior angels battle against evil forces led by **Satan**, who resembles Ahriman.

Following the Zoroastrian view, Judaism divides the universe into three parts: earth, **heaven**, and **hell**. Earth is the home of humans. Heaven is reserved for God and his angels. Hell is the dark world of Satan and his followers. Angels fulfill a similar role in the two religions, linking heaven with the world of humans and revealing God's plans and laws to humans. Their function is to serve God and carry out his will. They reward goodness and punish wickedness and injustice. They also help people understand God's will and take the souls of righteous individuals to heaven.

Christianity The Christian concept of a three-part universe came from Judaic and Zoroastrian ideas, as did Christian ideas of angels and their functions. In the Christian view, angels are God's messengers. Angels proclaimed the birth of Christ and continue to play an active role in the daily lives of Christians. They bring strength to those who are weak and comfort to those who suffer and carry the prayers of faithful Christians to God. According to legend, guardian angels watch over children.

Islam The Islamic idea of angels is similar to Judaic and Christian views. God is in heaven, and the angels serve him and carry out his will; however, while Judaism and Christianity generally divide spiritual beings into those who are with or against God, Islam divides such beings into angels, demons, and djinni (pronounced JIN-ee), spiritual beings or **genies**. The djinni may be either good or harmful. According to Islamic folklore, they were created out of **fire**, can be visible or invisible, and can assume various human or animal shapes.

Hierarchies of Angels Angels in different orders, or levels, were a part of the mythology of ancient Mesopotamia, a region between the Tigris and Euphrates Rivers located in present-day Iraq. Later, in the fifth century CE, an anonymous Christian theologian known as Pseudo-Dionysius (pronounced SOO-doh dye-o-NIH-shus) the Areopagite (pronounced ar-ee-OP-uh-jyte) described a hierarchy, or ranked order of importance, for angels. Based on his writings, angels are traditionally ranked in nine orders. The highest order of angels is the seraphim, followed by the cherubim, thrones, dominions (or dominations), virtues, powers, principalities, archangels, and angels.

According to Pseudo-Dionysius's hierarchy, the first circle of angels (the seraphim, cherubim, and thrones) devote their time to thinking about God. The second circle (the dominions, virtues, and powers) rule the universe. The third circle (principalities, archangels, and angels) carry out the orders of the superior angels.

Fallen Angels

Fallen angels were angels who had once been close to God but "fell" to a lower position. They tried to interfere with the relationship between human beings and God by encouraging individuals to sin. Fallen angels were also believed to cause such disasters as famine, disease, war, and earthquakes.

In Christian belief, the leader of the fallen angels is Lucifer, also known as Satan. He led a rebellion against God, for which he and the other fallen angels were cast into hell.

Angels in Context

Over the centuries, people have described the function of angels in various ways. The role of angels is developed in greatest detail in religions based on revelation, the communication of divine truth or divine will to human beings. These religions include Judaism, Christianity, and Islam, as well as Zoroastrianism.

In religions based on revelation, like Christianity, God and humans are distant from each other. Angels serve the purpose of bridging the gap between them. Angels praise God, carry out God's will, and reveal divine word. They may also help people attain salvation or receive special favors. Furthermore, acting for God, angels may influence human affairs through such deeds as rewarding faithful believers, punishing people who do evil, and helping people in need.

Angels tend to play a lesser role in polytheistic religions, or religions that feature many gods, such as the ancient Greek pantheon. The gods themselves may carry out angelic functions, often taking human forms. In religions based on the belief that all things are sacred and that the divine and the human share one essence, angels are less important. They are not needed to bridge a gap between the gods and humankind. However, even in these religions, angel-like spiritual beings may help people relate to the divine.

Key Themes and Symbols

At first, artists struggled with the problem of how to represent angels. Written descriptions were not very helpful. Artists tried various approaches before arriving at the image of a young male figure. Later they added two feathery wings to the figure's upper back. The wings suggested that angels were spiritual beings elevated above humans and associated with heaven. Besides wings, angels were sometimes portrayed with halos, long hair, and flowing white robes.

Over time, artists came to depict the different orders of angels in distinct ways. For instance, seraphim sometimes were shown with six wings and holding shields. Around the seraphim, flames burned to symbolize their devotion to God. Artists often portrayed the dominions bearing swords and spears as symbols of God's power.

Angels in Art, Literature, and Everyday Life

Since a large percentage of European art during the Middle Ages and the Renaissance depicted scenes from the Bible, angels appeared in many paintings of the period. Some of the most famous depictions of angels are found in Fra Angelico's *Annunciation* (c. 1440) and *Sistine Madonna* by Raphael (c. 1512). Angels often appeared as decorative sculptures on church exteriors as well.

The contemporary arts contain many depictions of angels. C. S. Lewis's *Out of the Silent Planet* (1938) was the first in a trilogy of books that took numerous Christian figures, including Eve, Satan, and angels, and re-imagined them in a science fiction setting. Films that portray angels include the Frank Capra classic *It's a Wonderful Life* (1946), *Angels in the Outfield* (1951 and 1994), and the 1998 film *City of Angels,* which starred Nicolas Cage as an angel named Seth.

Several television shows have also featured angels as main characters. Examples include *Highway to Heaven* (1984–1989) starring Michael Landon and *Touched by an Angel* (1994–2003).

Read, Write, Think, Discuss

According to a 2006 poll by the Associated Press, more than half of Americans surveyed said they believe in angels. How do you think this affects the portrayal of angels in popular media such as films, art, and television?

SEE ALSO Ahriman; Ahura Mazda; Persian Mythology; Semitic Mythology

Animals in Mythology

Theme Overview

Since the beginning of human history, people have lived in close contact with animals—usually as hunters and farmers—and have developed myths and legends about them. All kinds of creatures, from fierce leopards to tiny spiders, play important roles in mythology. A myth can give special meaning or extraordinary qualities to common animals such as frogs and bears. However, other creatures found in myths, such as many-headed monsters, **dragons**, and **unicorns**, never existed in the real world.

Major Myths

Many myths explore relationships between humans and animals. People may talk with animals, fight them, or even marry them. Sometimes animals perform services for humans, including guiding them through the **underworld** or helping them complete tasks. One large group of myths involving animals concerns transformations, or changes, between human and animal states. Other myths focus on the close connection between people and animals.

Myths of Transformation A princess kisses an enchanted frog and he becomes a handsome prince with whom, the fairy tale tells us, she will live "happily ever after." Such transformations, in which people turn into animals or animals turn into people, take place in myths and legends from around the world. Transformation myths are about crossing the boundaries that set humans apart from the rest of the world.

Native American mythologies describe a time in the past when the boundaries between people and animals were less sharply drawn and beings freely changed form. This is known as shape shifting. Bears were especially close to humans, and in some Native American stories, bears appear as humans wearing coats made of bearskins. The Tsimshian (pronounced CHIM-shee-an) people of southern Alaska and the northern coast of British Columbia tell about Asdiwal, a young man who follows a white bear up a mountain to the sky. He discovers that the beast is actually a beautiful woman dressed in a bear skin, and he marries her.

The ancient Greeks and Romans believed that the gods could blur the boundaries between different classes of beings. Ovid's *Metamorphoses* is a collection of Greek and Roman legends about mortals whom the gods turned into animals and plants. Both Chinese and Slavic mythologies include tales of people who, under some evil force, turn into werewolves.

The Scots have stories about selkies (pronounced SEL-keez), imaginary sea creatures that resemble seals and take on human form, marry men and women, and then return to the sea. In fact, the theme of animal wives or husbands comes up over and over again in mythology. Native Americans tell of girls marrying bears and men marrying deer. Eskimo and Chinese tales mention beautiful, seductive women who turn out to be foxes in disguise. In one Eskimo story, a woman enters the home of a hunter while he is out. She cooks for him and stays for some time, but eventually she puts on her fox skin and disappears. The well-known fable of Beauty and the Beast is a modern version of the myth of the animal husband whose beastly form cannot disguise his noble soul.

Sometimes transformations are forced on people by sorcerers, or magicians, or as punishment for offending the gods. When people voluntarily seek transformation, however, the change can be a sign of power. In many societies, individuals called shamans were thought to have supernatural abilities, including the power to communicate with animals or to transform themselves into animals. South American shamans were said to be able to change themselves into jaguars.

Connections Myths, legends, and folktales often highlight the close links between people and animals. West Africans and Native Americans, for example, believe that each person has a magical or spiritual connection to a particular animal that can act as a guardian, a source of wisdom, or an inspiration. Among the Plains Indians of North America, individuals had to discover their spirit animal through a mystical experience called a vision quest. Some Native American religions in Central America include *nagualism* (pronounced NA-wal-ism), the idea that each person's life is linked to an animal or object called a *nagual.* If the nagual is hurt or killed, the person suffers or dies. One myth says the naguals fought on the side of the Native Americans against invading Spaniards centuries ago.

Sometimes a family, a clan, or a whole society feels a special attachment to a certain kind of animal, usually one they consider to be an ancestor or protector. This connection, called totemism, defines social groups and their behavior. Hunters are sometimes forbidden to kill their group's totem animal, for example. Among the Native Americans of the Pacific Northwest, the beaver, the eagle, the raven, and the killer whale are all associated with particular clans. People display their identity and status with totem poles, which are tall standing logs carved with images of mythical animals. Totem poles mark village entrances, burial sites of chieftains, and the entrance of each clan house.

In many societies, people believed that shamans had animal helpers who guided them through the supernatural realm. This idea is similar to the common image of a witch's "familiar"—an animal, usually a black cat, that gives the witch certain powers. Traditional African religions had secret societies that performed rituals that involved wearing leopard skins. The men in these secret societies believed they took on a leopard's strength by performing these rituals. Animals offer helpful advice to ordinary people in many legends. Generally, those who ignore the animal's advice will fail to achieve their goal.

Many cultures have legends of human children raised by animals. The Romans claimed that a wolf mother had nurtured their legendary ancestors, **Romulus and Remus**. The story of Tarzan, who was raised by African apes, is a modern version of this ancient myth created by Edgar Rice Burroughs in the early twentieth century.

Roles in Myth and Legend Animals fill a wide variety of roles in myths and legends. Many stories explain the part that animals played in creating the world or in bringing **fire**, tools, or farming skills to humans. Animal stories also tell how things came to be the way they are or how animals got their appearance or characteristics. A story of the Seneca Indians, for example, says that the chipmunk's stripes were originally bear scratches.

Gods, Creators, and Heroes In some mythological traditions, the gods take on animal form. The ancient Egyptians portrayed their gods as animals or as humans with the heads of animals. **Bast** (pronounced BAST), for example, was a cat goddess, and **Horus** (pronounced HOHR-uhs) a hawk god. Although supernatural animals such as **Pegasus**, the winged horse of **Greek mythology**, were not gods themselves, they were often created, given power, or protected by the gods.

Some myths associate animals with the creation of the world. Asian and Native North American traditions place the earth on the back of an enormous turtle. Myths of Africa and elsewhere tell that the earth was formed from or supported by the body of a huge serpent. Some legends say that the earth's features, such as lakes or canyons, were carved by the digging of mythic beasts.

Animals are linked to human origins as well as to the origin of the world. Many Native American clans believed they were descended from animals, and the Yao people of southern China traced their origins to a dog ancestor. Animals also helped shape human existence by acting as messengers to the gods. An African myth tells that the gods sent two animals to Earth, one with a message of eternal life, one bringing death. The messenger of death arrived first, which explains why people die. The Pima Indians of North America say that a rattlesnake brought death into the world.

Animals can play a positive role as well, bringing people the gifts of civilization. Various African myths, for example, tell of a dog, chimpanzee, wasp, and praying mantis bringing fire to people. The Bambara people of Mali believe that a sacred antelope taught people to farm long ago. Zuni and Navajo myths show animals behaving heroically on behalf of people. In Chinese legends, monkeys perform brave deeds. In Mayan myth, they possess artistic talent, particularly in writing and sculpture.

Symbols Animals sometimes appear in myths and legends as symbols of certain characteristics they are believed to represent. Common phrases such as "sly as a fox" or "brave as a lion" are everyday examples of the practice of using animals to represent human qualities. The dog often appears as a symbol of loyalty in myths and legends, and the tiger stands for power and vitality. In **Celtic mythology**, the boar symbolized war, and its image was carved on helmets and coins. Many cultures have stories in which animal characters representing human qualities present moral lessons.

Animals can also be symbols of the gods. People traditionally saw owls as wise; therefore, **Athena**, the Greek goddess of wisdom, was often shown with an owl. Likewise, dolphins can represent the presence of the sea god **Poseidon**.

Tricksters Many myths feature animal **tricksters**, mischievous and unpredictable beings who use deceit, magic, or cleverness to fool others. Although some tricksters are just playing pranks, others act in harmful ways. Occasionally, the tricksters themselves wind up being tricked or trapped. Their limited magical powers may serve to show off the greater powers of the gods.

In Japanese legend, the kitsune are fox spirits who can take human form. Here a kitsune is betrayed when her shadow is seen to be that of a fox.
© MARY EVANS PICTURE LIBRARY/THE IMAGE WORKS.

In **Native American mythology**, the best-known trickster is the coyote, who has the power to take on human form. One of his favorite tricks involves masquerading as a hunter in order to sleep with the hunter's wife. Many African legends feature a trickster spider, tortoise, or hare that uses cunning to outwit larger or more powerful animals.

African slaves brought tales of the trickster hare to the United States, where it eventually became popular as the character **Brer Rabbit**.

Monsters From the great sea beast called **Leviathan** (pronounced luh-VYE-uh-thuhn) in the Bible to the mutant lizard Godzilla of modern science fiction movies, monstrous animals appear in many kinds of myths. Monsters represent our darkest fears: chaos, or disorder, and uncontrollable destruction. A monster is more than just a large or fierce animal. It is something abnormal, something that breaks the laws of society and the natural world.

An animal may be monstrous simply due to its abnormal size. The most dreadful monsters, however, do not correspond to anything known in the real world. Often they are hybrids, mixtures of different species, which represents another kind of blurring of natural boundaries. Dragons, for example, are usually shown as a snake or reptile with bat's wings and sometimes with a head resembling that of a horse. In some traditions, dragons have multiple heads or the ability to change shape.

Other hybrid creatures include the griffin, a creature with the head, forepart, and wings of an eagle and the body, hind legs, and tail of a lion. **Quetzalcoatl** (pronounced keht-sahl-koh-AHT-l), a god of Maya, Toltec, and **Aztec mythology**, is represented as a plumed serpent, a part bird, part snake hybrid. In addition, the pygmies of Central Africa tell stories about encounters with a living dinosaur, a beast the size of an elephant with a long neck and brownish-gray skin.

Some hybrids are human and animal combinations. The centaur (pronounced SEN-tawr) is half man, half horse; the Echidna (pronounced i-KID-nuh) is a snake woman; the **manticore** (pronounced MAN-ti-kor) is part human, part lion, part dragon; and the satyr (pronounced SAY-tuhr) is a man-like being with the lower body of a goat. In mythology, hybrid creatures often have qualities that are split between good and bad, much like their appearance.

Common Animals in Mythology Certain animals appear frequently in the myths and legends of different cultures, often with different meanings. Snakes or serpents, for example, can be helpful or harmful. The Romans regarded snake spirits as protection for their homes. The Hopi Indians, who live in a dry part of the American Southwest, have stories about a water snake that is associated with springs. Because the snake sheds its skin as it grows, some cultures see it as a symbol of rebirth and associate it with healing.

In the Bible, however, the snake is a treacherous creature that introduces **Adam and Eve** to sin. A Japanese myth tells of a huge snake with eight heads that holds a princess prisoner. Snakes and snake-like dragons play a similar evil guardian role in many other tales.

The bull is another animal that appears in many myths. It can represent either tremendous energy and power or frightening strength. In Celtic mythology, the bull was a sign of good fortune and fertility. In several Greek legends, bulls were associated with death and destruction. At different times, the hero **Theseus** (pronounced THEE-see-uhs) killed both a wild bull that was destroying farmers' fields and the **Minotaur**, a dangerous half-man, half-bull monster. Among Native Americans who traditionally survived by hunting buffalo, myths focus on the buffalo's fertility and generosity. The buffalo is also said to control love affairs and determine how many children a woman will bear. To the Celtic people, bulls stood for strength and power. Irish mythology tells of two famous beasts, the White-Horned Bull of Connacht (pronounced KAWHN-ut) and the Brown Bull of Ulster. The rulers of Connacht and Ulster each boasted of the size of their bulls; however, some said that the gods had sent the bulls to Ireland to cause trouble. Eventually, the two bulls met in a fierce battle that raged across all of Ireland. The Brown Bull won but then died. The death of the two magical bulls brought peace between Connacht and Ulster.

Dogs almost always appear in myths and legends in a positive light. Native American stories generally portray the dog as the symbol of friendship and loyalty. In Greek and **Roman mythology**, dogs often acted as guardians. The three-headed dog **Cerberus** (pronounced SUR-ber-uhs), for example, guarded the entrance to the underworld. Many cultures associated dogs with death as well as with protection. Both the ancient Egyptians and the Aztecs of Mexico believed that dogs guided the dead on their journey through the **afterlife**. Occasionally, dogs appear in negative roles, such as the hellhound Garm in **Norse mythology** or the fighting dogs belonging to the Greek goddess **Hecate** (pronounced HEK-uh-tee).

The goat is another animal with positive and negative qualities. Male goats are negatively linked with dangerous or uncontrolled sexual lust, while female goats appear as mother figures. In Greek mythology, a she-goat nursed the god **Zeus** when he was a baby boy. Goat images in mythology are often associated with sexuality and fertility.

Foxes in mythology are usually quick, cunning, and sneaky. Japanese legends tell of fox spirits called *kitsune* (pronounced keet-SOO-neh) who can turn themselves into people, are often deceitful, and have the powers of witches. In another example of the two-sided nature of animals, **Japanese mythology** also portrays the fox as the messenger of Inari (pronounced in-AHR-ee), the god of rice. The ancient Romans regarded foxes as fire demons, perhaps because of their reddish coats. In Christian mythology, the fox is associated with the devil.

The frog appears in many transformation stories, most likely because it goes through a transformation of its own, from tadpole to frog. Another animal that undergoes a physical transformation is the butterfly, which begins life as a caterpillar, rests in a cocoon, and emerges as a butterfly to spread its wings. The Greek word for butterfly, *psyche,* is also the word for soul, and in Greek mythology the butterfly was the symbol of the soul's transformation after the death of the body.

Mythological Animals in Context

The fact that animals play a role in the mythologies of all cultures demonstrates their universal importance to human society. Animals were and are an important source of food, labor, and even companionship to people everywhere. Domesticated animals such as one finds on a farm, in particular, were the backbone of agricultural societies, while more nomadic hunter societies relied on wild animals for food and for their skins. Although modern cultures continue to use animals for the same purposes as they did thousands of years ago, ancient cultures relied heavily on animals for survival, and lived closer to wild animals than people do today. This heavy reliance on, and physical closeness to, animals, resulted in a rich oral tradition in which animals both help and harm humans. They provide people with food, but they can also be dangerous. Animals represent the mystery and power of the natural world, which has the ability to create and destroy. Animals may serve as stand-ins for humans or human characteristics, as in the African and Native American trickster tales or the fables of the Greek storyteller Aesop. In some legends, animals perform heroic deeds or act as mediators or go-betweens for gods and humans. They may also be the source of the wisdom and power of a shaman, a person who has contact with the spiritual realm and uses magic to heal the members of his tribe.

Mythological Animals in Art, Literature, and Everyday Life

Mythological animals have always been a popular subject in art and literature, perhaps because they are often unlike any other creatures seen in the real world. This fascination with mythological creatures continues to this day, with modern fantasy stories such as C. S. Lewis's *The Chronicles of Narnia* (1950–1956), J. R. R. Tolkien's *The Lord of the Rings* trilogy (1954–1955), and J. K. Rowling's *Harry Potter* books (1997–2007) all containing creatures like those found in ancient myths.

Read, Write, Think, Discuss

Cultures typically developed myths around animals that were common to the area in which the people lived. For example, Native Americans developed myths about coyotes, deer, and bears, while Egyptians developed myths about crocodiles and cats. If you were to write a myth about an animal that represented your culture, which animal would you choose and what would the story be about?

SEE ALSO Anansi; Basilisk; Brer Rabbit; Centaurs; Cerberus; Dragons; George, St.; Gorgons; Griffins; Leviathan; Manticore; Minotaur; Pegasus; Sacrifice; Satyrs; Serpents and Snakes; Tricksters; Unicorns; Witches and Wizards

Antigone

Character Overview

In **Greek mythology**, Antigone (pronounced an-TIG-uh-nee) was the daughter of **Oedipus** (pronounced ED-uh-puhs), king of Thebes (pronounced THEEBZ), and his wife Jocasta (pronounced joh-KAS-tuh). A faithful daughter and sister, Antigone was caught between quarreling family members and was punished for her loyalty.

The story of Antigone is immortalized in the play *Antigone* by Greek playwright Sophocles (pronounced SOF-uh-kleez). It tells the tragic story of this young woman. In an earlier play by Sophocles, *Oedipus Rex,* Oedipus had unknowingly murdered his father and married his mother,

Nationality/Culture
Greek/Roman

Pronunciation
an-TIG-uh-nee

Alternate Names
None

Appears In
Sophocles' *Antigone,* Seneca the Younger's *Phoenissae,* Hyginus's *Fabulae*

Lineage
Daughter of Oedipus and Jocasta, King and Queen of Thebes

Jocasta. When they discovered what they had done, Jocasta hung herself and Oedipus blinded himself. His sons, Eteocles (pronounced i-TEE-uh-kleez) and Polynices (pronounced pol-uh-NYE-seez), drove Oedipus from Thebes and took over the kingdom.

Antigone and her sister Ismene (pronounced is-MEE-nee) accompanied their blind father on his wanderings around Greece. Meanwhile, Eteocles broke his promise to share power with Polynices and drove him from the kingdom as well. Polynices led an army against Thebes to regain the throne.

Their uncle, Creon (pronounced KREE-ahn), supported Eteocles in the conflict with his brother. An oracle (or person through which the gods communicated with humans) told Creon that whoever gave shelter to Oedipus would win the battle for Thebes. Creon therefore asked Oedipus, who had taken refuge in the city of Colonus, to return. When Oedipus refused, Creon sent soldiers to seize Antigone and Ismene to force their father to come back. **Theseus** (pronounced THEE-see-uhs), king of Athens, rescued Antigone and Ismene, but soon afterward Oedipus died and his daughters returned to Thebes.

Polynices attacked Thebes and in the battle that followed, the two brothers met in combat and killed each other. Creon became king. He gave Eteocles a hero's burial but refused to let anyone bury Polynices, whom he considered a traitor. Antigone, mindful of her duty to her brother, secretly crept out at night to bury Polynices. She was caught by Creon's soldiers and condemned to death for her disobedience. To avoid direct responsibility for her death, Creon ordered that Antigone be sealed alive in a cave with food and water. Creon's son Haemon (pronounced HEE-muhn), who was engaged to Antigone, pleaded unsuccessfully for her life.

A seer, or person who can see the future, then came to see Creon. He warned that the king had angered the gods by sealing up Antigone and refusing burial to Polynices. Creon immediately ordered that Polynices be buried and went to the cave to release Antigone. On opening the cave, however, he found that Antigone had hung herself. Haemon was overcome with grief. He tried to kill his father and then stabbed himself to death. When Creon's wife, **Eurydice** (pronounced yoo-RID-uh-see), learned of her son's suicide, she took her own life.

The Greek playwright Euripides (pronounced yoo-RIP-i-deez) tells a version of the story with a happier ending. In his play, Creon instructed Haemon to carry out Antigone's sentence. Haemon pretended to seal Antigone away as ordered but actually took her to the countryside. The couple stayed in hiding for many years, raising a son. After the son grew up, he went to Thebes to take part in an athletic event. There he stripped off his clothes to run in a race and revealed a birthmark that was found only on members of Antigone's family. Creon recognized the mark and sentenced Haemon and Antigone to death for disobeying his orders. The god **Dionysus** (pronounced deye-uh-NEYE-suhs), or, in some versions, the hero **Heracles** (known as Hercules to the Romans), pleaded with Creon to spare their lives. Creon agreed and the lovers were formally married.

Sophocles used the story of Antigone to comment on the conflict between the laws of the state and the laws of the gods. Creon's decree against burying Polynices is shown to be unjust and against the gods' wishes. Antigone's decision to perform her religious duty to her brother wins the sympathy of the audience.

Antigone in Context

The burial of the dead was an important practice in ancient Greece. Greeks believed that only by following proper burial procedure would the dead reach the **afterlife**. Burials were supposed to take place on the third day after death and were to be performed by a family member of the deceased. The preparation of the dead body was usually done by women, while the burial was done by men.

In the story of Antigone, Creon would normally be expected to bury his nephew Polynices. However, because Polynices is considered a traitor by Creon, the king forbids his burial. As Polynices's sister, Antigone feels a duty to perform the burial rite. When Creon punishes her for fulfilling her religious duty, he commits a double sin in Greek society: he first ignored his own duty to bury Polynices, and then he punishes someone else for trying to fulfill it. Although Greek rulers had tremendous power, they were not so powerful that they could ignore religious duty to serve their own political agendas without suffering consequences. The Greeks believed that violations of religious duty would result in destruction by angry gods, and so they believed that religious law was more important than political law.

Key Themes and Symbols

The name "Antigone" can be translated as "opposing family" or "against ancestors." This reflects Antigone's defiance against her uncle Creon, who has become both head of the family and the leader of Thebes.

Antigone could also be considered opposite in character to her ancestors. Unlike other members of her family, Antigone remains dedicated and loyal to her true family despite their quarrels with each other. She remains with her father after he is banished from Thebes by his sons. She also tries to secure a proper burial for her brother Polynices even though he is considered a traitor for his actions.

Antigone in Art, Literature, and Everyday Life

Sophocles and Euripides were the first of many writers to create works of art based on the story of Antigone. Among those who wrote plays about her were the European playwrights Jean Cocteau, Jean Anouilh, and Bertolt Brecht. Italian translations of the Greek plays were the basis for an opera by Christoph

Gluck in 1756, called *Antigono*. More recently, German composer Carl Orff wrote a "tragic play with music" about Antigone in 1949.

Read, Write, Think, Discuss

Antigone breaks a law of the state in order to care for her dead brother Polynices in the way she believes she must. Because we know of Antigone's devotion to her family, as well as the unfairness of the king's law regarding Polynices, it is easy to side with Antigone. In your opinion, should family traditions and beliefs be followed even when they result in breaking the law? Why or why not?

SEE ALSO Eurydice; Greek Mythology; Oedipus

Anubis

Character Overview

In the early days of ancient Egypt, Anubis (pronounced uh-NOO-bis), also known as Anpu, was the god of the dead. Later, when **Osiris** (pronounced oh-SYE-ris) took over this role, Anubis became the god who oversaw funerals. He was also the guardian of the **underworld**, or land of the dead, where he took the dead to the hall of judgment. Here he helped weigh each person's heart against the feather of truth before presenting the soul to Osiris.

Major Myths

Anubis was the son of the goddess Nephthys (pronounced NEF-this), who had tricked her brother Osiris into fathering her child. The goddess's husband, **Set**, hated Osiris and planned to murder the child when he was born. Nephthys therefore decided to abandon the infant at birth. She hid him in the marshes by the Nile River where he was found by **Isis** (pronounced EYE-sis), the wife of Osiris. Isis raised Anubis, and when he reached adulthood, he repaid her by becoming her protector.

Later, when Osiris set out to conquer the world, Anubis accompanied him. Osiris was murdered by his old enemy Set, who tore his body to pieces. Anubis helped find the pieces of Osiris's body and embalmed

Nationality/Culture
Egyptian

Pronunciation
uh-NOO-bis

Alternate Names
Anpu, Hermanubis

Appears In
The *Book of the Dead*

Lineage
Son of Nephthys and Osiris

The jackal-headed god of the dead, Anubis, weighed the hearts of the dead against the feather of truth while Ammit the Devourer watched. If the deceased did not pass the test, Ammit ate him. © CHARLES WALKER/TOPFOTO/THE IMAGE WORKS.

them, or preserved them so well that they never decayed. Because of his actions, Anubis is said to have performed the first Egyptian burial rites and to have introduced the practice of embalming the dead to Egyptian culture. The Greeks and the Romans also worshipped Anubis, whose name is actually the Greek form of the Egyptian name *Anpu.* Anubis was frequently merged with the similar Greek god **Hermes** (pronounced HUR-meez) and given the name Hermanubis.

Anubis in Context

Ancient Egyptians were experts at the practice of embalming, which involves preserving the remains of the dead so they last through the funeral or burial and beyond. The Egyptians developed an embalming process known as *mummification* in which a dead body is wrapped in strips of cloth and dried out for preservation. Ancient Egyptians believed that a person's body was still needed after death, since it transported the soul to the **afterlife**. For this reason, Anubis played a crucial role in the way ancient Egyptians dealt with death and the dead.

Key Themes and Symbols

Anubis is primarily associated with death and the dying. Images of Anubis depict him as a jackal, a type of wild dog, or as a man with the head of a jackal. Jackals prowled Egyptian cemeteries at night, looking for food and even eating corpses. The Egyptians believed that Anubis, in the form of a jackal, would keep real jackals away and protect the dead. In this way, Anubis represents a guardian and caretaker for Egyptians after they have died.

Anubis in Art, Literature, and Everyday Life

The image of Anubis appears on many ancient Egyptian tombs. In fact, the distinctive jackal-headed figure is one of the symbols most commonly identified with ancient Egypt. More recently, Anubis has appeared as a character in the television show *Stargate SG-1* (1997–2007).

Read, Write, Think, Discuss

Even though Anubis is considered a god of death and the guardian of the underworld, ancient Egyptians viewed him as a protector and guide. What does this suggest about the ancient Egyptian view of death and the afterlife? How do you think this is different from, or similar to, modern views on death?

SEE ALSO Egyptian Mythology; Isis; Osiris; Set

Aphrodite

Character Overview

The Greek goddess Aphrodite (pronounced af-ro-DYE-tee), one of the twelve Olympian deities, was associated with love, beauty, and fertility.

Nationality/Culture
Greek

Pronunciation
af-ro-DYE-tee

Alternate Names
Venus (Roman)

Appears In
Hesiod's *Theogony*, Homer's *Iliad*, Virgil's *Aeneid*

Lineage
Born of Uranus and the sea

The Romans later incorporated her into their pantheon, or collection of recognized gods and goddesses, and renamed her Venus.

Major Myths

According to one account, Aphrodite was born when the Titan **Cronus** cut off the sex organs of his father, **Uranus** (pronounced YOOR-uh-nuhs), and threw them into the sea. Aphrodite emerged fully grown from the foam (her name comes from *aphros,* the Greek word for foam) that gathered on the surface of the water. A different account of her birth makes her the daughter of the ruler of the gods, **Zeus** (pronounced ZOOS), and a minor goddess named Dione.

Aphrodite's connection with love is reflected in the numerous stories about her romantic affairs. She was married to **Hephaestus** (pronounced hi-FES-tuhs), the god of **fire** and blacksmiths. She had frequent love affairs and children with various other gods, including **Ares** (pronounced AIR-eez), **Hermes** (pronounced HUR-meez), **Poseidon** (pronounced poh-SYE-dun), and **Dionysus** (pronounced dye-uh-NYE-suhs), which angered her jealous husband. Among Aphrodite's many children were Deimos (pronounced DYE-mos; Greek for "terror"); Phobos (pronounced FOH-bos; Greek for "fear"), fathered by Ares; and Eryx (pronounced ERR-iks), the son of Poseidon. She was also the mother of the Roman hero **Aeneas**, whom she had with the shepherd Anchises.

The handsome youth **Adonis** (pronounced uh-DON-is) was another of Aphrodite's great loves. **Persephone** (pronounced per-SEF-uh-nee), the goddess of the **underworld**, also developed a passion for Adonis when he entered the underworld after being killed by a boar. Adonis' death did not dull Aphrodite's affection for him, and a bitter feud between the two goddesses erupted. Zeus resolved the conflict by instructing the youth to divide his time between them.

Aphrodite's role as the goddess of beauty was one of the factors that led to the start of the Trojan War. Zeus forced the Trojan prince Paris to decide which of three goddesses—**Hera**, **Athena**, or Aphrodite—was the fairest. Each goddess tried to bribe Paris with generous gifts, but he found Aphrodite's offer—to give him the most beautiful woman in the world—the best. Paris declared Aphrodite the fairest of the goddesses, and she kept her promise by helping him gain the love of **Helen**, the wife of King Menelaus (pronounced men-uh-LAY-uhs) of Sparta. Paris took Helen to Troy with him, and the Greeks' attempts to reclaim her resulted in the Trojan War.

Aphrodite continued to influence events during the ten years of the war. At various stages during the conflict she assisted the Trojan soldiers, particularly Paris. Meanwhile, Hera and Athena, who were still offended by Paris's choice of Aphrodite as the fairest, came to the aid of the Greeks.

Aphrodite in Context

The Greeks added Aphrodite to their pantheon later than the other gods. It is likely that the Greeks adopted Aphrodite from Eastern cultures with similar goddesses, such as the goddess Innana in ancient Sumer, the goddess **Ishtar** in ancient Babylonia, and the Canaanite goddess Astarte from ancient Syria. Aphrodite and Astarte both share similar myths regarding their attachment to a handsome young lover (Adonis in the Greek tradition, and Tammuz in the Canaanite tradition) who dies young but is allowed to divide his time between the underworld and the world of the living. This story connects Aphrodite as a fertility goddess with a vegetation god, whose cycle in and out of the world of the living represents the cycle of crops.

The ancient Greeks placed great importance on physical beauty because they believed the physical body to be a reflection of the mind and spirit. A beautiful person, according to the ancient Greeks, was more likely to have more desirable mental skills and personality traits. This is very different from more modern views on beauty, and shows that the ancient Greek focus of physical appearance was not quite as superficial as it appears.

Key Themes and Symbols

Throughout the Western world, Aphrodite is recognized as the symbol of love and beauty. But there are different interpretations of Aphrodite based on two different versions of her birth: as Aphrodite Urania—born from the sky god Uranus—she is a celestial figure, a goddess of spiritual love; as Aphrodite Pandemos—born from the union of Zeus and the goddess Dione—she is a goddess of love, lust, and pure physical satisfaction. Aphrodite is often associated with seafoam and seashells because of her origins, but she is also linked with doves, roses, swans, dolphins, and sparrows.

Aphrodite in Art, Literature, and Everyday Life

Aphrodite appears in the works of many ancient writers. The legend of her birth is told in Hesiod's *Theogony*. Aphrodite and her son Aeneas (pronounced i-NEE-uhs) are central to the action of Virgil's epic poem, the ***Aeneid***. The Greek playwright Euripides (pronounced yoo-RIP-i-deez) included the story of the judgment of Paris in his play *The Trojan Women,* and the Greek poet Homer described her role in the Trojan War in the ***Iliad***.

Aphrodite was the subject of the most famous work by the Greek sculptor Praxiteles (pronounced prak-SIT-uh-leez), who completed the *Aphrodite of Cnidos* in about 350 BCE. Although this statue is now lost, it is known through the many copies that were made during Roman times. Aphrodite was also the focus of one of Renaissance painter Sandro Botticelli's most famous creations, *The Birth of Venus* (1482–1486).

Aphrodite and her Roman counterpart Venus continue to represent the ideals of feminine beauty in modern Western culture; the name "Venus" is even used to market a brand of razors for women. She has appeared as a character in films, such as *The Adventures of Baron Munchausen* (1988), and on television as a character on the series *Xena: Warrior Princess* (1995–2001) and *Hercules: The Legendary Journeys* (1995–1999).

Read, Write, Think, Discuss

The ancient Greeks believed that physical beauty was important because it reflected an inner beauty. How do you think modern views on beauty compare to the ancient Greek perspective? In the modern world, are people who are considered beautiful also generally thought to be smart, friendly, or spiritual?

SEE ALSO Adonis; Aeneas; *Aeneid, The*; Ares; Cronus; Greek Mythology

Apollo

Character Overview

The most widely worshipped of the Greek gods, Apollo (pronounced uh-POL-oh) was the son of **Zeus** (pronounced ZOOS) and Leto (pronounced

Nationality/Culture
Greek/Roman

Pronunciation
uh-POL-oh

Alternate Names
Phoebus, Apulu (Etruscan)

Appears In
Homer's *Iliad*, Ovid's *Metamorphoses*, Hesiod's *Theogony*, Hyginus's *Fabulae*

Lineage
Son of Zeus and Leto

LEE-toh). He was also the twin brother of **Artemis** (pronounced AHR-tuh-miss), the goddess of the hunt. Apollo had many roles in **Greek mythology**, including god of the **sun**, god of the arts (especially music, poetry, and dance), god of medicine, protector of herdsmen and their flocks, and god of prophecy or predictions. His oracle at **Delphi** (pronounced DEL-fye) where humans could communicate with the gods through an appointed person, was the most famous in the world, and his reputation spread far beyond Greek culture.

Major Myths

According to legend, Apollo was born on the Greek island of Delos (pronounced DEE-loss) and grew to adulthood in just four days. To escape the island, he changed himself into a dolphin and caused a great storm on the sea. Apollo then threw himself on the deck of a ship in trouble and led it safely to shore. Having reached the mainland, Apollo set off for an important oracle of **Gaia** (pronounced GAY-uh), the earth goddess. A monstrous serpent named Pytho (pronounced PYE-thoh) not only guarded the place but also spoke the oracle's prophecies. Apollo killed Pytho and took the oracle for himself. The name of the site was called Delphi because Apollo had become a dolphin (*delphis* in Greek) in order to reach it. Delphi became the most famous and frequently visited oracle in the ancient world. Its location was considered to be the geographic center of the earth. The oracle's words were inspired by Apollo and delivered by a local female elder. She was called the Pythia (pronounced PITH-ee-uh) in honor of Pytho. As she spoke, priests interpreted her prophecies and wrote them down. The priests of Apollo claimed to be descended from the sailors aboard the ship that Apollo had led to safety in the storm.

Apollo's form was considered the ideal of male beauty; therefore, he had many love affairs and fathered many children. Despite his attractiveness, there are numerous stories of Apollo's failure to win the heart of a woman he desired. There are more stories of lovers being unfaithful to him.

In one story, Apollo fell in love with **Cassandra**, daughter of King Priam of Troy. In order to win her favor Apollo gave Cassandra the gift of prophecy. When she rejected him, Apollo punished her by declaring that her prophecies would be accurate but that no one would believe her. In another story, he courted the nymph (female nature god) Sinope (pronounced SEE-noh-pee), who asked him to grant her a favor before she accepted his proposal. When Apollo agreed, she asked to remain a virgin until her death.

One of Apollo's tragic loves was Daphne (pronounced DAF-nee), daughter of the river god Peneus (pronounced puh-NEE-uhs). Apollo fell in love with Daphne, but she did not return his affection. When Apollo chased her through the woods, she became so frightened that she cried out for her father to save her. Peneus turned Daphne into a laurel tree so that she could avoid Apollo's advances. The disappointed Apollo broke off a branch of the laurel and twisted it into a wreath to wear on his head in memory of Daphne. Thereafter, the laurel tree became sacred to Apollo's cult, devoted worshippers of the god. The laurel wreath also became a mark of honor to be given to poets, victors, and winners of athletic contests.

Some of Apollo's romantic misfortunes involved animals that became associated with him. One myth explains how the crow's feathers turned from white to black. In it, Apollo asked the crow to watch over the princess Coronis who was pregnant with his son; nevertheless, the crow failed to prevent Coronis from having an affair with another man. Angry at the crow, Apollo turned its feathers from white to black. He then asked his sister Artemis to kill Coronis. When Coronis lay burning on the funeral pyre (a large pile of burning wood used in some cultures to cremate a dead body), Apollo pulled his unborn son Asclepius (pronounced uh-SKLEE-pee-uhs) from her body. The boy later became the god of healing.

Apollo in Context

The worship of Apollo was widespread not only in Greece but also throughout the ancient world. Shrines could be found in places from Egypt to Anatolia (now northwestern Turkey). The Romans built their first temple to Apollo in 432 BCE, and he became a favorite Roman god. The Roman emperor Augustus was a devoted worshiper because the battle of Actium, in which he gained political supremacy, was fought near a temple of Apollo.

The worship of Apollo began outside of Greece. Early cults associated with the god developed in Asia Minor and in the lands north of Greece. Several tales link him to the city of Troy. One credits him with helping the sea god **Poseidon** (pronounced poh-SYE-dun) build the walls of Troy.

Scholars think that Apollo's original role may have been as protector of herdsmen and shepherds. He is often pictured holding a lyre, which is

a type of harp, and shepherds were known for playing music to pass their idle hours. Apollo's identification as god of music, archery, and medicine came after his oracle was established at Delphi. Only much later did he become the sun god.

Apollo represents "the light," both literal (the sun) and metaphorical, as in the light of reason and the intellect. Apollo's popularity clearly shows how important learning and the intellect were to the Greeks. They valued their soldiers, to be sure, but they also valued their thinkers. Philosophers, inventors, scientists, and artists all occupied places of honor in Greek society.

Key Themes and Symbols

To the ancient Greeks, Apollo represented order, reason, beauty, and self-control. Apollo is typically portrayed holding a bow and arrow, symbols of his role as the god of death and disease. Apollo is also often depicted holding a harp or lyre, representing his role as god of music and the arts or of shepherds. Another common symbol of Apollo is a tripod, a three-legged stool or altar normally reserved for oracles to use while communicating with the gods and predicting the future. Apollo was also associated with the wolf, the dolphin, the raven, the serpent, and other animals.

Apollo in Art, Literature, and Everyday Life

Like many important figures in myth and legend, Apollo is a favorite subject of art and literature. He first appears in Greek literature in the *Iliad*, Homer's epic, or long, grand-scale poem about the Trojan War. In the poem, Apollo is Troy's most consistent and enthusiastic champion against the Greeks. The *Iliad* opens with a fight between Apollo and **Agamemnon** (pronounced ag-uh-MEM-non), who took captive the daughter of Apollo's Trojan priest. Despite the priest's pleas and offers of ransom, Agamemnon refuses to return the girl. As punishment, Apollo sends a plague on the Greek army. Ultimately, Apollo kills the great Greek hero **Achilles** (pronounced uh-KILL-eez) by guiding the flight of an arrow shot by the Trojan warrior Paris into Achilles' heel, the only vulnerable spot on his body.

Ancient sculptures show Apollo as a handsome youth. One of the most famous is the *Apollo Belvedere,* a marble version of an ancient bronze statue found in Rome. The great German artist Albrecht Dürer used the proportions of the statue to create his "ideal male" figure. Apollo is featured in the poetry of Percy Bysshe Shelley and Algernon Charles Swinburne. He also served as the inspiration for a ballet by Igor Stravinsky. More than twenty operas have featured Apollo as a central figure.

"Apollo" was also chosen as the name of the U.S. space program that resulted in humankind's first successful moon landing.

Read, Write, Think, Discuss

The oracle at Delphi contained an important stone known as an *omphalos*. Using your library, the Internet, or other resources, research the *omphalos*. What is it? What does it represent? Why was it important to the ancient Greeks?

SEE ALSO Achilles; Agamemnon; Cassandra; Delphi; Greek Mythology; *Iliad, The*; Zeus

Arachne

Character Overview

In **Greek mythology**, Arachne (pronounced uh-RAK-nee) was a peasant girl who became an expert spinner and weaver of cloth. No human could spin or weave as well as Arachne, or produce finer cloth. She became famous throughout Greece for her singular talent.

Arachne grew arrogant about her skill, boasting that she was better than **Athena** (pronounced uh-THEE-nuh), the goddess of wisdom, who invented spinning and weaving. At first, Athena laughed off Arachne's claims. Then many people began to believe them and stayed away from Athena's temples and from festivals held in her honor. Athena decided she had to teach the boastful girl a lesson.

Disguised as an old woman, the goddess came to earth and challenged Arachne to a weaving contest. Athena wove scenes portraying the power of the gods and the fate of humans who dared to challenge them into her cloth. Arachne's tapestry contained scenes of the romantic misadventures of the gods, a subject which Athena felt made the gods look foolish. Arachne's work was equal to Athena's, and the goddess was impressed by its quality. However, Arachne could not resist boasting that her weaving surpassed that of Athena.

At that moment, the goddess revealed her true identity. She tore apart Arachne's weaving and beat the girl with the shuttle from her

Nationality/Culture
Greek/Roman

Pronunciation
uh-RAK-nee

Alternate Names
None

Appears In
Ovid's *Metamorphoses*

Lineage
Daughter of Idmon

weaving loom. In despair, Arachne took a rope and hung herself. Out of pity, Athena changed the rope into a web and turned Arachne into a spider, an animal known for its spinning and weaving skills. Today the class of animals to which spiders belong is called Arachnida (pronounced uh-RAK-nid-uh), after the girl who could weave so well.

Arachne in Context

In ancient Greece, all fabrics were created through handspinning and weaving. Almost every woman, regardless of social class, was expected to know how to spin and weave. For many women, weaving was as much a part of daily life as cooking or cleaning. Greek fabrics were often woven from wool that had been sheared from sheep, cleaned, and spun into yarn.

Key Themes and Symbols

Arachne is often associated with spiders and weaving looms because of her background. Like many Greek myths, Arachne's story can be seen as a warning against hubris, or overconfidence and arrogance about one's abilities. Although the goddess Athena was willing to admit that Arachne's work was as good as her own, Arachne insisted that her own work was better, which led to her downfall.

Arachne in Art, Literature, and Everyday Life

Arachne is often depicted as part-human and part-spider. One of the most famous images of Arachne is Gustave Doré's engraved illustration for Dante's *Divine Comedy*. In the *Divine Comedy*, Arachne is mentioned as one of the residents of Purgatory as penance for her sin of pride.

More recently, the name Arachne has been used to represent a superheroine, formerly known as Spider-Woman, in several Marvel Comics series. "Arachne" is also the name given to an Internet web browser, as well as an archeological database.

Read, Write, Think, Discuss

Arachne was turned into a spider, a creature that shared her astounding skill at weaving. Think about your own skills and interests. Based on those, what creature do you think you most resemble? Why?

SEE ALSO Athena; Greek Mythology

Ares

Character Overview

In **Greek mythology** Ares (pronounced AIR-eez), the son of **Zeus** (pronounced ZOOS) and **Hera** (pronounced HAIR-uh), waged battle as

Nationality/Culture
Greek

Pronunciation
AIR-eez

Alternate Names
Mars (Roman)

Appears In
Homer's *Iliad*, Ovid's *Metamorphoses*, Hesiod's *Theogony*

Lineage
Son of Zeus and Hera

the god of war. The Romans linked him with Mars, their war god, although the two gods were quite different in character. Ares liked to storm around the battlefields accompanied by his sister Eris (pronounced EE-ris), the goddess of discord, disagreement or lack of harmony; Enyo, a war goddess; and his twin sons Phobos (pronounced FOH-bos; Greek for "fear") and Deimos (pronounced DYE-mos; Greek for "terror"). He represented everything that was bad about warfare, such as **fire** and bloodlust, and nothing that was good, such as the glory of victory; despite Ares' fierce behavior, the goddess **Athena** often defeated him in battle.

The Roman version known as Mars, on the other hand, was a much more balanced representation of warfare. Mars was originally a fertility god, associated with spring and vegetation. The Romans celebrated major festivals to Mars in the spring, which also signalled the start of military campaigns. The founders of Rome, **Romulus and Remus**, were thought to be the sons of Mars.

Major Myths

Ares was not a major figure in Greek mythology, but some stories tell of his love affairs with the goddess **Aphrodite** and with human women. His sons became kings, warriors, and in one case a bandit. In one myth, **Poseidon**'s (pronounced poh-SYE-dun) son raped one of Ares' daughters, so Ares struck the youth dead. Poseidon insisted that the gods try Ares for murder at the place where the rape and the killing took place, on a hill outside the city of Athens. The gods found Ares not guilty. From that time on, Athenians referred to the hill outside their city as the Areopagus (pronounced ar-ee-OP-uh-guhs), or "Ares' hill."

Ares in Context

Generally described as bloodthirsty, cruel, and a troublemaker, Ares was not a popular god. Yet the people of ancient Greece saw war as an unpleasant but unavoidable fact of life: they were in a near-constant state of war with various neighbors. While they valued bravery and heroism, they also saw that hate, pain, and rage were also involved in battle. Ares represents that brutal battle-lust. It is important to note that Athena often bests Ares, which demonstrates the importance the Greeks laid on cool-headedness and honor over rage.

Key Themes and Symbols

Although Ares is usually associated with war, the ancient Greeks often
viewed Ares as the god of savage or violent warfare. In contrast, they
viewed Athena, half-sister of Ares, as the goddess of strategic and heroic
warfare. Vultures, who feed on the flesh of the dead on battlefields, were
regarded as Ares' sacred birds. Barn owls and woodpeckers were also
associated with Ares. Ares also represented **sacrifice**; aside from the

humans sacrificed in battle in Ares' name, animals were also sometimes sacrificed at his temples for good favor prior to the beginning of battle.

Ares in Art, Literature, and Everyday Life

Since Ares was not often the subject of worship, he is not featured as much as other Greek gods in sculpture and other ancient art. When shown, Ares is often portrayed holding a shield and a spear, his weapon of choice. In modern times, Ares has appeared as a major villain in both DC Comics and Marvel Comics. He also appears as a motorcycle-riding tough guy in Rick Riordan's 2005 *The Lightning Thief.* In the novel the young demigod Percy Jackson must fight Ares; he wins by outwitting the angry god.

Read, Write, Think, Discuss

The ancient Greeks make a distinction between savage and brutal warfare, represented by Ares, and strategic and noble warfare, represented by Athena. In your opinion, can all wars be classified easily into one of these two categories? Does one of the two gods more closely match your opinion of war? If so, which one and why?

SEE ALSO Athena; Greek Mythology; Zeus

Argonauts

Nationality/Culture
Greek/Roman

Pronunciation
AHR-guh-nawts

Alternate Names
None

Appears In
Apollonius Rhodius's
Argonautica

Lineage
Varied

Character Overview

In **Greek mythology**, the Argonauts (pronounced AHR-guh-nawts) were a band of **heroes** who sailed with **Jason** in his quest for the **Golden Fleece**. Their journey took them on numerous adventures and required the assistance of many different gods. Among the Argonauts were the sons of kings and of gods. According to some sources, one of the Argonauts was a woman, the huntress **Atalanta** (pronounced at-uh-LAN-tuh).

The Quest for the Fleece Jason was the son of Aeson, the king of Iolcus (pronounced ee-AHL-kuhs). When Aeson was overthrown by his brother Pelias, he sent Jason to be raised by the wise centaur (half-man, half-horse) called Chiron (pronounced KYE-ron). Later Jason returned to Iolcus to claim the throne. Pelias agreed to give it to him if he first found and brought back the Golden Fleece from the Kingdom of Colchis, which Pelias knew to be an almost impossible task.

The Golden Fleece was the hide of a golden ram sent by the gods to save Phrixus (pronounced FRIK-suhs) and Helle (pronounced HEL-ee), two royal children of the land of Iolcus. The children's lives were endangered by their stepmother. As the ram carried them to safety, Helle fell into the sea and drowned. The area where she fell became known as Hellespont. Her brother Phrixus reached Colchis safely. There he sacrificed the ram to **Zeus** (pronounced ZOOS). The fleece was hung on a tree in a grove sacred to **Ares**, guarded by a serpent that never slept.

Jason ordered a ship, the *Argo,* to be built and sent messengers throughout Greece to ask others to join him in his quest for the Golden Fleece. After assembling a group of fifty heroes, Jason set off. The Argonauts' first adventure happened on Lemnos, an island populated only by women. As a result of a dispute between husbands and wives, the women had killed all the men. The women received the Argonauts with great hospitality, and the heroes began to forget their quest; however, one of the Argonauts stood firm. This was **Heracles** (known as Hercules by the Romans), a hero known for his physical strength. Heracles persuaded the other Argonauts to return to the ship and their journey continued.

In another adventure, Heracles defended the *Argo* against six-armed **giants** who attacked the ship while the others were on land. Later, in a rowing contest, Heracles broke his oar. While cutting wood for a new oar, his squire, or male attendant, was kidnapped by a water nymph, or female nature deity. Heracles went in search of the boy and was eventually left behind by the Argonauts.

When the heroes stopped at the land of the Bebryces (pronounced be-BRYE-seez), the king, Amycus (pronounced AM-i-kuhs), challenged them, as he did all visitors, to a fight to the death. Pollux (pronounced PAHL-uhks), the son of Zeus, took up the challenge and killed Amycus.

The Argonauts then stopped to see Phineus (pronounced FIN-ee-us), the blind king of Thynia (pronounced thih-NEE-uh). Phineus was a prophet (a person able to see the plans of the gods), and the travelers needed advice on how to proceed. Phineus agreed to help them if they would rid him of the **Harpies**, fierce, part-woman, part-bird creatures who stole and spoiled his food. Jason ordered a feast to be prepared.

*Model of the **Argo**, the ship used by Jason and the Argonauts.* SCALA/ART RE-SOURCE, NY.

When the Harpies arrived to ruin the feast, two of the Argonauts, Calais (pronounced kuh-LAY-us) and Zetes (pronounced ZEE-teez; they were winged sons of Boreas, the North Wind) pursued them. Eventually, Zeus sent a message that the Harpies should be spared but that they should also leave Phineus in peace.

After reaching the entrance to the Black Sea, the Argonauts had to go through the Symplegades (pronounced sim-PLE-gah-deez). These were huge rocks that crashed together at random intervals, destroying any ship that tried to sail through them. Following Phineus's advice, the Argonauts released a dove and watched its course as it flew between the rocks. The dove made the passage, losing only a single tail feather when the rocks crashed together. As soon as the rocks began to part, the Argonauts pulled hard on their oars, following the path of the dove. When they had almost passed through, a great wave held them back. At that point, the goddesses **Athena** and **Hera** gave them a push and the ship made it to safety. Forever after, the Symplegades remained separated.

After more adventures, the Argonauts finally reached Colchis. Jason and several companions went to the court of King Aeëtes (pronounced aye-EE-teez) to request the Golden Fleece. The first to see Jason was **Medea** (pronounced me-DEE-uh), the king's daughter. Hera, who sponsored Jason's quest, asked fellow Olympian **Aphrodite** (pronounced af-ro-DYE-tee), the goddess of love, for her help. Aphrodite agreed and made Medea fall in love with Jason. Medea was a witch; therefore she was able to help Jason with the difficulties ahead.

Aeëtes had no intention of handing over the Golden Fleece, but he pretended to agree if Jason could pass several trials. Jason was to yoke two fire-breathing bulls to a plow, then plant a field full of dragon's teeth. As each dragon's tooth was planted, a fully armored warrior would spring up, which Jason would then have to kill. Medea gave Jason a magic ointment that he rubbed on himself to protect him from the fiery bulls. Next she told Jason to throw a boulder in the midst of the soldiers to confuse them and make them fight one another. Then he would have to fight only the survivors. Following her directions, Jason succeeded in completing the trials.

Aeëtes told Jason he would hand over the Fleece the next day, but Jason and Medea did not believe him. Promising to marry her, Jason once again asked for Medea's help. That night, she led him to the sacred grove and put the serpent to sleep with her magic. Jason easily took the Fleece and, with Medea and the Argonauts, set sail back across the Black Sea.

The Return Home Accounts of the Argonauts' journey home vary. According to the writer Apollonius Rhodius (pronounced ah-poh-LOH-nee-us ROW-dee-us), Medea's brother Apsyrtus (pronounced ap-SUR-tuhs) blocked the mouth of the Black Sea so the Argonauts had to find a different route back to Iolcus. Several versions of the legend agree that the heroes crossed the Black Sea to the Danube River. After sailing up the Danube, they traveled along various rivers before reaching the Mediterranean Sea. Some sources say the Argonauts went north to the Baltic Sea. Others relate that they followed the Rhine River to the Atlantic Ocean, or that they reached the Adriatic Sea. At the entrance to the Adriatic, they met Apsyrtus, who tried to convince Jason to give up Medea. Jason refused and killed Apsyrtus.

A Magic Ship

Jason's ship, the *Argo*, was made from the wood of a sacred oak and had the ability to think, to speak, and even to predict the future. The ship had one oar for each of the Argonauts, who rowed themselves to their adventures. When it was first built, the *Argo* refused to go into the sea until the musician Orpheus sang to it and played his lyre. During the quest, the ship traveled under the protection of Hera, Athena, and Apollo. Afterward, the *Argo* was dedicated to Poseidon and placed near his temple in Corinth. Eventually, the gods turned the ship into a constellation in the sky.

The Argonauts sailed up the Po River and down the Rhone. Having almost reached Greece, the *Argo* was blown off course to Libya. There a great wave stranded the crew in the desert. On the advice of the gods, the Argonauts carried the ship across the desert until the sea god Triton (pronounced TRY-tun) helped them launch it back on the Mediterranean.

As they sailed past the island of Crete, Talos (pronounced TAY-lohs), the bronze man appointed by King Minos to protect the island, threw rocks at the Argonauts. Medea responded by killing Talos with her witchcraft. The Argonauts' adventures continued. Nearing Greece, the ship was enveloped in a darkness so great they lost their way. **Apollo** sent a blazing arrow that showed them the way to an island where they could wait until the light returned.

At last, the *Argo* arrived home in Iolcus. The Argonauts were honored throughout Greece, and many noble families later claimed to be descended from them. Even though Jason presented Pelias with the Golden Fleece, he never became king.

Argonauts in Context

Over the centuries, many scholars have attempted to trace the route of the Argonauts as described by Homer and other writers. According to the story, the Argonauts began in Greece and ended up on the eastern shore of the Black Sea, in a region now known as Georgia. Many of the other places mentioned along the way, however, are not as easily identified. Historians are divided as to whether or not the fantastical journey of the Argonauts is meant to have occurred entirely in real places, or whether some of the locations were made up by the storytellers. Most ancient Greeks never traveled more than a handful of miles from their place of birth; the tales of the Argonauts both satisfied their desire to hear of exotic foreign lands, and cautioned them against wandering too far from what the Greeks considered civilized areas. The ancient Greeks were a sea-going people, and Jason and his crew represented for them the courage and curiosity required of sailors and explorers.

Key Themes and Symbols

The Argonauts symbolize the willingness to embrace adventure. When Jason puts out a call for heroes to join him on his quest, he gathers a variety of people who all seek excitement or glory. Each Argonaut leaves behind a safe, stable life in exchange for great dangers, the lure of riches, and the promise of new experiences.

Argonauts in Art, Literature, and Everyday Life

Many writers have been inspired by the subject of the Argonauts and Jason's quest for the Golden Fleece. Among the ancient Greek works are Pindar's *Pythian Ode*, Apollonius Rhodius's *Argonautica*, and Euripides' play *Medea*. The Roman poet Ovid mentioned the Argonauts in the *Metamorphoses*. In the Middle Ages, Chaucer retold the story in the *Legend of Good Women*, and in the 1800s, William Morris wrote the long narrative poem *Life and Death of Jason*. Robert Graves's novel *The Golden Fleece* was published in 1944, and John Gardner's *Jason and Medeia* was published in 1973.

The story of the Argonauts has also served as the basis for many films, most notably the 1963 movie *Jason and the Argonauts,* which featured groundbreaking visual effects by Ray Harryhausen.

Read, Write, Think, Discuss

The journey of the Argonauts can be described as a quest: they are searching for the location of a certain magical item that will restore Jason to his proper place as king of Iolcus. Can you think of another book, movie, or video game that also has a "quest" story structure? How is it similar to the tale of Jason and the Argonauts? How is it different?

SEE ALSO Atalanta; Harpies; Hera; Heracles; Jason; Medea

Ariadne

Nationality/Culture
Greek/Roman

Pronunciation
ar-ee-AD-nee

Alternate Names
None

Appears In
Hesiod's *Theogony*

Lineage
Daughter of Minos and
Pasiphaë

Character Overview

In **Greek mythology**, Ariadne (pronounced ar-ee-AD-nee) was the daughter of King Minos (pronounced MYE-nuhs) and Queen Pasiphaë (pronounced pa-SIF-ah-ee) of Crete. She fell in love with the Athenian hero **Theseus** (pronounced THEE-see-uhs) when he came to Crete. Theseus was one of a group of youths and maidens who were sent from Athens to be fed to the **Minotaur**. Half bull and half man, the Minotaur was kept in a maze called the Labyrinth. Before Theseus entered it, Ariadne helped him by giving him a ball of yarn. He used the yarn to leave a trail by which he could find his way out. Theseus succeeded in killing the Minotaur and escaping the Labyrinth. Ariadne then fled with Theseus when he sailed back to Athens.

There are different versions of the rest of Ariadne's story. In one, she was abandoned by Theseus on the island of Naxos (pronounced NAK-suhs) while she slept on the shore. Another suggests that Theseus did not abandon her, but was swept out to sea by a storm. Afterward, **Dionysus** (pronounced dye-uh-NYE-suhs) found Ariadne on the shore and decided to make her his wife. In yet another variation, after arriving on Naxos, Ariadne was killed by **Artemis** (pronounced AHR-tuh-miss), and then found by Dionysus, who asked **Zeus** (pronounced ZOOS) to make her immortal (able to live forever), so he could marry her. Dionysus and Ariadne were married on Naxos. Two festivals were held in honor of Ariadne: one celebrating her marriage and one mourning her death. The couple had three sons.

Ariadne in Context

Ariadne's parents were the rulers of Crete, the largest of the Greek islands. The Minoan civilization of Crete flourished from approximately 2600 BCE until 1400 BCE, making it the oldest known civilization in Europe. Excavations at Knossos have revealed a large, complex building that may have served as a palace or ruling center for Minos and other leaders of Crete. In addition, archaeologists have found some human remains that support the idea that the Minoans may have performed human sacrifices like those mentioned in Ariadne's story. The Athenian

Ariadne on the beach at Naxos. THE BRIDGEMAN ART LIBRARY/GETTY IMAGES.

Greeks viewed the Minoan culture as older and, in some ways, more powerful than their own. The tale of Ariadne's family and their Minotaur explained why the Minoans were able to secure tribute from Athenian Greeks.

Key Themes and Symbols

One item often associated with Ariadne is a ball of yarn or fleece, like the one she gave to Theseus so he could find his way out of the Labyrinth. In art, Ariadne is often portrayed sleeping near the seashore, as Dionysus is said to have discovered her. She has also been associated with the Corona Borealis constellation of stars.

Ariadne in Art, Literature, and Everyday Life

Ariadne was popularized in many ancient sculptures, usually with her husband Dionysus. The pair also appeared in paintings by artists such as Titian and Guido Reni. More recently, Ariadne has served as the subject for numerous operas, including the 1912 opera *Ariadne on Naxos* by Richard Strauss. In studies of logic, the term "Ariadne's thread" refers to a method of problem-solving that results in multiple possible solutions, such as one used to determine the correct path through a maze.

Read, Write, Think, Discuss

In the myth of Ariadne, Theseus, and the Minotaur, who do you think is the greater hero, Theseus or Ariadne? Think of at least two reasons that support your choice.

SEE ALSO Dionysus; Minotaur; Theseus

Ark of the Covenant

Nationality/Culture
Judeo-Christian

Alternate Names
None

Appears In
The Christian Bible, the Qur'an

Myth Overview

The Ark of the Covenant was the gold-covered wooden box that held the tablets on which the Ten Commandments were written. Its lid, called the Mercy Seat, had two gold statues of cherubim, or **angels**, kneeling in prayer. The Ark was carried by placing poles through the two rings on each side.

According to the Bible, the Hebrew people lived in slavery in Egypt until they were led to freedom by Moses, whom God told to take them to the Promised Land. God promised to protect the Hebrew people on their journey, and they agreed to obey His commandments. During their years of wandering in search of the Promised Land, the Hebrews set up a tabernacle, or house of worship, for the Ark at each stopping point. This was a tent with an inner room, called the Holy of Holies, where the Ark was placed. It was believed that the spirit of God dwelled there and sat upon the Mercy Seat. The Ark eventually guided the Hebrews to Canaan (pronounced KAIN-ahn), the Promised Land.

According to the first book of Samuel in the Bible, the Philistines, or natives of ancient Philistia, captured the Ark and carried it from town to town. Wherever the Ark went, people were struck with plagues. On the advice of Philistine priests and soothsayers, the Ark was placed on a cart and sent back to Canaan.

King David of Israel had the Ark moved to Jerusalem. His son, King Solomon, ordered a great temple to be built and placed the Ark within its Holy of Holies. In the 500s BCE, the Babylonians conquered the Hebrews and took the treasures from the temple. The fate of the Ark is not explained in the Bible, but it was probably lost or destroyed.

The Ark of the Covenant in Context

Some modern scholars and archaeologists believe that the Ark may have survived, at least partially, and have attempted to figure out its current location. Suspected locations include several sites throughout the Middle East and North Africa. Some even think that the Ark may have ended up in England. Although many possible locations have been offered, the Ark has never been located. The Ethiopian Orthodox Church in Axum (pronounced AK-sum), a city in northern Ethiopia, claims that it possesses the Ark of the Covenant, although church leaders refuse to display the artifact or allow experts to verify that it is genuine. Jewish and Christian followers consider the Ark of the Covenant to be important because it contains the original copy of the contract between the Hebrews and God, and it is likely the search for the Ark will continue for decades to come.

Unlike the cultures of their Canaanite enemies, the Hebrews did not believe in worshiping idols, or physical representations of their god. This is demonstrated in the Ten Commandments, which forbid making or worshiping idols, and in sections of the Hebrew Bible that refer to God in the abstract, rather than as someone in human form. The Ark of the Covenant was not a physical representation of God, but carried the actual presence of God, and was so sacred that even touching the Ark would result in immediate death. Hebrew monotheism (belief in just one god) was unique in a world where polytheism (the belief in many gods) was the norm; it was one way in which the Hebrews set themselves apart from the groups around them and preserved a unique identity. The capture of the Ark of the Covenant by their enemies was shameful to the Hebrews, not only because it signalled their military defeat but also because the capture was a sign of God's anger towards them because of their disobedience—they had turned the Ark into an idol and brought it into battle, hoping it would help them defeat their enemy. By blaming themselves, rather than their God, the Hebrews could explain how their all-powerful God was defeated by the inferior gods of their enemies.

Their God could continue to be the one true God, despite the conquest of the Hebrews by other nations.

Key Themes and Symbols

The Ark is a symbol of the covenant, or agreement, between God and the Hebrew people. It represents protection and guidance to the Hebrews, so they treat it as a sacred artifact. It is also a constant reminder of the rules, known as the Ten Commandments, that they have agreed to follow. The Ark is a symbol of God's power, illustrated by the plagues that followed it from place to place when it was captured by the Philistines.

The Ark of the Covenant in Art, Literature, and Everyday Life

Many replicas of the Ark of the Covenant can be found in tabernacle recreations around the world. One notable full-size recreation is found near Eilat (pronounced AY-laht), Israel. The 1981 Steven Spielberg film *The Raiders of the Lost Ark* is without a doubt the most well-known appearance of the Ark in modern popular culture. In the movie, Harrison Ford plays an archaeologist in the 1930s named Indiana Jones who locates the Ark and fights to keep it out of the hands of the Nazis.

Read, Write, Think, Discuss

Many people continue to look for the Ark of the Covenant because they consider it a holy artifact and a symbol of Hebrew identity. Human groups have always tried to create distinct identities for themselves through the use of artifacts, origin myths, and various symbols. Think about the images that represent your nation or ethnic group. Are these images mostly religious or nonreligious? What is it about these images that instills a sense of pride or allegiance in the members of a group? Write a personal essay about an image of your group that is especially appealing to you, and trace its history as far back as you can. Note the social factors that may have caused the image to change or transform throughout history.

SEE ALSO Angels; Semitic Mythology

Armageddon

Myth Overview

In the Christian tradition, Armageddon (pronounced ahr-muh-GED-in) is the final battle that will take place between the forces of God and the forces of **Satan**. The battle, in which evil will finally be defeated, will be followed by the Day of Judgment. On that day, Christ will judge all souls and decide whether to send them to **heaven** or to **hell**. Armageddon is mentioned just once in the Bible, in the sixteenth chapter of the New Testament book of Revelation. It is believed to refer to the final battle between good and evil, as well as its location. Although Armageddon brings about the destruction of most of the world, its destruction allows for the renewing of the earth into a better creation.

Armageddon in Context

The term *armageddon* is taken from a Hebrew phrase meaning "hill of Megiddo," Megiddo being an ancient town in present-day northern Israel. Megiddo stood at the crossroads of military and trade routes that connected Egypt, Israel, Phoenicia, Syria, and Mesopotamia. Numerous battles were fought at Megiddo because of its strategic location. The idea of Armageddon is important to Christians because it marks the final judgment of humanity, where believers are rewarded and nonbelievers are punished. It marks a validation of Christian beliefs, even though the idea of a "final battle" that destroys evil and makes way for a new and better life for the survivors is not unique to Christianity.

Key Themes and Symbols

Armageddon has come to symbolize an all-out war between good and evil. Over time, the word "armageddon" has been used to refer to any great or climactic battle, such as the First World War. Armageddon also represents the end of evil, since the forces of heaven will defeat the forces of hell.

Armageddon in Art, Literature, and Everyday Life

The subject of the end of the world has long been popular in literature, art, and films. One of the most famous artistic works on this subject is by

Nationality/Culture
Christian

Pronunciation
ahr-muh-GED-in

Alternate Names
Har-Magedon

Appears In
The New Testament

Tel Megiddo, the hill where the ultimate battle of Armageddon will take place, as described in the Book of Revelation. ERICH LESSING/ART RESOURCE, NY.

Michelangelo. His fresco in the Sistine Chapel known as *The Last Judgment* (1535–1541) depicts the final moments of humanity, where saved souls ascend to heaven and those not saved remain behind. *Armageddon* is also the name of a 1998 Michael Bay film in which Earth, and all life on it, is threatened with destruction by an approaching asteroid. Armageddon is also the subject of the popular Left Behind series by Jerry Jenkins and Tim LaHaye (published between 1995 and 2005).

Read, Write, Think, Discuss

The book *Armageddon Summer* by Jane Yolen and Bruce Coville (1999) tells the story of two teenagers who are part of a religious group that believes the world is about to end. In addition to focusing on belief and the possibility of the end of the world, the book deals with family, friendship, and the developing identities of its two main characters.

SEE ALSO Satan

Artemis

Character Overview

The Greek goddess Artemis (pronounced AHR-tuh-miss)—one of the twelve deities, or gods who lived on Mount Olympus—was the twin sister of **Apollo**. Fond of hunting, archery, and wild animals, she was also associated with childbirth, the harvest, and the moon. Artemis was considered the guardian of maidens and small children. The Romans worshipped her as Diana.

Artemis and Apollo were the children of **Zeus** (pronounced ZOOS) and Leto (pronounced LEE-toh). When Leto was about to deliver the **twins**, Zeus's jealous wife **Hera** declared that she would not allow them to be born in any land where the **sun** shone. For this reason, Zeus led Leto to a floating island and caused a wave to shade the shore, creating a place for the birth that was above ground but hidden from the sun.

Major Myths

Many myths about Artemis focus on her vengeful nature. She was known for punishing humans who offended or angered her. In one story, a young hunter named Actaeon (pronounced AK-tee-uhn) came upon Artemis while she was bathing in a stream. Although he knew better than to spy on a goddess, he was captivated by her beauty. Artemis caught sight of Actaeon and, not wanting him to boast of having seen her naked body, changed him into a deer. His own hounds then attacked and killed him. The nymph Callisto met a similar fate when Artemis punished her for losing her virginity by transforming her into a bear; Callisto's own son Arcas later unknowingly shot her while hunting.

Agamemnon (pronounced ag-uh-MEM-non), the leader of the Greek forces in the Trojan War, also felt the wrath of Artemis after he killed a deer that was sacred to her. In her anger, Artemis prevented the

Nationality/Culture
Greek

Pronunciation
AHR-tuh-miss

Alternate Names
Diana (Roman), Artume (Etruscan)

Appears In
Homer's *Iliad*, Hesiod's *Theogony*

Lineage
Daughter of Zeus and Leto

Greek fleet from sailing for Troy; it was only when Agamemnon promised to **sacrifice** his daughter Iphigenia (pronounced if-uh-juh-NYE-uh) to the goddess that Artemis let them go.

In another myth, Artemis and Apollo defended the honor of their mother, Leto. A woman named Niobe (pronounced NYE-oh-bee), who had six sons and six daughters, boasted that her offspring outshone

Leto's two children. Outraged, Leto sent Artemis and Apollo to punish Niobe. With their arrows, the twins shot and killed all of Niobe's children.

Artemis in Context

Like her brother Apollo, Artemis was a popular god among ancient Greeks. A fertility deity known as the "Lady of Ephesus" (pronounced EF-uh-suhs), worshipped by the people of Ephesus in Anatolia, or modern-day Turkey, was believed to be a foreign version of Artemis. The temple at Ephesus, built to honor Artemis, was considered one of the Seven Wonders of the Ancient World.

Artemis was regarded by the ancient Greeks as the goddess of the hunt. Hunting was an important part of ancient Greek life; although they developed sophisticated agriculture and animal domestication over the centuries, their cultural roots were closely tied to the hunting of wild animals as a means to survive. Hunters offered Artemis the heads, antlers, or skins of their prey, and fishermen likewise offered parts of their catch to her. The close connection between hunting and warfare resulted in her worship as a goddess of warfare in some Greek states.

Artemis was a patroness of young girls, and herself was a virgin goddess. She differed from the other Greek virgin goddess, **Athena**, in that she was considered the goddess of girls before they married, whereas Athena's virginity was considered to be asexual (without a sexual orientation). The followers of Artemis are known as "**nymphs**," and girls old enough to be married danced and sang at festivals that honored Artemis; it was one of the few opportunities in Greek culture for unmarried men and women to mingle. When girls married, Artemis continued to watch over them—this time as they gave birth. Artemis decided whether a woman lived or died in childbirth, and the Greeks believed that her arrows caused women to die from disease.

Key Themes and Symbols

Artemis is considered the goddess of wild things and the hunt. Because of this, she is often described as being young, wearing clothes she can run in—possibly made of animal skins—and carrying a bow and quiver of arrows. Strangely, though she is a huntress, she is also associated with protecting the forest and the creatures in it. The sister or twin of Apollo, the god of the sun, Artemis sometimes wears a crescent moon on her forehead to symbolize her connection to the moon and lunar cycles like the tide, and women's mysteries and phases such as childbirth, puberty, and motherhood.

Artemis in Art, Literature, and Everyday Life

In works of art, Artemis is often shown carrying her bow and arrows, surrounded by her hounds. She appears in many literary works including Homer's *Iliad*, Ovid's *Metamorphoses*, and Euripides' *Hippolytus*.

More recently, Artemis has appeared as a character in comic books published by both Marvel Comics and DC Comics, and the superheroine Wonder Woman is named Diana (the Roman name for Artemis) in honor of the goddess.

Read, Write, Think, Discuss

In ancient Greece, most hunting was done by men. Why do you think Artemis, as a female, was considered to be the goddess of hunters?

SEE ALSO Apollo; Athena; Greek Mythology; Zeus

Arthur, King

Nationality/Culture
Romano-British/Celtic

Alternate Names
None

Appears In
Geoffrey of Monmouth's *History of the Kings of Britain*, Malory's *Le Morte d'Arthur*, Tennyson's *Idylls of the King*

Lineage
Son of Uther Pendragon and Igraine of Cornwall

Character Overview

King Arthur was a legendary ruler of Britain whose life and deeds became the basis for a collection of tales known as the **Arthurian legends**. As the leading figure in British mythology, King Arthur is a national hero and a symbol of Britain's heroic heritage. But his appeal is not limited to Britain. The Arthurian story—with its elements of mystery, magic, love, war, adventure, betrayal, and fate—has touched the popular imagination and has become part of the world's shared mythology.

The Celts blended stories of the warrior Arthur with those of much older mythological characters, such as Gwydion (pronounced GWID-yon), a Welsh priest-king. Old Welsh tales and poems place Arthur in traditional Celtic legends, including a hunt for an enchanted wild pig and a search for a magic cauldron, or kettle. In addition, Arthur is surrounded by a band of loyal followers who greatly resemble the disciples of **Finn**, the legendary Irish hero.

As time went on, the old Celtic elements of King Arthur's story were buried under new layers of myth. Some versions claimed that Arthur was descended from **Aeneas** (pronounced i-NEE-uhs), the legendary founder of Rome. This detail linked British mythology with that of ancient Greece and Rome. As Britain came under Anglo-Saxon rule, Arthur became an idealized leader, a symbol of national identity who had once united all the warring chiefdoms of the British Isles. In some accounts, he led his armies across Europe, much like Alexander the Great of the ancient world.

Christianity also played a role in the stories about Arthur. Some scholars have compared Arthur, a good man betrayed by those closest to him, to Jesus, who was betrayed by his trusted disciple Judas. In time, Arthur's story would be interpreted as a tale of Christian virtues and vices.

Literary Development Modern scholars can trace the changes in King Arthur's story through the works of particular medieval writers. The most important of these writers was Geoffrey of Monmouth, who lived and worked between about 1100 and 1155. His *History of the Kings of Britain* contains the most detailed account of King Arthur written up to that time. Geoffrey drew upon Welsh folklore and possibly upon earlier histories; but his Arthur, a conquering national hero, is mainly his own literary creation.

Geoffrey's work introduced King Arthur to a wide audience. Soon, English and European writers were producing their own versions of Arthur's life and adding new characters, adventures, and details. Sir Thomas Malory, an English writer, wove various strands of myth and history into a lengthy volume called *Le Morte d'Arthur* (The Death of Arthur) that placed King Arthur firmly in the medieval world. Published in 1485, it became the best-known and most widely read account of the legendary king. Modern images of Arthur—illustrated in books, movies, comic books, and cartoons—are largely based on Malory's story.

Arthur's Life and Deeds Arthurian legends are filled with themes common to ancient stories shared around the globe. Although supernatural elements, such as magic, wizards, and **giants**, play key roles in the story, at its heart is the simple drama of a man struggling to live by the highest standards in a world of human weakness. According to Malory, Arthur was the son of a king named Uther (pronounced OO-ther) Pendragon, who fell in love with Igraine (pronounced EE-grain), wife of Duke Gorlois (pronounced gor-LOW-iss) of Cornwall. With the aid of a wizard named **Merlin**, Uther disguised himself as Gorlois and conceived a child with Igraine. (Some versions say that Uther married Igraine after Gorlois died.) Their child, born at Tintagel (pronounced tin-TAJ-uhl) Castle in Cornwall, was named Arthur.

Merlin took charge of the boy's upbringing, arranging for a knight named Sir Hector to raise Arthur as his foster son. When King Uther died, he left no known heir to the throne. It was said that the person who succeeded in pulling the magical sword Excalibur from the stone that held it would be the next king. The greatest knights in the land accepted the challenge, but none managed to extract the sword. When Sir Hector brought young Arthur to London, the boy was able to withdraw the sword with ease, thus proving that he was meant to be king of England; at a later point in Arthur's story, however, Malory says that he received the sword from a mysterious figure called the **Lady of the Lake**. Either way, Arthur became king and gained possession of Excalibur. The wise magician Merlin helped him defeat the rebellious lesser kings and nobles who did not want Arthur to be king.

King Arthur was visited by Morgause (pronounced mor-GAWZ), wife of King Lot of the Orkney Islands. Morgause, a daughter of Igraine, was Arthur's half-sister. Among her children was Gawain (pronounced gah-WAYN), Arthur's nephew, who later became one of his loyal supporters. Morgause then bore a younger son, **Mordred**. In some versions of the story, Mordred was Arthur's child, the result of a relationship with his half-sister.

The Fate of the King Arthur fell in love with **Guinevere** (pronounced GWEN-uh-veer), daughter of King Leodegrance (pronounced lee-oh-duh-GRANTZ) of Cameliard, in southern England. But Merlin said that Arthur must fight in France before he could marry. As a result, Arthur and Guinevere were married after his triumphant return from France. As a present, Guinevere's parents gave Arthur a large round table for the knights who made up his court. This Round Table became the symbol of the fellowship of the brave knights who went on quests to defeat evil, help those in danger, and keep the kingdom safe. Among their quests was the search for the **Holy Grail**, the cup used by Jesus at the Last Supper.

King Arthur made **Camelot** the seat of his court, and Merlin built a castle with a special chamber for the Round Table. After a time, though, trouble arose. Queen Guinevere and Sir **Lancelot**, Arthur's best friend and champion, became lovers. Mordred accused the queen of having an affair, an offense punishable by death. Lancelot defended her honor successfully, but the conflict destroyed the unity of the court. Some knights sided with Arthur, and others with Mordred. After several battles, Guinevere returned to Arthur.

Arthur left Mordred in charge of the kingdom while he went off to fight a military campaign. While the king was away, Mordred plotted against him, planning to marry Guinevere and become ruler of Britain. When Arthur returned and learned of the plot, he challenged Mordred to a battle.

Arthur and Mordred assembled their armies near the town of Salisbury, in southern England. While the two commanders discussed peace terms, someone saw a snake in the grass and drew his sword. In a flash, all the knights drew their weapons and started to fight. Arthur killed Mordred but suffered his own mortal wound in the process. He asked the sole survivor of the battle, Sir Bedivere, to take Excalibur and throw it into a particular lake. At first Sir Bedivere hesitated, but eventually he followed Arthur's command. As he did so, a hand rose from beneath the water, the hand of the Lady of the Lake, and caught the sword. Then a mysterious barge appeared. Sir Bedivere placed King Arthur on the barge, which carried him away to Avalon, a mythical and sacred isle in the west. There he would be cared for by Morgan Le Fay and healed of his wounds. Legend said that he would return one day when England once again needed him.

King Arthur in Context

King Arthur was born somewhere in the misty region where history and imagination meet. The original legends may have been based on a real person, but scholars have yet to determine who that person was. Whether real or imaginary, the story of Arthur has been shaped by the ancient myths and literary creations that developed around him. The courtly medieval king who appears in the best-known versions of Arthur's story is a creation of a later time.

Almost fifteen hundred years after the first known reference to Arthur was written, scholars still debate whether or not Arthur was based on a real person. Some believe that King Arthur may be based on a Romano-British war leader, possibly named Artorius, who defended the native Celtic people of Britain against Anglo-Saxon invaders after Rome withdrew its troops from the British Isles in 410 CE. References to this hero appear in a book written around 550 by a Celtic monk named Gildas; in a work by Nennius, a Celtic historian of around 800; and in a genealogy from Wales compiled around 955 from earlier sources. According to these accounts, Artorius fought a series of battles against the Saxons sometime between 500 and 537.

A British researcher named Geoffrey Ashe proposed a different identity for Arthur. He based his theory on a letter that a Roman nobleman wrote around 460 to a British king named Riothamus. Linking this letter with medieval accounts of Arthur's deeds in France, Ashe suggested that Riothamus, who led a British army into France, was the man upon whom the Arthurian legends are based.

King Arthur has also been linked with Glastonbury in southwestern Britain. Old traditions claimed that early British Christians founded Glastonbury Abbey in the first or second century CE, with the earliest stone structure established in the seventh century. The abbey stood until a **fire** destroyed it in 1184. According to legend, Arthur and his queen, Guinevere, were buried nearby. Arthur's tomb bore these words: "Here lies Arthur, king that was, king that shall be." Some chronicles say that King Henry II ordered the tomb opened in 1150 and that it contained Arthur's skeleton and sword. Modern scholars, though, have been unable to separate fact from legend.

Key Themes and Symbols

One of the main themes of the King Arthur legend is the notion that "might makes right," or that strength and power can be used to enforce a moral code. This moral code was known as chivalry, and included traits such as generosity, bravery, courtesy, and respect toward women. For a time, Camelot, the seat of King Arthur's court, seemed to be a perfect realm, free from wickedness. The Round Table represented the unbroken unity of the knights and their common purpose; however, the very knights charged with maintaining a moral standard ended up failing to uphold the standard themselves.

King Arthur in Art, Literature, and Everyday Life

Aside from the numerous retellings of the legend of King Arthur in classic literature, the character has remained popular in contemporary culture and art. His traditional story has been brought to newer generations by books such as T. H. White's *The Once and Future King* (1958) and John Steinbeck's *The Acts of King Arthur and His Noble Knights* (1976), which attempted to modernize the language of the tales for contemporary audiences.

King Arthur has also proven to be a popular character in film. Several versions of his legend have been created, including the 1963 Disney animated version *The Sword in the Stone* (based on T. H. White's novel) and the more historically based 2004 film *King Arthur. Camelot* (1960) was a successful Broadway musical production that was adapted to film in 1967. *Excalibur,* a 1981 John Boorman film based on the writings of Thomas Malory, is considered by some to be the finest adaptation of the King Arthur legend.

Many other books and films are based far more loosely on the legend of King Arthur, or simply include King Arthur as a character. Examples include Mark Twain's novel *A Connecticut Yankee in King Arthur's Court* (1889), and films such as *Monty Python and the Holy Grail* (1975) and *Shrek the Third* (2007).

Read, Write, Think, Discuss

King Arthur and his court pledged themselves to behave in accordance with the code of chivalry. The code bound the knights to defend women from harm and treat them with honor as part of their knightly duties. Some modern feminists have criticized this attitude because it suggests that women are too weak to defend themselves and are dependent on men for help. At the same time, the modern phrase "Chivalry is dead" expresses a regret that men no longer treat women with the kind of respect that was once part of the code of chivalry. Can society have it both ways? Is it possible to treat all members of society with respect without fostering inequality? Some have argued that the death of chivalry is an unavoidable outcome of greater equality between the sexes. Do you agree? Why or why not?

SEE ALSO Arthurian Legends; Camelot; Celtic Mythology; Guinevere; Holy Grail; Lady of the Lake; Lancelot; Merlin

Arthurian Legends

Nationality/Culture
Romano-British/Celtic

Alternate Names
None

Appears In
Matter of Britain, *Le Morte d'Arthur*, *Idylls of the King*

Myth Overview

The Arthurian legends are stories about the character of King **Arthur**. They form an important part of Britain's national mythology. Arthur may be based on a real person from history, possibly a Celtic warlord of the late 400s CE. The legends, however, have little to do with history. They blend **Celtic mythology** with medieval romance, and feature such well-known elements as the magic sword Excalibur, the Knights of the Round Table, and the search for the **Holy Grail**, the cup from which Jesus drank during the Last Supper. Arthur's court at **Camelot** has been idealized as a kind of perfect society, with a just and wise king guiding his happy people.

The Arthurian legends exist in numerous versions and can be interpreted in various ways. They include tales of adventure filled with battles and marvels, a tragic love story, an examination of what it means to be king, and an exploration of the conflict between love and duty. The legends tell the story of the mighty King Arthur who brought order to a troubled land. He might have gone on to rule the world if passion and betrayal had not disrupted his perfect realm and contributed to his death.

Like many **heroes** of myth and legend, Arthur is of royal birth; however, until he comes of age and claims his throne, he does not know the truth about who he is. Arthur must defeat many enemies before becoming king. Some of these defeated kings and noblemen are so impressed by him that they swear to remain his loyal servants.

Like **Finn**, the legendary Irish hero, Arthur is surrounded by a band of devoted followers. In early versions of the tales, these were warriors and chieftains, but once the tales were set in the Middle Ages, his followers became courtly knights. Their number varies from a dozen to more than a hundred, depending on the source. A few of the knights, especially Gawain (pronounced gah-WAYN), **Galahad**, and **Lancelot**, emerge as distinct personalities with their own strengths and weaknesses.

Not all the legends focus on King Arthur. Many deal with the Knights of the Round Table, who ride out from King Arthur's court at Camelot to do good deeds and perform brave feats. The most honorable and difficult of all their actions is the search for the Holy Grail. Of all the knights, only Galahad is pure enough to succeed in this quest.

Magical Power and Human Weakness Supernatural beings and events play an important part in the Arthurian legends. Before Arthur is born, his destiny is shaped by the wizard **Merlin**, who later serves as the king's adviser and helper. Another powerful magical figure is the witch Morgan Le Fay, who works for good in some versions of the legends and for evil in others. She is sometimes referred to as Arthur's half sister.

Arthur becomes king by gaining possession of the enchanted sword Excalibur. There are two versions of how Arthur gets the sword. In one, Excalibur is in a stone, and all believe that whoever can pull the sword from the stone will be the true king. Arthur pulls the sword from the stone and claims the throne. In the other version, Arthur is given the sword by the "**Lady of the Lake**" (a water spirit probably of ancient Celtic origin).

Arthur and the Knights of the Round Table battle a number of **giants** and monsters—supernatural creatures that figure often in the legends—but the tragic aspect of the legends arises not from spells cast by wicked sorcerers or the actions of vicious enemies but from the behavior of people closest to the king. **Guinevere** (pronounced GWEN-uh-veer), Arthur's queen, and Lancelot, his beloved friend and best knight, betray Arthur by becoming lovers. Like the appearance of the serpent in the Garden of **Eden**, their betrayal introduces disorder and deception into what had been a perfect world.

Mordred, Arthur's jealous nephew, uses Guinevere's affair to destroy the unity of the Round Table. Eventually, Mordred goes to war against Arthur. Some versions of the story make Arthur and his half sister Morgause (pronounced mor-GAWZ) Mordred's parents, placing part of the blame for the fall of Camelot on the king's youthful sin of incest.

Arthurian Legends in Context

The earliest Arthurian legends blended Celtic history and myth. Scholars have not been able to determine if King Arthur is based on a person who really existed, even though several early histories of Britain mention him. These histories suggest he may have been a Celtic war leader who helped defend Britain against Anglo-Saxon invaders in the 400s or 500s CE.

The role of Celtic mythology in the early Arthurian legends is much more definite. Many of the characters and adventures associated with Arthur come from older myths. Arthur himself may be based on the legendary Welsh priest-king Gwydion (pronounced GWID-yon), and

Irish Arthur

Arthurian legends are primarily rooted in the mythology of Wales, but Arthur also appears in Irish folklore and literature. In early tales, he is the son of the king of Britain. He steals dogs belonging to Finn, a legendary Irish hero drawn from the same ancient Celtic sources as Arthur himself. During the Middle Ages, Irish storytellers and writers produced their own versions of the Arthurian tales. They also used Arthurian characters in later Irish stories. In one such story from the 1400s CE, Sir Gawain helps the king of India, who has been turned into a dog, to recover his proper form.

Merlin clearly comes from Myrddin (pronounced MIRTH-in), who appears as both a prophet and a madman in Welsh and Scottish lore. Scholars believe that the Arthurian legends took shape sometime after about 500 CE, when the Celts began to attach familiar myths to new stories about a war hero named Arthur.

Key Themes and Symbols

The Round Table is a key symbol in the legends of King Arthur. It represents the unbroken bond between the knights, all of whom are dedicated to the same goals. Since the table does not have a "head," each knight is given a position of equal importance. The idea of equality was important to the knights of Arthurian legend.

Another important theme in Arthurian legend is the idea of Arthur as an eternal, or timeless king. When Arthur finally falls in battle, he is carried away to the mythical and sacred isle of Avalon, off the west coast of Wales. Arthur's wounds heal on Avalon and he returns to Britain to help solve a future crisis. Some scholars have seen similarities between Arthur and **sun** gods who die and sink into the west only to be reborn.

Arthurian Legends in Art, Literature, and Everyday Life

Writers during the Middle Ages created new versions of the Arthurian legends. In the early 1100s, an Englishman named Geoffrey of Monmouth produced the *History of the Kings of Britain,* which presented Arthur as a national hero. New influences, such as Christianity, transformed the ancient legends. An old Celtic Arthurian tale about the search for a magic

King Arthur's Knights of the Round Table. © ARCHIVO ICONOGRAFICO, S. A./ CORBIS.

cauldron, or kettle, for example, became a quest for the Christian Holy Grail. Another key influence was the medieval concept of chivalry, the code of conduct that inspired the courtly behavior of the Knights of the Round Table.

Numerous versions of the Arthurian legends were produced during the Middle Ages. French writer Chrétien de Troyes wrote poems on Arthurian subjects between 1155 and 1185. He focused on magic and marvels and introduced the theme of the quest for the Holy Grail. The Grail also inspired Wolfram von Eschenbach, a German who wrote his epic poem *Parzival* around 1200. Other romances of the period developed the character of Merlin and featured the romantic entanglement of Lancelot and Guinevere.

In 1485 Sir Thomas Malory, an Englishman, wove together many strands of the Arthurian legends in a volume called *Le Morte d'Arthur* (The Death of Arthur). The best-known version of the legends, Malory's work has served as the basis of most modern interpretations. Many writers since Malory have adapted the Arthurian legends. In 1859 the English poet Alfred, Lord Tennyson published the first part of *Idylls of the King,* a book-length poem about Arthur and his knights. Between 1917 and 1927, the American poet Edwin Arlington Robinson published three poems on Arthurian subjects: *Merlin*, *Lancelot*, and *Tristram*.

One of the most popular modern Arthurian novels is T. H. White's *The Once and Future King* (1958), which originally appeared in four separate volumes over the course of two decades. Other writers, such as Mary Stewart and Marion Zimmer Bradley, have retold the Arthurian story from different points of view, including those of the women in Arthur's life. The legends have also inspired the Broadway musical *Camelot* (1960), made into a film in 1967, and the films *A Connecticut Yankee in King Arthur's Court* (1949) and *Excalibur* (1981).

Read, Write, Think, Discuss

The three years during which President John F. Kennedy led the United States (1961–1963) are sometimes referred to as "Camelot." Using your library, the Internet, or other available resources, research the brief but memorable administration of President John F. Kennedy. Why do you think this administration was referred to as Camelot? What similarities or differences do you see between it and the Camelot of Arthurian legend? Are there elements, such as the fate of Arthur, that seem to be mirrored in these historical events?

SEE ALSO Arthur, King; Camelot; Celtic Mythology; Finn; Galahad; Guinevere; Holy Grail; Lady of the Lake; Lancelot; Merlin

Astarte

See **Ishtar.**

Atalanta

Character Overview

In **Greek mythology**, Atalanta (pronounced at-uh-LAN-tuh) was a skilled huntress and swift runner. As an infant, she was abandoned by her father, King Iasius of Arcadia, who was disappointed that she was not a boy. The goddess **Artemis** sent a female bear to nurse the child until some hunters took her in. A prophecy (or prediction learned from the gods) foretold that Atalanta would be unhappy if she married, so she decided to remain a virgin and dedicate herself to hunting. While still a girl, she used her bow and arrows to kill two **centaurs** (half-man, half-horse creatures) who tried to rape her.

Atalanta became famous in the Calydonian boar hunt. Meleager (pronounced mel-ee-EY-jer), the son of the king of Calydon (pronounced KAL-i-don), organized a great hunt to kill a huge boar. Atalanta joined the hunt, and Meleager fell in love with her. Atalanta was the first to wound the boar; Meleager was the one to kill it. Meleager gave Atalanta the beast's hide, the prize of the hunt, despite the protests of the other hunters who did not want it to be given to a woman.

Later Atalanta tried to join **Jason** on his quest for the **Golden Fleece**. Some sources say she sailed as one of the **Argonauts**, Jason's loyal band of **heroes**. Other sources state that Jason refused to accept her, fearing that a woman in the crew would create problems among the men.

When Atalanta's fame spread, her father invited her to return home. He wanted to see her properly married. She agreed to forfeit her life as a virgin and take a husband under one condition: the suitor would have to beat her in a foot race, or die if he lost. Many young men tried and died. Finally, a young man named Hippomenes (pronounced hi-POM-uh-neez) prayed to **Aphrodite** for help. The goddess gave him three golden apples and instructed him to throw them across Atalanta's path at different times during the race. The apples distracted her, so Hippomenes was able to pull ahead and win. He and Atalanta were married and had a son. They later angered Aphrodite, who responded by turning them into lions.

Nationality/Culture
Greek

Pronunciation
at-uh-LAN-tuh

Alternate Names
None

Appears In
Ovid's *Metamorphoses,* Hyginus's *Fabulae*

Lineage
Daughter of Iasius and Clymene

Atalanta in Context

In ancient Greece, women were generally not allowed to participate in hunting or warfare. Despite this, the goddesses Artemis and **Athena** are both often associated with hunts and battles. Other ancient cultures that existed near Greece, such as the Scythians (pronounced SI-thee-ehns), did allow women to participate in warfare and hunting. This suggests that the ancient Greeks could respect women's abilities, but they regarded female dominance or aggression as something outside their own social norms.

Aphrodite's transformation of Atalanta and Hippomenes into lions was significant to ancient Greeks. They believed that male and female lions could not mate with each other, but instead had to mate with leopards of the opposite sex. By turning Atalanta and Hippomenes into lions, Aphrodite ensured that the two would never be together again.

Key Themes and Symbols

Atalanta stands with Artemis and Athena as a symbol of the strength and skill a woman can achieve in male-dominated areas. This theme is even more compelling with Atalanta, who—unlike Artemis and Athena—is human. The Calydonian boar is a symbol of strength and masculinity, which Atalanta conquers. The golden apples used by Hippomenes represent temptation, and lure Atalanta away from the race, helping Hippomenes to win. As is the case in many ancient Greek myths and legends, trickery and cunning help the hero achieve his goals, even in the face of a superior opponent.

Atalanta in Art, Literature, and Everyday Life

In art, Atalanta is usually shown running in her famous race against Hippomenes. The composer George Frideric Handel wrote the opera *Atalanta* in 1736 in her honor. In 1903, sociologist and civil rights pioneer W. E. B. DuBois put the legend of Atalanta to use in his essay "Of the Wings of Atalanta," which was published in *The Souls of Black Folks*. He compared the black citizens of Atlanta, Georgia, to Atalanta and worried they would be tempted by material success into abandoning more important goals. In 1974, an animated television special (which has gone on to be a cult classic) titled *Free to Be You and Me* featured a retelling of the Atalanta legend in which Atalanta and Hippomenes finish their race side by side. In the animated television series *Class of the Titans* (2005), the character of Atlanta is a descendant of Atalanta. Atalanta was also a character on the television series *Hercules: The Legendary Journeys* (1995), starring Kevin Sorbo as Hercules.

Read, Write, Think, Discuss

Atalanta and the Arcadian Beast by Jane Yolen and Robert J. Harris (2003) tells the tale of young Atalanta's search for the monster that killed the hunter who raised her. *Quiver* by Stephanie Spinner (2002) is a retelling of the story of Atalanta that covers her later years, including the famous race against Hippomenes.

SEE ALSO Argonauts; Artemis

Aten

Character Overview

Aten (pronounced AHT-n), or Aton, was an ancient Egyptian god who was worshipped during the reign of the pharaoh, or Egyptian king, Akhenaten in the Eighteenth Dynasty or 1350s to 1330s BCE. Unlike earlier pharaohs who had worshipped many gods, Akhenaten claimed that Aten was the one supreme god. This may have been the earliest example of monotheism, or the belief in a single god as opposed to many gods, in the ancient Near East.

Aten was the **sun** disk, once an aspect of **Ra**, a much older Egyptian deity. Aten is described as the giver of all life, and as both male and female. Much of what is known about Aten worship comes from the *Great Hymn to the Aten,* a joyful poem inscribed on the walls of ancient tombs at Amarna, which is located on the east bank of the Nile River in Egypt. The hymn, whose authorship is attributed to Pharaoh Akhenaten himself, describes Aten as the only supreme being and creator. It says that Akhenaten and his wife, Queen Nefertiti, are the only people capable of understanding the god and expressing his wishes. The hymn speaks of Aten as a loving god who brings order and beauty to the world.

Nationality/Culture
Egyptian

Pronunciation
AHT-n

Alternate Names
Aton

Appears In
The Tale of Sinuhe, Great Hymn to the Aten

Lineage
Creator of all living things

The pharaoh Akhenaten and his family worshiping Aten, represented as the sun. ERICH LESSING/ART RESOURCE, NY.

Major Myths

Aten, as the sun disk, had no body, no wife, and no children. Although he was recognized as containing the elements of other gods such as Ra and **Horus** (pronounced HOHR-uhs), he was not the direct subject of any currently known myths. This may be due to the fact that he was not popular for long; it may also reflect the efforts of later Egyptian leaders to remove all traces of the god from the Egyptian cultural record.

Aten in Context

Originally named Amenhotep (pronounced ah-men-HO-tep), Pharaoh Akhenaten changed his name to mean "right hand of Aten." Akhenaten was determined to promote Aten as the only supreme god and not to honor other gods. To this end, he tried to get rid of images of other gods and to reduce the power of the priests who led the worship of other gods. He built temples to Aten and established a new capital city, called Akhetaten, or Horizon of Aten. Today that city is known as Amarna.

The worship of Aten as the sole supreme being lasted only for the years of Akhenaten's reign. The Egyptian people could not accept the idea of one supreme god and returned to their old belief in many gods after Akhenaten died in about 1336 BCE. They destroyed the temples to Aten, and the once supreme being became a minor god among all the other gods. The rise and fall of Aten is an example of how the pharaohs controlled public practice through their powers; Akhenaten promoted his particular favored god in an effort to rally the masses to demonstrate his power, while pharaohs that followed virtually eliminated Aten as a form of protest against the previous pharaoh's rule.

Key Themes and Symbols

Aten was depicted as a disk representing the sun. Rays of light ending in hands extended from the disk and reached down to the king, his family, and the natural world. Unlike other Egyptian gods, Aten was never pictured in human form.

Aten in Art, Literature, and Everyday Life

Although Aten was the most popular god during the reign of Akhenaten, his popularity all but disappeared after the pharaoh died. The Pharaoh Tutankhamun, who assumed control after Akhenaten's death, abandoned the city built in Aten's honor and returned to worshipping gods that were popular before Akhenaten's reign. Many monuments and much of the art that honored Aten were destroyed, defaced, or recycled over the centuries. In modern times, the *Great Hymn to the Aten* was used as lyrics for a song in the 1984 opera *Akhnaten* by Philip Glass.

Read, Write, Think, Discuss

In many cultures, the sun is associated with the supreme god or creator. Why do you think the sun is recognized as such an important symbol in cultures around the world?

SEE ALSO Amun; Egyptian Mythology

Athena

Character Overview

Nationality/Culture
Greek

Pronunciation
uh-THEE-nuh

Alternate Names
Athene, Pallas Athena, Minerva (Roman)

Appears In
Hesiod's *Theogony*, Ovid's *Metamorphoses*, Hyginus's *Fabulae*

Lineage
Daughter of Zeus and Metis

In **Greek mythology**, Athena (pronounced uh-THEE-nuh) was the goddess of wisdom, warfare, and crafts. She was the favorite child of **Zeus** (pronounced ZOOS) and one of the most powerful of the twelve Olympian gods. Although Athena was worshiped in many cities, the Athenians considered her to be their special protector and named their city after her; no other Greek god has such a specific association with a city. Many rulers sought her wisdom in both government and military matters. The Romans called her Minerva (pronounced mi-NUR-vuh).

Like **Artemis** (pronounced AHR-tuh-miss), the goddess of the hunt, Athena was a virgin goddess. Unlike Artemis, she did not reject men. Athena took an active part in the lives of many **heroes** and enjoyed their bravery in battle. As a goddess of battle, she stood alongside warriors she favored and gave them courage in the fight; she particularly favored those warriors who were both strong and intelligent. Her main weapon was the *aegis,* a shield that inspired panic in her enemies when she raised it in battle.

Balancing her role as a goddess of warfare is her role as the goddess of the arts and domestic crafts such as sewing. In both aspects of her character, Athena represents rational organization, moderation, and intelligent preparation. She is therefore closely associated with social organization in its ideal form, and the welfare of the community was of particular interest to her.

Major Myths

Athena was the daughter of Zeus and of the Titan Metis (pronounced MEE-tis), known for her knowledge and wisdom. Metis had tried to avoid Zeus's advances by changing herself into different animals, but her tactic failed, and she became pregnant. Zeus learned from an oracle (or person through which the gods communicated with humans) that Metis was expecting a girl. The oracle also predicted that if Metis and Zeus had a male child, the boy would overthrow his father when he grew up, just as Zeus had overthrown his father. To protect himself from this possibility, Zeus swallowed Metis after she changed herself into a fly. Some sources say that Zeus did this mainly because he wanted to possess her wisdom.

Time passed and one day Zeus developed a terrible headache. He cried out in pain, saying he felt as if a warrior were stabbing him from inside with a spear. **Hephaestus** (pronounced hi-FES-tuhs), the god of metalworking, finally understood what was wrong and split Zeus's head open with an ax. Athena sprang out, fully grown and dressed in armor. By all accounts she was a dutiful daughter. For his part, Zeus tended to indulge Athena, which made the other gods jealous and angry.

The goddess was active in the lives of many warriors, kings, and heroes. She gave **Bellerophon** (pronounced buh-LAIR-uh-fun) the magic bridle that enabled him to ride **Pegasus** (pronounced PEG-uh-suhs), the winged horse. She showed the shipbuilder Argus how to build a magic ship for **Jason** and then protected the boat on its travels. She helped **Perseus** (pronounced PUR-see-uhs) kill the monster **Medusa** (pronounced meh-DOO-suh). She supported **Heracles** (pronounced HAIR-uh-kleez; also known as Hercules) through the twelve labors he was made to perform.

Athena also played a role in the Trojan War. She was one of three goddesses who took part in a beauty contest that led to the war. During the conflict, she fought on the side of the Greeks. In particular, she inspired **Odysseus** (pronounced oh-DIS-ee-uhs) to come up the idea of the Trojan Horse, which brought about the defeat of the Trojans. When the fighting was over, she helped Odysseus return home. Although Athena favored the Greeks, she was also important to the people of Troy. They erected a statue of her and called it the Palladium. The Greeks believed that as long as it remained in Troy, the city could not be conquered. Before they were able to win the Trojan War, the Greeks had to creep into the city to steal the statue.

To become the protector of Athens, Athena had to win a contest against **Poseidon** (pronounced poh-SYE-dun), god of the sea. The clever

Athenians asked each god to devise a gift for the city. With his trident (a three-pronged spear), Poseidon struck the Acropolis, the hill in the middle of the city, and a saltwater spring began to flow. Athena then touched the Acropolis with her spear, and an olive tree sprang forth. The people decided that the goddess's gift was the more valuable and chose her as their protector. To avoid angering Poseidon, they promised to worship him too. In ancient times, visitors to Athens were taken to see Athena's olive tree and the rock that Poseidon had struck.

Despite her virgin status, Athena ended up raising a child. According to one myth, Hephaestus became attracted to her and tried to force his attentions on her. The powerful Athena resisted him, and Hephaestus's seed fell to the ground. From that seed was born the half-man, half-snake Erichthonius (pronounced ir-ek-THONE-ee-uhs). Athena put the baby in a box and gave him to the daughters of Cecrops (pronounced SEE-krahps), king of Athens. She told them to care for him but not to look in the box. Two of the daughters looked inside and, driven mad, jumped off the Acropolis to their deaths. Athena then took Erichthonius to her temple and raised him herself. Later he became king of Athens and honored her greatly.

Patron of Crafts, Civilization, and Wisdom Athena created many useful items, including the potter's wheel, vase, horse bridle, chariot, and ship, which explains why she was regarded as the goddess of handicrafts. She was the patron (meaning protector or supporter) of architects and sculptors, too, and the inventor of numbers and mathematics, which influenced many aspects of civilization. Athena took a special interest in agricultural work, giving farmers the rake, plow, and yoke, and teaching them how to use oxen to cultivate their fields. Athena also invented spinning and weaving.

Athena even tried her hand at musical instruments. She created the flute to imitate the wailing of the **Gorgons**, a trio of beastly women with snakes for hair. When the goddess saw her reflection playing this new instrument with her cheeks puffed out, she was disgusted with her appearance. She threw the flute away and put a curse on the first person to pick it up. The satyr Marsyas (pronounced mahr-SEE-uhs) picked up the flute and suffered the consequences when he dared to challenge **Apollo** to a musical contest. Some sources say that Athena threw away the flute because the other gods laughed at her for looking so ridiculous.

The goddess Athena is considered the patron of the arts. Here she is shown teaching the art of sculpture to the people of Rhodes.
RÉUNION DES MUSÉES NATIONAUX/ART RESOURCE, NY.

Athena was generally a kind goddess. She promoted good government and looked after the welfare of kings who asked for her guidance. Athena was a goddess of justice tempered by mercy. Her work led Athens to adopt trial by jury.

Like the other gods, however, Athena did not tolerate lack of respect. She turned **Arachne** (pronounced uh-RAK-nee) into a spider after Arachne boasted that she could weave more skillfully than Athena. She also blinded Tiresias (pronounced ty-REE-see-uhs) when he happened upon a stream where she was bathing and saw her nude. Because his fault was accidental, she softened his punishment by giving him the gift of prophecy, or the ability to see the future.

Athena in Context

The Acropolis is a hill rising 500 feet above the city of Athens. On it stands the remains of some of the finest temples of ancient Greece. The largest and most famous of these temples is the Parthenon (pronounced

PAR-thuh-non), which was built to honor Athena. This magnificent white marble building is surrounded by columns. A huge statue of Athena, made of gold and ivory, used to stand inside. Athena, as the protector of Athens, was no doubt a figure whose importance was tied directly to Athens's importance as a Greek center of power. Her qualities reflect the qualities that Athenians saw in themselves, as well as the qualities that they aspired to achieve.

Several festivals, some tied to the growing season, were held in honor of Athena. Processions of priests, priestesses, and other members of society, particularly young girls, often formed part of the celebration. The goddess's most important festival was the Panathenaea (pronounced pan-ath-uh-NEE-uh). Started as a harvest festival, this annual event gradually evolved into a celebration of Athena. A great parade of people from Athens and surrounding areas brought the goddess gifts and sacrifices. Athletic competitions, poetry readings, and musical contests rounded out the festival. The Panathenaea came to rival the Olympic Games in popularity.

Key Themes and Symbols

Athena is one of the most well-regarded deities in Greek mythology. Although she sometimes struck down those who showed arrogance or disrespect, she was generally considered a wise and dutiful protector. She is often associated with owls, a traditional symbol of wisdom. Athena is also described as having gray eyes, which Greeks considered to be a sign of wisdom. The olive tree is another important symbol of Athena, representing her gift to the people of Athens.

Athena in Art, Literature, and Everyday Life

In works of art, Athena is usually portrayed as a warrior. She wears a helmet and breastplate and carries a spear and a shield adorned with the head of Medusa. An owl generally sits on her shoulder or hand or hovers nearby. The Romans frequently depicted the goddess wearing a coat of armor.

Athena inspired numerous paintings and statues. The great Athenian sculptor Phidias (pronounced fi-DEE-uhs) produced several works in the fifth century BCE, including a thirty-foot bronze piece and an ivory and gold statue that was housed in the Parthenon. The statue of Athena kept in the Roman temple of the goddess Vesta was said to be the Palladium of Troy, taken by the Trojan prince **Aeneas** (pronounced i-NEE-uhs) when he fled the burning city.

Athena and her stories appear in many literary works as well. In Greek literature, she is a prominent character in Homer's ***Iliad*** and the ***Odyssey***, and her influence is felt throughout the plays of Aeschylus (pronounced ES-kuh-luhs), Sophocles (pronounced SOF-uh-kleez), and Euripides (pronounced yoo-RIP-i-deez). The goddess also plays a leading role in the works of Roman writers Virgil and Ovid.

In the realm of science, one genus of owls has been classified under the name *Athene,* an alternate spelling of the goddess's name.

Read, Write, Think, Discuss

Bright-Eyed Athena: Stories from Ancient Greece by Richard Woff (1999) is a collection of eight of the most popular myths associated with Athena. In addition, the book features photos of many ancient artifacts related to Athena.

SEE ALSO Arachne; Artemis; Bellerophon; Helen of Troy; Heracles; *Iliad, The*; Jason; Medusa; Odysseus; Pegasus; Perseus; Poseidon; Titans; Zeus

Atlantis

Myth Overview

According to the ancient Greeks, Atlantis was an island located in the Atlantic Ocean beyond the Straits of Gibraltar (pronounced jih-BRAWL-ter). It was an island paradise that sank into the sea one day. Since ancient times, many people have tried to explain the legend of Atlantis or to discover what remains of the island.

The tale of Atlantis comes from the Greek philosopher Plato (pronounced PLAY-toh), who lived from 427 to 347 BCE. In two of his written works, *Timaeus* (pronounced tih-MEE-us) and *Critias* (pronounced CRY-tee-us), Plato relates that the famous Athenian lawgiver Solon had heard the story of Atlantis when he visited Egypt. In the very distant past, according to the story, a great island as large as North Africa and the Near East put together existed in the Atlantic Ocean. The island

Nationality/Culture
Greek

Pronunciation
at-LAN-tis

Alternate Names
None

Appears In
Plato's *Timaeus* and *Critias*

Paradise Lost

Many cultures have stories that tell of a "golden age" in the distant past when people were happy and lived without strife. Usually the earthly paradise was lost as a result of greed. The golden age of the ancient Greeks was ruled by Cronus (pronounced KROH-nuhs, called Saturn by the Romans). When Zeus took over, the Silver, Bronze, and Iron Ages followed, each less happy and less prosperous than the one before it. Persian mythology tells how Masha and Mashyoi lost their paradise after being fooled by an evil spirit. A Mayan myth tells of perfect people, made out of cornmeal, who became too proud. Their downfall came when the gods put a mist before their eyes to weaken their understanding.

belonged to the god **Poseidon** (pronounced poh-SYE-dun), who fell in love with and married a young woman of the island named Cleito (pronounced KLAY-toh). Poseidon built a city on the island, and on a mountain in the center of the city, he built a palace for Cleito. The couple had ten children and, in time, Poseidon divided the island among them, giving each a section to rule.

Atlantis was a paradise. No one had to work hard, every type of wonderful food grew there, and animals were plentiful. Poseidon had created a stream of hot water and a stream of cold water for the island. It had a glorious culture with wonderful palaces and temples. The kings were rich in gold, silver, and other precious metals. The people of Atlantis lived in a golden age of harmony and abundance.

Then things began to change. The gods started to intermarry with humans. The Atlanteans became greedy for more than they had. They decided to conquer the lands around the Mediterranean. Angered by the Atlanteans' behavior, **Zeus** (pronounced ZOOS) sent an earthquake, or perhaps a series of earthquakes, that caused Atlantis to sink into the sea over the course of one day and one night.

Atlantis in Context

Scholars of the Middle Ages and the Renaissance believed that Plato was recounting a real event. They were curious about the location of Atlantis. After the discovery of the Americas, some Europeans made a connection between the newly found lands and Atlantis. Some thought that the Native Americans might be descendants of the people of Atlantis who fled their destroyed island. The legend of Atlantis also inspired writers and thinkers. Sir Francis Bacon, an English philosopher of the early seventeenth century, wrote a political fable called *The New Atlantis* (1626) that described an ideal world.

In the 1800s, the myth regained popularity. Scholars and popular writers both tried to use scientific evidence to support the existence of Atlantis; however, many used only the evidence that supported their ideas and conveniently ignored the rest. Although geological studies of the ocean floor revealed no sunken islands or continents at the bottom of the Atlantic Ocean, the legend persisted. In fact, people from lands as diverse as Scotland, the Basque region of Spain, and Scandinavia have claimed Atlanteans as their ancestors.

Since 1960, geological, meteorological, and archeological studies have supported the legend, though not in its original form. Many scientists now think that Atlantis was actually the island of Thera, located in the Mediterranean Sea near the island of Crete. Thera (part of the Santorini archipelago) was one of the colonies of the rich Minoan civilization of Crete. The Minoans built luxurious palaces and temples and traded all over the Mediterranean. Geologists and meteorologists have established that around 1600 BCE, Thera's volcano erupted and part of the island sank into the sea. Subsequent earthquakes and tsunamis destroyed life on Crete, 70 miles to the south. Archaeologists have studied Thera and have found the remains of a large Minoan town built around the volcano. The town has a palace and waterways that seem to match the general plan described by Plato.

Regardless of which culture is fascinated by it, the myth of Atlantis provides comfort in the idea that a perfect human society is possible. This offers hope that achieving such a perfect society is possible again in the future.

Key Themes and Symbols

Atlantis represents a perfect world that is eventually destroyed by human failings. In this way, it resembles the Garden of **Eden** from biblical legend as well as King **Arthur**'s **Camelot**. Atlantis is often used as an example of a utopia, or a place of social, economic, and political perfection. The divisions of the island may have been meant to represent the Greek city-states that shared the rule of Greece in ancient times.

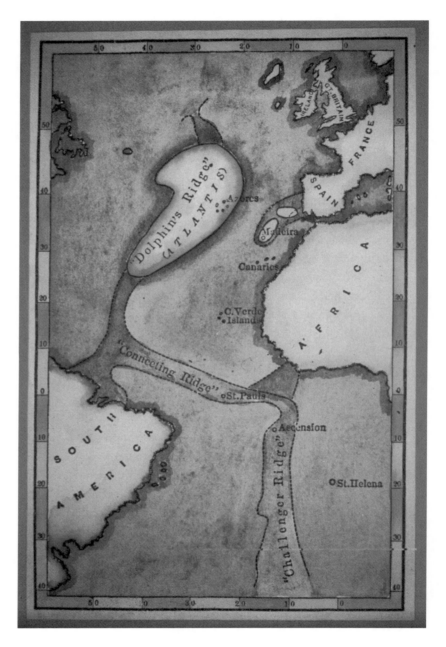

Atlantis in Art, Literature, and Everyday Life

Atlantis is one of the most well-known mythological places. Although many writings about Atlantis were unknown or lost during the Middle

Ages, the legend resurfaced during the Renaissance. Much later, *Atlantis: the Antediluvian World* (1882), a nonfiction book written by Ignatius L. Donnelly, an author and congressman from Minnesota, helped to bring Atlantis into the imagination of Americans. Many modern fantasy writers have included Atlantis as a setting for their books, or have offered their own versions of the legend. These authors include Sir Arthur Conan Doyle, J. R. R. Tolkein, H. P. Lovecraft, and Jules Verne.

Several films and television shows have focused on the Atlantis myth. Recent examples include the 2001 Disney animated film *Atlantis: The Lost Empire,* as well as the 2004 science fiction series *Stargate Atlantis,* in which the real Atlantis is located on a planet in the Pegasus Galaxy.

Read, Write, Think, Discuss

Atlantis is often regarded as a utopia, or a perfect society. What elements do you think would be most important in a perfect society? Do you think creating such a society is possible? Why or why not?

SEE ALSO Eden, Garden of; Poseidon

Atlas

Character Overview

In **Greek mythology**, Atlas (pronounced AT-luhs) was a Titan, a son of **Titans** Iapetus (pronounced eye-AP-uh-tus) and Clymene (pronounced KLEM-eh-nee), also known as Asia. After the Titans lost a war against the upstart younger god **Zeus** (pronounced ZOOS), Atlas was condemned to stand forever holding up the heavens.

Atlas belonged to an illustrious, or widely known, family. One of his brothers was **Prometheus** (pronounced pruh-MEE-thee-uhs), god of **fire** and creator of humankind. Atlas's daughters included the Pleiades (pronounced PLEE-uh-deez), a group of seven stars that announce good spring weather; the Hyades (pronounced HIGH-uh-deez), the stars that announce the rainy season; and the nymph Calypso (pronounced kuh-LIP-soh). Atlas was also either the father or the grandfather of the

Nationality/Culture
Greek

Pronunciation
AT-luhs

Alternate Names
None

Appears In
Hesiod's *Theogony*, Ovid's *Metamorphoses*, Hyginus's *Fabulae*

Lineage
Son of Iapetus and Clymene

Hesperides (pronounced hee-SPER-uh-deez), **nymphs** who, according to Greek legend, guarded a tree bearing golden apples.

Major Myths

Many different stories are told about Atlas. One story features **Heracles** (pronounced HAIR-uh-kleez; also known as Hercules), the great-grandson of **Perseus** (pronounced PUR-see-uhs). One of the labors of Heracles was to obtain some of the golden apples that were guarded by the Hesperides. Heracles asked Atlas to help him get the apples. Seeing an opportunity to escape from the burden of holding up the heavens, Atlas asked Heracles to take over while he obtained the apples. Heracles agreed. When Atlas returned with the apples, he told Heracles that he would deliver them for him. His intention was to leave Heracles to support the heavens; however, Heracles asked Atlas to take back the heavens for just a moment so that he could adjust his burden. When Atlas did this, Heracles walked away with the apples.

Another story concerns Perseus, son of Zeus and slayer of the Gorgon **Medusa** (pronounced meh-DOO-suh). Because of a prophecy, or prediction, that a son of Zeus would one day steal the golden apples of the Hesperides, Atlas refused to offer Perseus hospitality when he came to visit. Insulted, Perseus showed him the severed head of Medusa, which had the power to turn all who looked at it into stone. Atlas was therefore turned into stone. The stone became the Atlas Mountains in what is now the country of Morocco.

Atlas in Context

A collection of maps has been called an atlas since the sixteenth century when cartographer, or mapmaker, Gerardus Mercator (pronounced muhr-KAY-tuhr) put a picture of Atlas holding up the earth, not the heavens, on the title page of his book. Because the place where Atlas stood to perform his task was the westernmost end of the world known to the ancient Greeks, the ocean near him was named the Atlantic in his honor.

For the ancient Greeks, Atlas was an attempt to explain how certain things existed the way they did. It was obvious that something thrown into the sky would eventually fall back down, so how did the heavens remain above the Earth? The answer was Atlas, a Titan who held the heavens in place with his enormous strength.

Key Themes and Symbols

Because of the task he performs of holding up the heavens, Atlas has become a symbol of strength, power, and, most importantly, endurance. Atlas also symbolizes the unseen forces at work in the world that allow humans to exist. In the story of Atlas and Heracles, Atlas represents a cunning trickster who attempts to deceive Heracles into performing his thankless task.

Atlas in Art, Literature, and Everyday Life

Atlas has become a popular icon in art, and is usually depicted holding a celestial sphere or the earth upon his shoulders. Sculptures of Atlas have appeared in front of many prestigious buildings, including Rockefeller Center in New York City and the World Trade Center in Amsterdam. The comic book publishing company known as Marvel Comics was previously called Atlas Comics, and the Marvel Comics universe features a super-villain named Atlas.

Read, Write, Think, Discuss

Readers can find new sympathy for the difficulty of Atlas's job after reading Rick Riordan's 2007 novel *The Titan's Curse*, the third in his Percy Jackson series.

SEE ALSO Heracles; Medusa; Prometheus; Titans

Aurora

Nationality/Culture
Roman

Pronunciation
aw-RAWR-uh

Alternate Names
Eos (Greek)

Appears In
Hesiod's *Theogony* (as Eos), Ovid's *Metamorphoses,* Homer's *Odyssey* (as Eos)

Lineage
Daughter of Hyperion and Theia

Character Overview

Aurora (pronounced aw-RAWR-uh), according to **Roman mythology**, was the goddess of the dawn. The Greeks called her Eos, though she has come to be more commonly known by her Roman name. She was the daughter of the **Titans** Hyperion (pronounced hy-PEER-ee-on) and Theia (pronounced THEE-uh), and the sister of Helios (pronounced HEE-lee-ohs; the **sun** god) and Selene (pronounced suh-LEE-nee; the moon goddess). Every morning, Aurora arose from the sea and rode in her horse-drawn chariot across the sky ahead of the sun, carrying a pitcher from which she sprinkled dew upon the earth.

Major Myths

Aurora's first husband was the Titan Astraeus (pronounced ah-STRAY-uhs). They had several sons: the winds Boreas, Eurus, Notus, and Zephyrus, as well as the morning star Eosphorus and the evening star Hesperus. Aurora's beauty caused Mars, the Roman god of war, to take an interest in her. This angered Venus, who caused Aurora to fall in love with a number of mortals. She even married one of them, Tithonus (pronounced tih-THOHN-uhs), and begged **Zeus** (pronounced ZOOS) to make him immortal. Zeus granted Aurora's wish, but she forgot to ask for Tithonus's eternal youth too. As a result, he continued to age until he became a shriveled old man. Aurora shut him away in his room until the gods finally took pity on him and turned him into a grasshopper.

Aurora in Context

The terms "aurora borealis" and "aurora australis" are used to refer to bands of colored light sometimes visible in the night sky, especially near the North or South Poles. This phenomenon is also known as the "northern lights" and the "southern lights." Although Greece and Italy are not very close to the North Pole, several ancient Greek and Roman writers documented sightings of the northern lights over the years. Although some attempted to explain these appearances using scientific principles, it is likely that many ancient Greeks and Romans considered these strange and beautiful bands of light to be the work of the goddess of dawn.

The goddess Aurora in her chariot. © MARY EVANS PICTURE LIBRARY/THE IMAGE WORKS.

Key Themes and Symbols

As the goddess of dawn, Aurora came to be associated with the glow in the sky seen before sunrise, as well as the early morning dew. She represents the boundary between day and night, which are her siblings. In the story of Tithonus, Aurora represents someone who is ruled more by her heart than her head.

Aurora in Art, Literature, and Everyday Life

Although Aurora was not as popular as some other goddesses, she was the subject of paintings by artists such as Guido Reni, Nicolas Poussin, Guercino, and Simon Julien. She is mentioned by name in William Shakespeare's play *Romeo and Juliet* (1597). The name "Aurora" has also been used by a number of fictional characters not directly related to the myth, including a Marvel Comics super-heroine and the princess who serves as the main character in the Disney animated film *Sleeping Beauty* (1959).

Read, Write, Think, Discuss

In ancient cultures, natural events such as the northern lights were often believed to have supernatural or divine causes. Using your library, the Internet, or other resources, research a natural event such as thunder or earthquakes. Write a scientific description of the process that causes this event to happen. Can you find an example of an ancient culture that believed this event to be caused by the gods?

SEE ALSO Heracles; Titans

Australian Mythology

Australian Mythology in Context

Australia, a vast land dominated by desert and semi-desert landscapes, was first inhabited by the Aborigines (pronounced ab-uh-RIJ-uh-neez). The mythology of Australia comes from these people and has been influenced by their very close relationship with the natural environment. Most of the myths deal with the features of the landscape, how they were created, and their importance to the Aborigines.

In Australian mythology, there are no standard versions of individual myths. Instead, a tale about a particular character varies from region to region. The reason for these variations in the mythology lies in the lifestyle of the Aborigines.

The first humans to inhabit Australia, the Aborigines, may have arrived more than fifty thousand years ago. They probably came from the islands north of the Australian continent, now known as Indonesia, or from islands in the Pacific Ocean. Some scholars believe that the earliest inhabitants traveled overland across a land bridge that once connected

Australia and southeastern Asia. Later people arrived by raft or boat after the ocean rose, covering the land route.

The early inhabitants were semi-nomads who survived by hunting wild animals, fishing, and gathering fruits and plants. Each group had a home territory where their ancestors had originally settled; however, most groups moved with the seasons as they ran out of food and fresh water. This semi-nomadic lifestyle exposed some Aborigines to new regions and brought various groups into contact with one another.

For thousands of years, the Aboriginal way of life was hardly touched by outside influences. Then, in the late 1700s and early 1800s, European colonists began to arrive in Australia. Today the Aborigines make up little more than 2 percent of Australia's population, and few of them maintain their traditional way of life. Aware that the breakdown of their semi-nomadic lifestyle and oral traditions could lead to a loss of their heritage, some Aborigines are making an effort to collect and record their myths and legends for future generations.

By participating in certain rituals, individuals are able to reenact the journeys of their ancestors. The ritual reenactment of a myth is as important as the story itself. The rituals involve singing, dancing, and painting, which, according to the Aborigines, nurtures the land, the people, and the ancestral beings. The individuals who perform the ritual call upon the ancestral beings and later sing a song to return them to their place of emergence.

Aboriginal rituals also include the creation of mythological designs, such as the body paintings, ground paintings, rock paintings, and engravings found throughout Australia. The Aborigines decorate sacred objects and weapons to represent certain myths. They chant a myth to attach it to the object being decorated. When a sacred object or place is touched, struck, or rubbed, it releases the spirit that inhabits it. Such rituals are preserved and repeated to establish ties between past, present, and future generations.

Core Deities and Characters

The Australian Aborigines are comprised of many different tribes across Australia, and their deities vary widely from region to region. Underlying this variation, however, is the belief in the mythical era known as the **Dreamtime**, when the ancestor spirits created the world. These spirit ancestors continue to affect Aboriginal life today in the Dreaming rituals.

Song chants, dances, and art retell the stories of the Dreamtime and assure the continuity of life, cultural values, and law.

The Dreamtime ancestors were totem figures—animal or human mythological ancestors to whom the contemporary Aboriginal groups trace their ancestry. As familial ancestors, they will continue to provide for their descendents as long as the proper rituals are performed. The great Rainbow Serpent was one of the creator ancestor spirits who emerged from the ground in the Dreamtime and is an important mythological figure today. As a protector of water resources, the Rainbow Serpent constantly battles with the Sun to preserve water holes in the sometimes dry Australian landscape. If not properly respected through ritual, however, the Rainbow Serpent can inflict punishment on the people.

An aboriginal bark painting showing the wandjina from Australian mythology. JENNIFER STEELE/ART RESOURCE, NY.

Major Myths

Aboriginal myths fall under different categories. Some are public and may be shared with all members of a group. Others are restricted; only people who have participated in certain special ceremonies may hear them. Some sacred stories may only be told and heard by men, while others are restricted to women or to the elder members of the community.

The Aborigines believe that the world began during a mythical period called the Dreamtime. During this time, powerful ancestral beings that slept beneath the ground emerged from the earth. They created the landscape, made people, established the laws by which people lived, and taught them how to survive. They also established the correct relationships between the many Aboriginal clan groups, between people and animals, and between people and the land. After the ancestral beings' work was done, they returned underground. The Aborigines actively recall the events of the Dreamtime through myth and ritual.

Scene from *The Aeneid*: Departure of Aeneas and Death of Dido

After Aeneas left Carthage to follow his destiny, his lover Dido committed suicide, as shown in this illustration from a 1469 edition of the Roman epic *The Aeneid. See Aeneid, The.*

Priests Carrying the Ark of the Covenant

The Ark of the Covenant was sacred to ancient Hebrews, who believed that the presence of God dwelled in it. The Ark also held the Tablets of the Law, the Ten Commandments given to the Hebrews by God. *See* Ark of the Covenant.

Alinari/Art Resource, NY.

Norse Warriors in Valhalla

Norse warriors who died in battle went to Valhalla, a mythical place where they could enjoy feasting, singing, and indulging in mock combat. *See* Afterlife.

The Death of King Arthur

After he was mortally wounded in battle, King Arthur travelled by ship to mythical Avalon, where Morgan Le Fay (center, holding a book) and other fairy queens treated his wounds. According to legend, he will return from Avalon some day when England needs him. *See* Arthur, King.

The Basilisk

In European mythology, the basilisk was a small serpent that could kill any living thing with its glance or its breath. It was usually represented as a creature with a dragon's body and wings, and a serpent's head. *See* Basilisk.

Erich Lessing/Art Resource, NY.

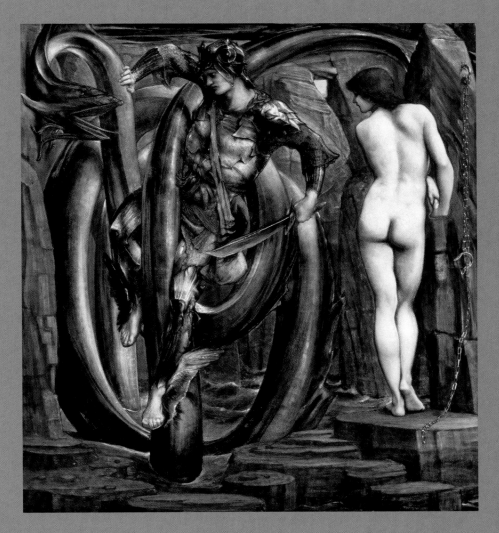

Andromeda's Rescue from the Sea Serpent

Condemned to be a sacrifice to a sea serpent, Andromeda escaped her fate thanks to the hero Perseus. He killed the serpent and freed her. *See* Andromeda.

Amaterasu Emerges From the Cave

Angry at her brother's behavior, the sun goddess Amaterasu shut herself in a cave, depriving the world of sunlight. The other gods tricked her into coming back out so light would return to the world. *See* Amaterasu.

Hippomenes Wins the Race Against Atalanta

Desiring to remain unmarried, Atalanta agreed to marry only the man who could beat her in a foot race. She was so fast that no man had ever succeeded—until Hippomenes beat her by distracting her with golden apples he threw on the course. *See* Atalanta.

Achilles Dragging the Body of Hector

In revenge for the death of his friend, Patroclus, Achilles killed Hector in battle and then dragged the body behind his chariot, preventing the Trojans from giving Hector a proper funeral. *See* Achilles.

Vanni/Art Resource, NY.

Paris Awards the Apple of Discord to Aphrodite

Asked to judge a beauty contest between the Greek goddesses Hera, Athena, and Aphrodite, the Trojan prince Paris offered the prize—the Apple of Discord—to Aphrodite after she promised to give him the most beautiful woman in the world as his wife. *See* Aphrodite.

THE APPLE OF DISCORD

Baucis and Philemon Give Hospitality to Gods

The elderly couple Baucis and Philemon offered hospitality to the Greek gods Hermes and Zeus, thinking they were humble travellers. The gods rewarded them for their good deed by transforming their cottage into a palace. *See* Baucis and Philemon.

Aboriginal myths often tell of a big flood, with local variations. The Worora people in western Australia describe an enormous flood that destroyed the previous landscape. It was caused by ancestral figures called the *wandjina*, who spread throughout the land establishing a new society. Other groups say the flood was brought by a great serpent that still exists in deep pools of water or off the coast.

The Tiwi, from islands off the northern coast, tell of the old woman Mudungkala who rose up from the ground carrying three children. These children were the ancestors of all the islands' inhabitants. As Mudungkala walked across the landscape, water rose up behind her and cut the islands off from the mainland. According to some myths, the people of the land were created by two sisters and a brother called the **Djang'kawu**, who traveled throughout the land. Their journey is recalled in a cycle of more than five hundred songs.

Ayers Rock, also known as Uluru, is a huge dome-shaped rock in central Australia. According to Aboriginal myths, the gullies and holes on the south side of Ayers Rock were scars left over from a battle between snake men, or serpent beings. To the southwest of the rock are some stands of oak trees. These were said to be young warriors waiting silently to join in the battle.

Aboriginal beliefs about the origin of death vary. One tale about death refers to an argument between Crow and Crab about the best way to die. Crab crawled off into a hole, shed her shell, and waited for a new one to grow. Crow said that this took too long and that he had a better way. He rolled back his eyes and fell over dead. The Murinbata people have a ritual dance that compares the two types of death. It shows that Crow's way is the better way.

Other popular mythical figures include the Seven Sisters. According to a version of their story told in central and southern Australia, the sisters fled from central Australia to Port Augusta on the south coast to escape a man named Wati Nehru who wanted to rape the oldest sister. They traveled over hundreds of miles, and many features of Australia's current landscape are associated with their journey. For example, legend has it that a low cliff near Mount Conner is a windbreak they constructed, and a cave is a hut they built. One of the wild fig trees nearby is the oldest sister. At the end of the journey, the sisters turned into the constellation popularly known as the Pleiades (pronounced PLEE-uh-deez), and Wati Nehru became the constellation commonly known as **Orion**.

Sacred Land and the Dreamtime

Australian Aborigines view the land as sacred because it was created by their ancestor spirits during the Dreamtime and continues to be inhabited by them. The Gagudju, an Aboriginal tribe in northern Australia, believe that, after the ancestors created the land, they transformed themselves into various objects, like rocks and water pools. These parts of the landscape are full of power and energy and are sacred sites to the Gagudju. If these sites are destroyed, the ancestors inhabiting them will also be destroyed, and the Gagudju will also suffer. This view of land as sacred can be found among tribal groups throughout the world.

Tales about **tricksters** who often cause trouble are believed to be among the earliest Aboriginal myths. Tricksters typically appear as characters who upset the natural order of things. They do this by stealing, or by causing humans to fight or engage in other unpleasant behavior. People of the Kimberley region in northwestern Australia say that a race of tricksters called the Wurulu-Wurulu use flowers mounted on sticks to steal honey from bees' nests. An empty nest is said to be a sign that the Wurulu-Wurulu have been there.

Key Themes and Symbols

Australian myths deal with the creation of the world, **floods**, drought, and other natural disasters, as well as major events in the life cycle, such as birth and death. Most myths explain the origins of features of the land, including hills and valleys, water holes, and places of safety or danger. By listening to the stories, the Aborigines learn about the local geography and reinforce their bonds to their land, their group, and their heritage.

In Aboriginal culture, many types of information, including myths and legends, are transmitted orally. Storytellers rely on techniques like repetition and special expressions that always take the same form. They use songs, chants, and sand paintings to help relate their stories. Journeys, the subject of many Aboriginal stories, are described by explaining what happened at each place along the way.

Australian Mythology in Art, Literature, and Everyday Life

Aboriginal mythology has long been passed down from generation to generation through myth and art. Aboriginal art, often based on intricate and sophisticated motifs, includes rock paintings, body art, sculpture, wood carvings, tree bark paintings, and decorative and ritual items. These designs and motifs are also functional, as they trace land rights and relationships to the ancestral beings. Songs and stories were not written down, but spoken aloud and memorized. In recent years, thanks to interest from art collectors and tourists alike, some Aboriginal artists have been able to support themselves and their communities by creating traditional artwork that reflects their culture and belief system.

Read, Write, Think, Discuss

Dreamtime: Aboriginal Stories by Oodgeroo Noonuccal (1994) is divided into two halves: in the first, author Noonuccal relates personal stories of growing up as an Aboriginal girl on an island just off the Queensland coast; in the second half, Noonuccal tells several of the most important Aboriginal myths of her childhood. The book also features illustrations by Bronwyn Bancroft.

SEE ALSO Animals in Mythology; Creation Stories; Djang'kawu; Dreamtime; Tricksters

Aztec Mythology

Aztec Mythology in Context

The mythology of the Aztec civilization, which dominated central Mexico from the 1300s through the early 1500s CE, described a universe that was both grand and dreadful. Worlds were created and destroyed in the myths, and splendid gods warred among themselves. Everyday items, like colors, numbers, directions, and days of the calendar, took on special meaning because each was associated with a deity, or god. Aztec religious life ranged from keeping small pottery statues of the gods in homes to attending elaborate public ceremonies involving human **sacrifice**.

The Aztecs migrated to central Mexico from the north in the 1200s CE. According to their legends, they came from a land called Aztlán, the source of their name. The Aztecs were not a single people but several groups, including the Culhua-Mexica, the Mexica, and the Tenocha. In the early 1300s, these groups formed an alliance and together founded a city-state called Tenochtitlán (pronounced teh-nowch-TEE-tlan) on the site of present-day Mexico City. The people of Tenochtitlán rose to power and ruled a large empire during the fifteenth century.

The Aztecs were newcomers to a region long occupied by earlier civilizations such as the Olmecs and the Toltecs, who had developed a pantheon, or worship of a collection of gods, and a body of their own myths and legends. The Aztec culture absorbed the deities, stories, and beliefs from these earlier peoples and from the Maya (pronounced MYE-ah) of southern Mexico. As a result, Aztec mythology contained religious and mythological traditions shared by many groups in Mexico and Central America. Under the Aztecs, certain aspects of the religion, notably human sacrifice, came to the forefront.

When Spanish colonists defeated the Aztecs and settled in the area, they destroyed as many Aztec documents and images as they could. They did this because they believed the Aztec religion was evil. Much of what we know about Tenochtitlán and Aztec customs comes from accounts of Spanish writers who witnessed the last days of the Aztec empire.

Core Deities and Characters

In the Aztec view of the universe, human life was small and insignificant. An individual's fate was shaped by forces beyond his or her control. The gods created people to work and fight for them. They did not offer favors or grant direct protection, although failure to properly serve the gods could lead to doom and destruction.

Duality, or the presence of two opposing forces in one thing, was the basic element of the deity Ometecuhtli (pronounced oh-me-teh-KOO-tle). This god had a male side called Ometeotl (pronounced oh-me-TEH-oh-tl) and a female side known as Omecihuatl (pronounced o-me-SEE-wah-tl). The other gods and goddesses were their offspring. Their first four children were **Tezcatlipoca** (pronounced tehs-cah-tlee-POH-cah), **Quetzalcoatl** (pronounced keht-sahl-koh-AHT-l), **Huitzilopoch-tli** (pronounced wee-tsee-loh-POCH-tlee), and **Xipe Totec** (SHE-pay TOH-tek), the creator gods of Aztec mythology.

Originally a Toltec god, Tezcatlipoca, Lord of the Smoking Mirror, was god of the night sky. The color black and the direction north were associated with him. He had a magical mirror that allowed him to see inside people's hearts. The Aztec people considered themselves his slaves. In his animal form, he appeared as a jaguar. His dual nature caused him to bring people good fortune at some times, misery at others.

Tezcatlipoca's great rival and opponent in cosmic battles, as well as his partner in acts of creation, was Quetzalcoatl, the Feathered Serpent, an ancient Mexican and Central American deity absorbed into Aztec mythology. His color was white and his direction west. Some stories about Quetzalcoatl refer to him as an earthly priest-king, which suggests there may have been a Toltec king by that name whose legend became mixed with mythology.

As a god, Quetzalcoatl had many different aspects. He was the planet Venus (both a morning and an evening star), the god of **twins**, and the god of learning. The Aztecs credited him with inventing the calendar. A peaceful god, Quetzalcoatl accepted sacrifices of animals and jade, but not of human blood. When he was defeated by Tezcatlipoca, Quetzalcoatl sailed out into the Atlantic Ocean on a raft of serpents. The legend arose that he would return over the sea from the east at the end of one of the Aztecs' fifty-two-year calendar cycles. When the white-skinned Spanish invader Hernán Cortés landed in Mexico in 1519, some Aztecs thought he was Quetzalcoatl come again, a belief Cortés encouraged.

Huitzilopochtli, Hummingbird of the South, is a deity that originated with the Aztecs. He was the **sun** and war god. The souls of warriors who died in battle were said to become hummingbirds and follow him across the sky. Blue was his color and south his direction. The Aztecs claimed that an idol of Huitzilopochtli had led them south during their long migration and told them to build their capital on the site where an eagle was seen eating a snake. The worship of Huitzilopochtli was especially strong in Tenochtitlán, where he was regarded as the city's founding god.

Xipe Totec, the Flayed Lord, had a dual nature. He was a god of vegetation and life-giving spring growth. At the same time, he was a fearsome god of torture and sacrifice. His intense duality reflected the Aztec vision of a universal balance in which new life had to be paid for in blood. Xipe Totec's color was red, his direction east.

The Aztecs also incorporated the worship of **Tlaloc** (pronounced TLAH-lok), an important god of rain and fertility long known under

In this depiction of an Aztec human sacrifice, a priest holds up the still-beating heart of a victim. © PRINT COLLECTOR/ HIP/THE IMAGE WORKS.

various names in Mexico and Central America. He governed a host of lesser gods called Tlaloques (pronounced TLAH-loh-kes), who made thunder and rain by smashing their water jars together. Other deities, such as Huitzilopochtli's mother, the earth goddess **Coatlicue** (pronounced koh-aht-LEE-kway), Lady of the Serpent Skirt, probably played key parts in the religion of the common people, who were mainly farmers. Many minor deities were associated with flowers, summer, fertility, and **corn**.

Major Myths

Many Aztec myths tell all or part of the story of the five suns. The Aztecs believed that four suns, or worlds, had existed before theirs. In each case, catastrophic events had destroyed everything, bringing the world to an end. Many stories related the Loss of the Ancients, the mythic event in which the first people disappeared from the earth. One version says that Tezcatlipoca stole the sun and Quetzalcoatl chased him and knocked him back down to earth with a stick. Tezcatlipoca then changed into a jaguar and devoured the people who lived in that world. The Aztecs combined versions of this story to explain the disappearance of people at the end of each of the four worlds that had existed before theirs. Carvings on a stone calendar found in 1790 tell how, one after another, jaguars, wind, **fire**, and flood destroyed the Ancients.

According to Aztec myth, at the beginning of this world, darkness covered the earth. The gods gathered at a sacred place and made a fire. Nanahuatl (pronounced nah-nah-WAH-tl), one of the gods, leaped into the fire and came out as the sun. However, before he could begin to move through the sky, the other gods had to give the sun their blood. This was one of several myths that described how the gods sacrificed themselves to set the world in motion. Through bloodletting and human sacrifice, people imitated the sacrifices made by the gods. The example of the deities taught the Aztec people to believe that feeding the sun with blood kept it alive.

Tezcatlipoca created the first sun, known as Nahui-Ocelotl, or Four-Jaguar. It came to an end when Quetzalcoatl struck down Tezcatlipoca, who became a jaguar and destroyed all the people. Quetzalcoatl was the ruler of the second sun, Nahui-Ehécatl, or Four-Wind. Tezcatlipoca threw Quetzalcoatl off his throne, and together the fallen god and the sun were carried off by a hurricane of wind. People turned into monkeys and fled into the forest.

The third sun, Nahuiquiahuitl (pronounced nah-wee-kee-ah-WEE-tl) or Four-Rain, belonged to the rain god Tlaloc. Quetzalcoatl destroyed it with fire that fell from the heavens. The water goddess Chalchiuhtlicue (pronounced chal-choo-TLEE-quay) ruled the fourth sun, called Nahui-Atl (pronounced nah-wee-ATL) or Four-Water. A fifty-two-year flood destroyed that sun and the people turned into fish. Quetzalcoatl gave life to the people of the fifth sun by sprinkling his own blood over the bones of the only man and woman who had survived the flood. The gods created the world with blood and required the sacrifice of human blood to keep it intact. One day, however, the fifth sun would meet its end in a destructive earthquake.

The Aztecs lived in the world of Nahui-Ollin (pronounced nah-wee-oh-LEEN; Four-Movement), the fifth sun. They believed the earth was a flat disk divided into north, east, south, and west quarters, each associated with a color, special gods, and certain days. At the center was Huehueteotl (pronounced hway-hway-tay-OH-tul), god of fire. Above the earth were thirteen heavens. Below the earth were nine underworlds, where the dead dwelled, making nine an extremely unlucky number. A myth about Tezcatlipoca and Quetzalcoatl tells how the world was quartered. They made the earth by seizing a woman from the sky and pulling her into the shape of a cross. Her body became the earth, which, angered by their rough treatment, devoured the dead.

Another myth tells of Tezcatlipoca and Quetzalcoatl working together to raise the sky. After the flood ended the fourth sun, the sky collapsed onto the earth. The two gods became trees, pushing the sky up as they grew. Leaving the trees supporting the sky, one at each end of the earth, they climbed onto the sky and met in the Milky Way.

Key Themes and Symbols

The idea that people were servants of the gods was a theme that ran through Aztec mythology. Humans had the responsibility of keeping the gods fed, otherwise, disaster could strike at any time. The food of the gods was a precious substance found in human blood. The need to satisfy the gods, especially the sun god, gave rise to the related theme of human sacrifice.

Priests conducted ceremonies at the temples, often with crowds in attendance. Masked performers acted out myths using song and dance, and priests offered human sacrifices. To prepare for the ceremonies, the priests performed a ritual called bloodletting, which involved pulling barbed cords across their tongues or other parts of their bodies to draw blood. Bloodletting was similar to a Mayan ceremony known as the Vision Quest. Peoples before the Aztecs had practiced human sacrifice, but the Aztecs made it the centerpiece of their rituals. Spanish explorers reported witnessing ceremonies in which hundreds of people met their deaths on sacrificial altars. The Aztecs sacrificed prisoners, which contributed to their drive to conquer their neighbors.

Sacrifice was linked to another theme, that of death and rebirth. The Aztecs believed that the world had died and been reborn several times and that the gods had also died and been reborn. Sometimes the gods even sacrificed themselves for the good of the world. Though death loomed large in Aztec mythology, it was always balanced by fertility and the celebration of life and growth.

Another important idea in Aztec mythology was that the outcome of a person's life was already determined by the gods. The Aztec ball game, about which historians know little, may have been related to this theme. Aztec temples, like those belonging to other cultural groups throughout Mexico and Central America, had walled courts where teams of players struck a rubber ball with their hips, elbows, and knees, trying to drive it through a stone ring. Some historians believe that the game represented the human struggle to control their destiny, or future path in life. It was a religious ritual, not simply a sport, and players may have been sacrificed after the game.

The theme of fate was also reflected in the Aztecs' use of the calendar. Both the Aztecs and the Maya developed elaborate systems of recording dates. They used two calendars: a 365-day solar calendar based on the position of the sun, and a 260-day ritual calendar used for divination, or predicting the future through supernatural means. Each day of the ritual calendar was influenced by a unique combination of gods and goddesses. Divination involved interpreting the positive or negative meanings of these influences, which determined an individual's fate. Priests also used the ritual calendar to choose the most favorable days for such activities as erecting buildings, planting crops, and waging war.

The 365-day and 260-day cycles meshed, like a smaller wheel within a larger one, to create a fifty-two-year cycle called the Calendar Round. At the end of a Calendar Round, the Aztecs put out all their fires. To begin a new Calendar Round, priests oversaw a ceremony in which new fires were lit from flames burning in a sacrificial victim's chest.

A third key theme of Aztec myth was that of duality, a balance between two equal and opposing forces. Many of the Aztec gods and goddesses were dualistic, which meant they had two sides, or roles. Deities often functioned in pairs or opposites. Further, the same god could appear under multiple names or identities, perhaps because Aztec mythology drew elements from a variety of sources.

Aztec Mythology in Art, Literature, and Everyday Life

The legacy of Aztec mythology remains strong within Mexico. Aztec images and themes continue to influence the arts and public life. In the late 1800s, Mexico won independence from Spain but had yet to establish its own national identity. Civic and cultural leaders of the new country began forming a vision of their past that was linked with the proud and powerful Aztec civilization. Symbols from Aztec carvings, such as images of the god Quetzalcoatl, began to appear on murals and postage stamps. Mexico's coat of arms featured an eagle clutching a snake in its beak, the mythic emblem of the founding of the Aztec capital.

During the 1920s, Mexico's education minister invited artists to paint murals on public buildings. The three foremost artists in this group were Diego Rivera, José Clemente Orozco, and David Alfaro Siqueiros. Although their paintings dealt mainly with the Mexican Revolution and the hard life of Indians and peasants, the artists also drew upon Aztec mythology for symbols and images to connect Mexico's present with its ancient past. In one mural, for example, Rivera combined the images of the earth goddess Coatlicue and a piece of factory machinery. Although early colonists tried to eliminate it, Aztec mythology has increasingly become an important part of Mexico's national identity.

Read, Write, Think, Discuss

Letters from Mexico (2001) is a new translation of the letters written by Hernando Cortés, Spanish conqueror of the Aztecs, to the king of Spain. The letters detail Cortés's deeds (in a way that made himself look good) and provide a glimpse of the Aztec culture at the time of Spanish invasion in 1519.

SEE ALSO Coatlicue; Huitzilopochtli; Mayan Mythology; Quetzalcoatl; Sacrifice; Tezcatlipoca; Tlaloc

B

Character

Deity

Myth

Theme

Culture

Nationality/Culture
Canaanite

Pronunciation
BAY-uhl

Alternate Names
Hadad, Belos

Appears In
The Hebrew Bible, the
Baal cycle

Lineage
Son of El

Baal

Character Overview

Baal (pronounced BAY-uhl) was one of the most widely worshipped gods in ancient Canaan (pronounced KAY-nuhn), the early name for present-day Israel and neighboring regions. Associated with fertility and rain, Baal was the son of **El**, the supreme god of the Canaanites, and the husband and brother of Anat, the ferocious goddess of war.

Baal is a common Semitic word that means "lord" or "owner." The title was given to the local god of nearly every city in Canaan. Because of the importance of rain to life in the dry lands of the Near East, these local gods were usually associated with fertility and the cycle of wet and dry seasons. Baal developed into a single, widely known god, called Lord of the Earth and Lord of the Rain and Dew. Clay tablets found at the ruins of the ancient town of Ras es-Shamrah (in present-day Syria) contain a series of stories about how Baal became the rain god and gained power over the waters of earth. These stories are known as the Baal cycle.

Major Myths

According to the myths, Yam, the sea god, demanded that Baal be made his slave. He sent messengers to Baal, asking him to surrender, but Baal attacked the messengers and drove them away. Baal then fought with

157

Yam and, using two magic weapons, defeated him and seized control of the waters.

Other myths about Baal relate to fertility and the cycle of the seasons. One such story tells of the battle between Baal and Mot, the god of death and infertility. After conquering Yam, Baal complained that he had no house like the other gods did. El agreed to let the crafts god Kothar build Baal a fine house. When it was finished, Baal held a great feast, but he did not invite Mot or send him respectful presents. Greatly insulted, Mot asked Baal to come to the **underworld**, or land of the dead, to dine. Although he was afraid, Baal could not refuse the invitation. The food served at Mot's table was mud, the food of death, and when Baal ate it, he was trapped in the underworld.

While Baal was in the underworld, famine struck the earth, and El searched for someone to replace Baal. Asherah (pronounced ASH-er-ah), a fertility goddess, convinced El to give Baal's throne to her son Ashtar. But when Ashtar, the god of irrigation, sat on the throne, his feet did not even touch the floor. Realizing he could not fill Baal's place, Ashtar gave up the throne.

Meanwhile, Baal's wife and sister, the fierce goddess Anat, traveled to the underworld. After splitting Mot with her sword, she separated his pieces with her fan, burned the pieces in a **fire**, ground them in a mill, and planted them in the ground. These actions brought Baal back to life. Mot was later restored to life, and the two gods battled each other again. In the end, the **sun** goddess Shapash separated them, Baal regained his throne, and the land became fertile again.

Baal in Context

Worship of Baal was widespread in the ancient Near East. The clay tablets of Ras es-Shamrah, which relate the Baal cycle, date from about 1500 BCE. Baal was also popular in Egypt from about 1400 to 1075 BCE. In Mesopotamia, Baal was known to the Babylonians and Assyrians and was identified with their national gods **Marduk** and Ashur. The Greeks called the god Belos and identified him with **Zeus** (pronounced ZOOS).

Like the other inhabitants of Canaan, the ancient Hebrews worshipped local gods called Baal and honored their children with names ending with *baal,* such as Ishbaal, the son of King Saul. In fact, the Hebrew god Yahweh (pronounced YAH-way) appears to have shared many of Baal's characteristics.

As the worship of Yahweh became more important, Baal fell out of favor with the Hebrews. In the 800s BCE, a queen of Israel named Jezebel introduced a cult of Baal borrowed from the Phoenicians. She set up the cult as a rival to the official worship of Yahweh. Opposition to Baal grew so strong that over the next century the name *Baal* was replaced with the

Beelzebub, Lord of the Flies

In the New Testament of the Bible, *Beelzebub* is one of the names Jesus gave Satan. In some places, he is Satan's main assistant rather than Satan himself. The name comes from *Baalzebub*, the name of the god of the Philistine city of Ekron. *Baalzebub*, which means "lord of the flies," is probably a distorted version of *Baal*, or "lord of the house." The origin of the word is unknown.

term *boshet,* meaning shame. In later texts, the name of Saul's son was changed from Ishbaal to Ishbosheth. Later still, Christians considered *Baal* to be a name for a devil.

Key Themes and Symbols

In the story of Yam and Baal, Yam represents the destructive nature of water, as in rivers and seas flooding the land and ruining crops. Baal represents water's positive powers, including how rain and dew provide moisture needed to make crops grow. The myth of Baal and Mot emphasizes the importance of rain to the land. Baal represents the fertility of spring rains, while Mot represents the drought of the summer months. The actions taken by Anat against Mot, such as splitting, winnowing, burning, grinding, and planting, are steps taken by farmers when they harvest wheat. They prepare it for use as food during the winter and sow it to create more crops the next year. By defeating the drought, represented by Mot, the rains, represented by Baal, renew the earth each year and allow life to flourish in the dry climate of the Near East.

Baal in Art, Literature, and Everyday Life

Though some ancient examples of art and sculpture depicting Baal exist, the deity fell out of favor and was seldom depicted in recent times. The later Christian view of Baal as a demon or king of **hell** has become the most enduring image of the deity. Baal is represented as a demonic character in role-playing games such as *Magic: the Gathering*, and appeared as a character in the TV series *Stargate SG-1* (1997–2007). *Baal* is also the title of a 1923 play by Bertolt Brecht, though the play's main character, also named Baal, is neither a god nor a demon but a murderous poet.

Read, Write, Think, Discuss

Baal was considered a very important god in the region of Canaan, in the arid Middle East. How do you think the geography and climate of this region helped to shape Baal's position and popularity?

SEE ALSO Devils and Demons; El; Satan; Semitic Mythology; Underworld

Babel, Tower of

Myth Overview

According to the monotheistic religions (religions in which the people believe in only one god) of the Middle East, arrogant people built the Tower of Babel. In turn, they were made humble by losing their common language. The story of the Tower of Babel is told in the first book of the Old Testament of the Bible. In it, some people decided to build a city on the plains of southern Mesopotamia. The city they envisioned would feature a massive tower that reached up into the heavens. Their plan was to gain recognition for themselves as a people and to be able to stay together. When God saw what they were doing, however, he concluded that they were simply trying to gain power. To make planning difficult for them, he made them speak many different languages. Unable to communicate with each other at the building site, the people gave up the project and scattered to different lands. The remains of the city became known as Babel.

The Tower of Babel in Context

The story of the tower may have developed from the way later visitors interpreted the ruins of the old cities of the region. In Hebrew, the word *Babel* is a misinterpretation of the name *Babylon,* which meant "the gate of God." In fact, archaeologists have found evidence of several tall ziggurats, or step-sided temples, in the ancient city of Babylon.

Nationality/Culture
Judeo-Christian

Pronunciation
TOW-ur uv BAY-buhl

Alternate Names
None

Appears In
The Book of Genesis in the Old Testament

Key Themes and Symbols

The Tower of Babel is often viewed as a lesson of humility, or being modest before God. The Hebrew word *balal,* similar to "babel," means "confusion." Today the image of the Tower of Babel is used to indicate confusion and failure to communicate.

The Tower of Babel in Art, Literature, and Everyday Life

The Tower of Babel is one of the most popular myths of the Old Testament. It has been depicted in artwork by Pieter Brueghel the Elder,

Gustave Doré, and M. C. Escher, among others. Science fiction author Ted Chiang wrote a thought-provoking short story about this myth, "Tower of Babel," which won the Nebula Award in 1990. Another science fiction writer, Douglas Adams, gave the name "Babel fish" to a creature that appears in his 1979 novel *The Hitchhiker's Guide to the Galaxy*. The fish-like creature can live inside the ear and instantly translate any language into any other language.

It is possible that the term "babble," meaning to speak nonsense or say things without meaning, is related to the story of the Tower of Babel; however, etymologists, or experts in the history of words, have not been able to establish a clear link between the two.

Read, Write, Think, Discuss

Over half of Europeans speak two languages (or more), but only nine percent of Americans speak two languages. English is so widely spoken throughout the world that, even when traveling abroad, Americans can often get by with little knowledge of the language of the country they are visiting. Do you think the American educational system should put more stress on teaching foreign languages? Why or why not? What are the benefits of knowing more than one language? Is the rapid spread of English as a common language of business around the world desirable or undesirable?

SEE ALSO Semitic Mythology

Bacchus

See **Dionysus.**

Balder

Character Overview

In **Norse mythology**, Balder (pronounced BAWL-der) was the son of **Odin** (pronounced OH-din), the supreme Norse deity, and of **Frigg**

Nationality/Culture
Norse

Pronunciation
BAWL-der

Alternate Names
Baldr, Baldur

Appears In
The Prose Edda, the Poetic Edda

Lineage
Son of Odin and Frigg

(pronounced FRIG), goddess of marriage and motherhood. Balder was the most beautiful of the gods and the one most beloved by Odin.

Major Myths

As a youth, Balder led a happy life and eventually married Nanna. Soon, however, Balder began to suffer from terrible dreams that threatened death. Fearing for his safety, Frigg asked everything in creation, including animals, birds, stones, wood, and metal, to promise not to hurt Balder. There was only one thing she did not ask to make such a promise: the mistletoe plant. Frigg thought that the mistletoe was too young to take an oath.

After everyone and everything had taken Frigg's oath, the gods amused themselves by throwing things at Balder because they knew nothing could harm him. However, the evil god **Loki** (pronounced LOH-kee) decided to find a way to hurt Balder. Loki transformed himself into an old woman and went to visit Frigg. The old woman asked if it was true that all things had taken an oath not to hurt Balder. Frigg admitted that she had not asked the mistletoe to take the oath. Loki then went to the place where the mistletoe grew and took a twig from it.

Next, Loki approached Balder's blind brother Höd (pronounced HAWTH) and asked why he was not throwing things at Balder like everyone else. Höd replied that he could not see Balder, and besides, he had nothing to throw. Loki then handed Höd a dart he had made from the mistletoe and offered to guide Höd's hand as he threw it. The dart struck Balder, killing him instantly. The gods were shocked and confused. Frigg begged someone to go to the **underworld**, or land of the dead, and pay a ransom to bring back her son.

Hermódr, another of Odin's sons, volunteered to recover Balder. Hermódr journeyed to the underworld where he found **Hel**, the goddess of death. She told Hermódr that if everything under **heaven** shed a tear for Balder, she would allow him to return; however, if even one thing, living or dead, spoke against Balder or refused to weep for him, he would have to remain in the underworld. The gods sent messengers to every part of world to ask everything to weep for Balder. They thought they had succeeded until they found an old hag named Thökk sitting in a cave. They asked her to weep for Balder, but she refused. Most accounts

suggest that Thökk was none other than Loki, the trickster god, in disguise. Frigg eventually recovered Balder.

Balder in Context

The Poetic Edda, also called the Elder Edda, is a collection of ancient poems known mostly from the discovery of a single manuscript, the *Codex Regius.* Although the manuscript is believed to have been written in the thirteenth century CE, many of the poems may have existed for centuries before that.

The Prose Edda, also called the Younger Edda, was written in the thirteenth century CE by an Icelandic academic named Snorri Sturluson. The author based much of his work on the poems of the Elder Edda. The stories and poems of the two Eddas relate the most popular and important tales of Norse mythology, including stories featuring Balder. They remain the best sources of information regarding Norse myths.

The myth of Balder and the deadly mistletoe may be seen as a way of communicating the poisonous nature of mistletoe among the Norse people. Unlike the berries of many other plants, the raw berries from mistletoe are highly toxic, and can cause vomiting, seizures, and cardiac arrest.

Key Themes and Symbols

In Norse mythology, Balder is seen as a symbol of innocence, purity, and beauty. According to legend, the tears Frigg shed after Balder's death became the berries on the mistletoe plant. The tradition of kissing under the mistletoe commemorates Frigg's joy upon recovering Balder from the dead, and the plant has become a symbol of love. The link between mistletoe and love gave rise to the tradition of kissing under a sprig of mistletoe during the winter holiday season.

Balder in Art, Literature, and Everyday Life

In early mythological texts, Balder was often shown at or just before his moment of death by mistletoe. In more recent times, Balder is not as popular in art or literature as other Norse gods such as Odin and **Thor**. Balder has appeared as a superhero in several Marvel Comics series since 1964. The comic book character shares many traits with the Norse deity, including his vulnerability to mistletoe. The *Baldur's Gate* video game series, created by BioWare in 1998, is set in a fantasy world that references Norse mythology. In northern Europe, one species of mayweed, a flowering plant in the sunflower family, is known as Balder's brow. It is so called because its bright white flowers are said to match Balder's light complexion.

Read, Write, Think, Discuss

In some ways, the story of Balder is similar to the story of **Achilles** from Greek myth. Compare the two. How did each become almost invincible?

How did the other gods play a part in the downfall of Balder and Achilles? Are their personalities similar or different? How is this reflected in each myth?

SEE ALSO Frigg; Hel; Loki; Norse Mythology; Odin

Banshees

Character Overview

Banshee (pronounced BAN-shee) is the English spelling of *bean sídhe,* the name of a female fairy of Irish and Celtic folklore. Banshees were omens of death and let out a howl that chilled listeners to the bone. The banshee's nighttime howling warned people that a death was about to take place. When an important or holy person was about to die, several banshees would wail or sing together. According to some legends, the banshees were accompanied by a large black coach carrying a coffin and pulled by headless horses. When the coach arrived at a house, blood was thrown at the person who opened the door. On the other hand, if a banshee loved a person who was near death, she would sing a gentle song that predicted death but also comforted the dying person and family members.

Banshees in Context

The legend of the banshee may have gotten its start in the Irish and Scottish tradition of "keening." When a person in the community passed away, it was customary for a chosen woman, known as a keener, to sing a song of lament, or grief, at the person's funeral. Some keeners were believed to be descended from fairies.

Key Themes and Symbols

Banshees represent the certain approach of death, since their wail means that someone will die. For this reason, they are usually feared and seen as messengers from the land of the dead. However, they may also represent comfort and peace in the face of approaching death.

Nationality/Culture
Irish/Celtic

Pronunciation
BAN-shee

Alternate Names
Banshie, Bean Sídhe

Appears In
Irish and Celtic folktales

Lineage
None

Banshees in Art, Literature, and Everyday Life

Banshees are among the best-known beings from Irish mythology, appearing in the literary works of William Butler Yeats and modern fantasy novelist Terry Pratchett. They were also featured in the Disney film *Darby O'Gill and the Little People* (1959). Banshees are represented in many fantasy role-playing games, including the *Dungeons & Dragons* and *Warcraft* series. The term "banshee" has been used in the names of many different products, from vehicles to sunglasses.

Read, Write, Think, Discuss

As mentioned above, keening was a common part of Irish and Scottish funerals at one time. Using your library, the Internet, or other available sources, research "keening" as a funeral tradition in Ireland and

Scotland. What does the keener usually sing about? Is keening still performed in modern times? Why or why not?

SEE ALSO Celtic Mythology

Basilisk

Character Overview

In European mythology, the basilisk (pronounced BAS-uh-lisk) was a small serpent that could kill any living thing with its glance or its breath. It was usually represented as a creature with a dragon's body and wings, and a serpent's head. Early myths related that weasels and roosters were enemies of the basilisk. It was believed that a basilisk would die if it heard a rooster crowing. Another way to destroy a basilisk was to hold a mirror up to its face. The creature would die immediately after seeing its reflection. Travelers often carried roosters, weasels, or mirrors for protection when they traveled to regions where basilisks were thought to live.

The Basilisk in Context

The basilisk first appeared in legends from ancient Greece and Rome. Its name is derived from the Greek *basileus,* or "little king." The basilisk was described in detail by the author, naturalist, and philosopher Pliny the Elder in the first century CE. In the 1100s CE, St. Hildegard wrote of a serpent coming out of an egg sat upon by a toad. Early descriptions of the basilisk indicate that it was simply a small but very lethal serpent. Some historians believe that the legend may have been based on the deadly family of snakes known as cobras.

Key Themes and Symbols

Called the king of serpents, the basilisk was often associated with the devil and symbolized the deadly sin of lust. The fact that it was a serpent born from an egg incubated by a toad was an indication of its unnatural and unholy nature.

Nationality/Culture
Greek

Pronunciation
BAS-uh-lisk

Alternate Names
Regulus (Roman)

Appears In
Pliny the Elder's *Natural History*

Lineage
Born of a serpent's egg incubated by a rooster or toad

The Basilisk in Art, Literature, and Everyday Life

The basilisk appears in many European cultures across different religions and mythologies. Jesus is even depicted fighting one in medieval art. The basilisk is mentioned in literature by the English writers Geoffrey Chaucer and Edmund Spenser, and is referred to in William Shakespeare's plays *Romeo and Juliet* and *Richard III*. More recently, the basilisk has appeared in several role-playing games and the 1998 novel *Harry Potter and the Chamber of Secrets* by J. K. Rowling. The basilisk has also lent its name to a variety of tropical lizards known for their ability to run quickly across the surface of water using only their hind legs.

Read, Write, Think, Discuss

The basilisk is a creature that is often described as having parts similar to a mixture of other creatures. Create your own mythical creature using parts of existing animals and write a description of it. Describe any special powers you think it should have, and be sure to name it.

SEE ALSO Devils and Demons; Serpents and Snakes

Bast

Nationality/Culture
Egyptian

Pronunciation
BAST

Alternate Names
Bastet, Ubasti, Pasht

Appears In
Papyrus texts and engravings in Lower Egypt, Herodotus's *Histories*

Lineage
Sometimes referred to as the daughter of Isis and Osiris

Character Overview

Bast is best known as the cat-headed goddess of ancient Egypt. Evidence of Bast has been dated as early as 2600 BCE. Early myths suggest that she was the daughter of the **sun** god **Ra**, though later she was popularly known as the daughter of the goddess **Isis** (pronounced EYE-sis) and the god **Osiris** (pronounced oh-SYE-ris). In these later myths, she was also believed to be the sister of the god **Horus**.

Bast became closely associated with Sekhmet, a lion-headed goddess from Upper Egypt. Sekhmet was considered a warrior goddess, while Bast, being symbolized by a domesticated cat rather than a lion, was a gentler goddess who brought good fortune. Bast was the protector of cats and children, as well as the royal house of the pharaoh, or ruler of Egypt.

Because of her early association with Ra, Bast was considered a sun goddess; however, later Greek descriptions of Bast referred to her instead as a goddess of the moon.

Major Myths

In one early myth, Bast protected Ra from his mortal enemy, a serpent named Apep. For her service, she was given the serpent of wisdom known as Uraeus (pronounced your-AY-us). Symbols of this serpent became associated with the pharaohs, and were worn as headpieces to indicate that they were protected by Bast and Ra.

Bast in Context

The ancient Egyptians were among the first to document the domestication, or taming, of cats so they could live with humans. As far back as 4000 BCE, Egyptians used cats to keep rodent populations under control near areas of stored grain. Cats proved so important to maintaining grain supplies that they were considered sacred, or worthy of religious respect. They became common in many households, and when a family's cat died, the family went into a period of mourning. In fact, cats held a special place in the hearts of ancient Egyptians even after death: in 1888, a farmer near Beni Hasan uncovered a tomb containing tens of thousands of dead cats that had been mummified, or dried and preserved, thousands of years before.

Key Themes and Symbols

As the protector of cats, the main symbol associated with Bast is the cat. Another important symbol is the sistrum, a handheld musical instrument containing discs of metal that make

Statue of the Egyptian goddess Bast. THE ART ARCHIVE/ MUSÉE DU LOUVRE PARIS/ GIANNI DAGLI ORTI/THE PIC- TURE DESK, INC.

noise when shaken. In ancient Egyptian art, Bast is often depicted with a human body and the head of a cat, holding a sistrum in one of her hands.

Bast in Art, Literature, and Everyday Life

The goddess Bast was mentioned in Book 2 of *Histories* by the Greek historian Herodotus in the fifth century BCE. Herodotus described the annual festival held at Bubastis, the city named in honor of Bast. Icons of Bast, depicting the cat-headed goddess, remain popular in modern times as decorative symbols of ancient Egypt. Bast appeared as a character in various Marvel comic book series beginning in 1966, and was the subject of a graphic novel trilogy entitled *The Sandman Presents: Bast* (2003). The goddess is mentioned in the 2004 film *Catwoman* as the source of Catwoman's unusual powers.

Read, Write, Think, Discuss

In many ways, the ancient Egyptians treated cats much like modern pet owners do. Some historians claim that cats were important to Egyptians only because they controlled rodent populations. Why do you think domesticated animals such as cats and dogs remain popular in modern times? What functions, if any, do you think pets serve? Do you think we give our pets as much respect and adoration as the ancient Egyptians did?

SEE ALSO Egyptian Mythology; Horus; Isis; Osiris

Nationality/Culture
Greek/Roman

Pronunciation
BAW-sis and fi-LEE-muhn

Alternate Names
None

Appears In
Ovid's *Metamorphoses*

Lineage
Unknown

Baucis and Philemon

Character Overview

Baucis (pronounced BAW-sis) and Philemon (pronounced fi-LEE-muhn), an old couple from the land of Phrygia (pronounced FRIJ-ee-uh), showed hospitality toward the gods and were rewarded.

According to Greek myth, the gods **Zeus** (pronounced ZOOS) and **Hermes** (pronounced HUR-meez) assumed human form and visited earth disguised as poor travelers. When they reached Phrygia, an ancient kingdom located in the west-central part of Anatolia, they looked for shelter but were turned away by everyone except Philemon and his wife, Baucis.

The old couple gladly shared their small amount of food and wine with the strangers. Baucis and Philemon realized that their guests were gods after noticing that the wine jug never ran out and their poor wine was replaced by wine of the finest quality. Once refreshed, Zeus and Hermes led the couple to a hill above Phrygia and sent a flood to destroy the land to punish the people who had turned them away. Only the old couple's house remained undamaged. Zeus made the house a temple to the gods and awarded Baucis and Philemon two wishes: to serve as priest and priestess of the temple and, when the time came, to die together. Many years later, when the moment of their deaths came, Baucis and Philemon were transformed into trees, one linden (also known as lime) and one oak, with intertwined branches.

Baucis and Philemon in Context

Phrygia, where Baucis and Philemon lived, was a region that covered a large inland portion of present-day Turkey. Phrygian culture was distinct from Greek culture, and the Phrygian people worshipped many gods different from the Greeks. The Greeks often associated these Phrygian gods with their own. For example, the Phrygian nomadic horseman god Sabazios was usually linked to Zeus or **Dionysus**. Much of what is known about Phrygian culture is taken from existing Greek works, such as Homer's *Iliad*.

Key Themes and Symbols

The linden, or lime, tree is considered by many European cultures to be a symbol of love and fertility. The oak tree is widely considered to be a symbol of strength and steadfastness, and was even used as a symbol of Zeus. Both trees are known to have lifespans of many centuries. The intertwining branches symbolize a bond between the two that promises to gain strength as the trees continue to grow.

In the myth, Baucis and Philemon are the only people in Phrygia to help the two gods disguised as strangers. For this reason, Baucis and Philemon also symbolize hospitality to travelers.

Baucis and Philemon in Art, Literature, and Everyday Life

Baucis and Philemon have very limited appearances in Greek myth, but their tale remains a popular one among later artists and writers. Ovid's original tale was translated by John Dryden in 1693, and Jonathan Swift wrote his own poetic update to the myth, setting it in England around 1709. The bestselling novel *Cold Mountain* by Charles Frazier (1997) uses the tale of Baucis and Philemon as a counterpoint to the Civil War–era couple that serve as his main characters.

Read, Write, Think, Discuss

Using the library, the Internet, or other resources, find Jonathan Swift's poem "Baucis and Philemon" (1708) and read it. (The poem is freely available on Web sites that offer public domain works of literature.) How does Swift's poem differ in tone and message from the original myth? How is the ending different? Which version do you prefer and why?

SEE ALSO Greek Mythology; Hermes; Zeus

Bellerophon

Nationality/Culture
Greek

Pronunciation
buh-LAIR-uh-fun

Alternate Names
Bellerophontes

Appears In
Homer's *Iliad*, Hesiod's *Theogony*

Lineage
Son of King Glaucus of Corinth

Character Overview

In **Greek mythology**, Bellerophon (pronounced buh-LAIR-uh-fun) was a hero and warrior who accidentally killed his own brother. He tamed the winged horse **Pegasus** (PEG-uh-suhs) and fought a ferocious beast called the Chimaera (pronounced kye-MEER-uh).

After accidentally killing his brother and another man, Bellerophon sought protection from King **Proteus** (pronounced PRO-tee-uhs) of Tiryns (pronounced TEER-ins), who granted Bellerophon shelter. Proteus's wife, Anteia (pronounced ahn-TAY-uh), tried to seduce Bellerophon, but he resisted her. Angry at being rejected, Anteia told her husband that Bellerophon had tried to rape her. Proteus was furious but did not want to kill his guest. Instead, he sent Bellerophon to Anteia's father, King Iobates (pronounced eye-OH-buh-teez) of Lycia

(pronounced LISH-ee-uh). He also sent a note explaining what had happened and asking Iobates to kill Bellerophon.

Iobates, too, was reluctant to kill his guest, so he sent him on dangerous missions instead. First, he asked Bellerophon to kill the Chimaera, a fire-breathing monster with the head of a lion, the body of a goat, and the tail of a serpent. With the help of the gods, Bellerophon tamed the winged horse Pegasus and then used it to fight the Chimaera. He still could not get near the beast because of its fiery breath, but the gods helped him formulate a plan. He put a block of lead on the end of his spear and lodged it into the Chimaera's throat. The heat of its breath melted the lead, which went down the creature's throat and suffocated it. After the defeat of the Chimaera, Iobates ordered Bellerophon to defeat two armies, including the fierce **Amazons**. Bellerophon succeeded in these missions as well.

Afterward, Bellerophon told the sea god **Poseidon** (pronounced poh-SYE-dun) that Iobates seemed ungrateful for his help. In response, Poseidon caused a great flood to strike Lycia. Iobates finally realized that Bellerophon must be innocent of the charges against him. When he discovered that his guest did not rape Anteia, Iobates gave Bellerophon one of his daughters as a bride and made him heir to the throne of Lycia.

Proud of his success, Bellerophon tried to ride Pegasus to Mount Olympus (pronounced oh-LIM-puhs), home of the gods. **Zeus** (pronounced ZOOS) sent a fly to bite Pegasus, who bucked and threw Bellerophon to the ground. Bellerophon survived the fall but was crippled for life. He spent the rest of his days wandering the earth as a beggar.

Bellerophon in Context

During the Middle Ages and Renaissance, a more popular Greek hero was credited for taming Pegasus, which was one of Bellerophon's main accomplishments. The artwork of the period showed **Perseus** (pronounced PUR-see-uhs) taming Pegasus, which led to this version of the story becoming the one most generally accepted in modern culture.

Key Themes and Symbols

One of the important themes in Bellerophon's tale is the danger of *hubris,* or excessive pride that clouds one's judgment. Bellerophon, because of his great heroism, believes that he deserves to go to Mount Olympus. The powerful Olympian gods disagree, and Zeus causes Bellerophon to fall and become crippled for life.

Bellerophon in Art, Literature, and Everyday Life

Bellerophon was one of the more celebrated **heroes** in ancient Greece. He was usually depicted riding Pegasus and slaying the Chimaera.

Fratricide

Killing a brother, or fratricide, is considered an unthinkably horrible crime in many cultures. In Christian mythology, Cain, the son of Adam and Eve, kills his brother Abel. God curses him and banishes him from the society of others. The story also appears in the holy book of Islam, the Qur'an.

Euripides' (pronounced yoo-RIP-i-deez) tragedy, *Bellerophontes,* details his story, only fragments of which still remain. During the Middle Ages and Renaissance, Bellerophon's role became less important as depictions of Perseus became more popular among artists and writers.

Read, Write, Think, Discuss

Compare the myth of Bellerophon with the myth of **Heracles** and his twelve labors. How are the two myths similar? How are they different? Does each one have a different theme or lesson?

SEE ALSO Amazons; Pegasus; Proteus; Zeus

Beowulf

Myth Overview

Beowulf (pronounced BAY-uh-woolf) is the earliest existing Anglo-Saxon epic, or a long, grand-scale poem. It tells the story of Beowulf, a Norse hero and warrior who fought and conquered several monsters that terrorized Denmark and Sweden.

 Beowulf is divided into two parts. The action in the first part takes place in Denmark, where Hrothgar (pronounced ROTH-gar) is king. Beowulf, a mighty warrior from Sweden, comes to help the king destroy a monster that is terrorizing the local people. The second part, set in Sweden, provides an account of Beowulf as an old man who must rid his country of a fearsome dragon.

Nationality/Culture
Anglo-Saxon

Pronunciation
BAY-uh-woolf

Alternate Names
None

Appears In
The epic *Beowulf*

Grendel As part one of the story opens, readers are introduced to King Hrothgar. He has built a great assembly hall called Heorot (pronounced HAY-oh-roht), where his warriors gather to eat, drink, and receive treasure after their victories in combat. Lurking in the dark swamps of Hrothgar's kingdom is a cruel and brutal monster named Grendel (pronounced GREN-dl). Grendel lives in a cave with his mother, also a monster, and cannot be harmed by the weapons of humans. As Grendel roams the marshes and swamps, he hears the joyful sounds of song and laughter from Heorot. They fill him with envy and hatred for Hrothgar and his warriors. One night, Grendel goes to Heorot and finds the warriors asleep after a great deal of drinking and celebration. He snatches up thirty sleeping men, kills them, and carries their bodies home to eat.

In the morning, Hrothgar sees the bloody aftermath of Grendel's attack. Loud wails and cries replace the joyful singing of the previous night. The Danes see Grendel's footprints, but do not think he will return; however, the next night Grendel comes back and kills even more warriors. The Danes gather in their temples and pray for protection from Grendel, but their prayers do not help. For twelve years Grendel continues to terrorize the warriors. Afraid to sleep at Heorot, they abandon the great hall.

Stories of Grendel's raids spread to the surrounding kingdoms, eventually reaching the land of the Geats in southern Sweden. When a mighty Geatish warrior named Beowulf—a man who has slain **giants** and sea monsters and is known for his strength, courage, and skill in battle—hears of Grendel's deeds, he decides to sail to Denmark and help Hrothgar rid his kingdom of the monster.

Beowulf prepares a ship and chooses fourteen brave warriors to accompany him. They set sail for Denmark, arriving the next day. At Heorot, the Geats are welcomed by Hrothgar, who has known Beowulf since he was a child. The king throws a feast for the Geatish warriors. At the feast, a Danish warrior named Unferth insults Beowulf by suggesting that he is too boastful and not a great enough warrior to kill Grendel. Beowulf responds by noting that he has heard no tales of Unferth's bravery. He says that if Unferth were as fierce as he believes himself to be that Grendel would not now be terrorizing the Danes. Pleased by Beowulf's defiant attitude, Hrothgar is confident that the Geatish warrior will slay Grendel and free the kingdom from the monster's evil.

What's a Life Worth?

The story of Beowulf features a concept, common in early Germanic societies, known as *wergild* (pronounced WAIR-geld). This was the price set on a person's life based on that person's value to society. If an individual was killed, the family received wergild to compensate for the loss. In *Beowulf*, Hrothgar presents Beowulf with wergild for the Geatish warrior who was killed fighting Grendel. According to Germanic law, the system of wergild was meant as an alternative to seeking revenge for the loss of a loved one.

That night, the Geats stay at Heorot. Grendel soon appears and, before Beowulf can stop him, kills one of Beowulf's own men. Grendel then grabs Beowulf, but the mighty warrior seizes the monster's arm with his powerful grip. Beowulf and Grendel struggle until Grendel finally manages to wrench himself away, leaving his arm in Beowulf's grasp. The monster staggers back to his cave to die. The severed arm is hung in Heorot as a trophy for all to see. Hrothgar showers Beowulf with gifts and honors him with another feast. The Danes believe they will finally be able to sleep in peace at Heorot again.

Grendel's Mother The Danes' troubles are not over. When Grendel's mother sees her dying son, she vows revenge. She goes to Heorot at night and surprises the Danish warriors. After killing the king's most trusted adviser, she leaves with Grendel's arm. Again the Danes call upon Beowulf for help.

Beowulf and several warriors track the monster to her lair in the swamps. They find it at the base of a cliff at the bottom of a pool bubbling with blood and gore. Unferth, who has by now changed his opinion of Beowulf, lends him Hrunting, his sword. Brandishing it, Beowulf leaps into the slimy waters. Grendel's mother grabs Beowulf and pulls him into a cave where the water cannot enter. Beowulf strikes at the monster with Hrunting, but the sword does not hurt her. The two wrestle, and Grendel's mother almost kills Beowulf, but his armor saves him. Then he sees a giant sword hanging on the wall of the cave. He grabs it and, with one mighty swing, cuts off the monster's head. At the back of the cave, he sees Grendel's corpse.

Using the same sword, he cuts off Grendel's head and returns to the surface with it. He also brings the remains of the sword. Beowulf and his men return to Heorot in triumph, and Hrothgar again rewards them. Finally, the Geats go home to Sweden where Beowulf eventually becomes king.

Beowulf and the Dragon As the second part of the epic begins, Beowulf has ruled for fifty years, and his kingdom has prospered. A winged dragon lives in the land, protecting an ancient treasure buried hundreds of years earlier. One day, a slave who had been punished by his master runs away and finds the cave where the treasure is buried. To earn his master's forgiveness, the slave steals a golden cup and takes it to his household. When the dragon inspects the treasure, as he did every day, he quickly notices the missing cup. To punish the Geats for stealing from him, the dragon flies over the countryside breathing **fire** on the villages and setting homes ablaze.

Though he is now an old man, Beowulf decides to fight the dragon. He and eleven warriors find the dragon's cave, but Beowulf insists on fighting the dragon alone. Early in the battle, Beowulf discovers that his iron shield will not protect him against the dragon's fiery breath. Just as Beowulf is about to be killed, a warrior named Wiglaf, Beowulf's young kinsman, rushes to his aid. With Wiglaf's help, Beowulf slays the dragon. Mortally wounded in the battle, the king asks Wiglaf to bring out the treasure so that he might see it before he dies.

In accordance with Norse burial customs, Beowulf's body is burned in a great fire on a cliff overlooking the sea. The treasure is placed in the fire with Beowulf as a **sacrifice**. A large burial mound is built over the remains of the fire to serve as a reminder of the great king, and to provide a landmark for seafarers. The poem ends with a ceremony of praise for Beowulf.

Beowulf in Context

The manuscript containing the story of Beowulf was discovered in England in the 1600s. It was written in Old English, the language of the Anglo-Saxon invaders who settled in England between 450 and 600 CE. There is some debate about when *Beowulf* was written and who wrote it. Although the manuscript dates from around 1000, the poem was composed much earlier, sometime between 700 and 950.

As Beowulf and Grendel struggle, Beowulf rips off the monster's arm. © MARY EVANS PICTURE LIBRARY/THE IMAGE WORKS.

Certain references in the text suggest that the author was a Christian who modeled the story after pagan (non-Judeo-Christian) tales of past Norse and German **heroes**. The writer was probably either a monk or a poet connected to a nobleman's court in central or northern England.

Beowulf is set in a much earlier time than the period in which it was written, and the action takes place in Denmark and Sweden. The story shows the warrior culture of ancient Germanic peoples, where wars were so common that many men held steady jobs as fighters. The king supplied these warriors with food, shelter, land, and weapons. In return, they promised to be loyal and obedient to the king.

Key Themes and Symbols

Beowulf emphasizes values that were important to Norse warriors, such as courage, loyalty to one's king and comrades, and honor for those who fight and die bravely. The story emphasizes how fragile life and fame can be. Like any person, Beowulf must find meaning in his world while accepting the fact that he will eventually die. He meets that challenge by facing danger bravely and trusting that the story of his deeds will cause him to live on in the memories of those who hear it.

Beowulf in Art, Literature, and Popular Culture

Beowulf has endured over the centuries as a prime example of a Western European hero. He is different from many Greek and Roman heroes in that even though he possesses great strength and skills, he is fully human, and his successes do not depend upon help from the gods. The story of Beowulf has been translated and adapted by many writers over the centuries. Numerous movies have also been made about the hero, such as the motion-capture computer-animated *Beowulf* (2007).

Read, Write, Think, Discuss

John Gardner's novel *Grendel* (1971) is a retelling of the story of Beowulf from Grendel's point of view. Gardner calls into question the heroism of Beowulf, and offers a starkly different account of the events described in the epic poem.

Think about how point of view affects the telling of a story. What factors can cause a single set of events to be described in two vastly different ways?

SEE ALSO Dragons; Norse Mythology; Witches and Wizards

Bhagavad Gita

Myth Overview

Written more than two thousand years ago, the *Bhagavad Gita* is probably the most widely read of the Hindu scriptures and contains some of the basic ideas of Hindu culture. The poem is actually part of a larger Hindu epic (long poem) called the **Mahabharata**, which tells the story of the struggle between two closely related families, the Kauravas and the Pandavas. The *Bhagavad Gita* begins just before the start of the great battle between the families. It is written in the form of a conversation between one of the warriors, Prince Arjuna, and his chariot driver, **Krishna**—actually a god in disguise.

As the poem opens, the two armies are lined up facing each other across the battlefield. Prince Arjuna questions his part in the war. He wonders whether he should follow his duty and fight, even though this would mean killing friends, relatives, and teachers in the opposing army, or whether he should throw down his arms and let himself be killed. Krishna reminds Arjuna that everyone has certain duties in society. As a member of the warrior caste (the second highest level in India's complex social class system), Arjuna's duty is to fight and protect. Yet, while he is required by duty to act, his actions must be "right" actions, meaning they must be guided by devotion and selflessness.

The *Bhagavad Gita* in Context

The *Mahabharata* (pronounced muh-hah-BAHR-ruh-tuh), the great epic of which the *Bhagavad Gita* is a part, is one of the longest poems in the world, with over 1.5 million words and almost seventy-five thousand verses. The sage Vyasa (pronounced vee-YAH-sah), who may or may not have been a real person, is believed to be its author, but he probably just collected and compiled the many stories in the epic. Originally the *Mahabharata* was passed down through oral tradition, changing and developing from generation to generation. The *Bhagavad Gita* was probably added to the original epic sometime between the fifth and second centuries BCE. If the *Mahabharata* describes an actual historical war, scholars place it around the beginning of the ninth century BCE.

Nationality/Culture
Hindu

Pronunciation
BAH-ga-vad GEE-ta

Alternate Names
The Gita, The Song of God

Appears In
The *Mahabharata*

Page from the **Bhagavad Gita,** *the most widely read of the Hindu scriptures.* © ART MEDIA/HIP/THE IMAGE WORKS.

Key Themes and Symbols

Selfless devotion to duty is the major lesson in the *Bhagavad Gita*. Each caste has its own specific duty, and society as a whole benefits when all members perform their duty properly. Through the conversation between Arjuna and Krishna, the reader also learns of many ways to express religious belief, including meditation, worship, and work. The poem teaches that Krishna is a loving god who is concerned about people's welfare and who appears on earth to help during times of trouble.

The *Bhagavad Gita* in Art, Literature, and Everyday Life

Throughout history, religious and political leaders in India have written commentaries on the *Bhagavad Gita* and translated it into many Indian languages. Mahatma Gandhi, a major figure in the Indian independence movement, referred to the *Bhagavad Gita* as his "spiritual dictionary." Since 1785, the text has also been translated into English and European languages. The *Bhagavad Gita* was the inspiration for the former Beatle George Harrison's posthumous album, *Brainwashed* (2002). Robert Redford's 2000 film *The Legend of Bagger Vance*, starring Will Smith, Matt Damon, Jack Lemmon, and Charlize Theron, was based on Steven

Pressfield's 1995 novel of the same name that takes place in the *Bhagavad Gita*. In both the film and the novel, Bagger Vance is a Krishna figure who guides the main character through difficult times.

Read, Write, Think, Discuss

The Bhagavad Gita: A Walkthrough for Westerners by Jack Hawley (2001) is one way to enjoy the tale with the help of an expert. This book presents the tale in a simple, easy-to-read format and explains the significance of elements to those unfamiliar with Hinduism and Indian culture.

SEE ALSO Hinduism and Mythology; Krishna; Vishnu

Bragi

Character Overview

In **Norse mythology**, Bragi was the god of poetry. He was the son of **Odin** (OH-din) and the husband of **Idun** (EE-thoon), the goddess of fertility. Described as an old man with a long beard, Bragi welcomed to **Valhalla** the warriors who had died in battle.

Major Myths

Bragi condemned the trickster god **Loki** for his role in causing the death of the much-loved god **Balder**. The two exchanged threats despite the other gods' attempts to calm them down until finally Loki predicted the destruction of the gods and left them.

Bragi in Context

Some scholars think that the figure of Bragi might have come from Bragi Boddason, a Norwegian poet of the ninth century CE. In his *Prose Edda*, author Snorri Sturluson mentions Bragi Boddason as a real historical figure who served a number of Swedish kings and was a well-known poet in his time. He could have inspired a legend that grew over the centuries because the culture of this time period placed high value on poets, who

Nationality/Culture
Norse

Pronunciation
BRAH-gee

Alternate Names
None

Appears In
The Eddas

Lineage
Son of Odin

were considered second only to kings in esteem. However, throughout his writings, Sturluson—who wrote about four hundred years after Bragi Boddason lived—does not indicate that the two Bragis are related.

Key Themes and Symbols

Bragi is usually depicted with a harp, an important accompanying instrument for a poet who reads his work aloud. He is always shown with a long beard. He is sometimes described as having runes, or characters from an ancient and magical alphabet, carved on his tongue. Bragi was associated with royal funeral services, when a "cup of Bragi" was used to drink to the honor of a dead king. This cup also figured in the taking of oaths, as anyone taking an oath would do so over a cup of Bragi.

Bragi in Art, Literature, and Everyday Life

Bragi does not often appear outside the classic works of Norse mythology. The most well-known images of Bragi are from the nineteenth century: an illustration by Carl Walbohm, and a painting by Nils Blommér.

Read, Write, Think, Discuss

Legends are sometimes based on a real historical figure. Think of someone whom you admire; it can be someone famous, or someone you know. Write a description of that person as a figure of legend. What characteristics do you think would be remembered and exaggerated? What aspects of their appearance would be emphasized? Are there any particular legends for which the person would be remembered?

SEE ALSO Idun; Odin; Valhalla

Brahma

Character Overview

In Hindu mythology, Brahma was the first god in the sacred Hindu trinity, or Trimurti. The other gods were **Vishnu**, the Preserver, and

Nationality/Culture
Hindu

Pronunciation
BRAH-muh

Alternate Names
None

Appears In
The Puranas, the Brahma-Samita

Lineage
Born from the navel of Vishnu

Shiva, the Destroyer. Brahma was the creator god, but his role was not as great as that of creator gods in other mythologies. Brahma's ability to create is a skill he uses at the request of greater gods when something needs to be created; typically, he creates by thinking something into being. When Brahma comes under the influence of darkness, he creates demons; under the influence of goodness, he creates gods. He can also grant immortality, and his tendency to grant immortality to demons causes significant problems for Vishnu and Shiva, who must overcome them. Brahma is not involved in matters concerning death.

Major Myths

There are many different accounts of the origin of Brahma. According to one story, the creator made the cosmic waters and put a seed in them. The seed turned into a golden egg. After one thousand years, the creator himself emerged from the egg as a younger Brahma. He then made the universe and all things in it. Another legend says that Brahma was born in a lotus flower that sprouted from Vishnu's navel. He went on to create the fathers of humankind, as well as all other things in the universe.

According to legend, Brahma had four faces that came into being from his desire to gaze at a beautiful goddess he created. Brahma originally had five heads, but the god Shiva destroyed one of them when Brahma spoke to him disrespectfully.

Brahma in Context

In the early literature of Hinduism, Brahma was one of the major gods. However, he plays little part in the modern Hindu religion. Over time, Vishnu and Shiva became more important than Brahma and are more widely worshipped today. While Shiva and Vishnu are each worshipped at thousands of sites throughout India, Brahma alone is worshipped at only a handful of temples. Various legends suggest that Brahma was cursed by either Shiva or a high priest, the curse being that no person would ever worship him. Some scholars believe that Brahma's one-sided focus on the act of creation is why he is not as important as the other gods, who deal with both creation and with death; worshippers seek to follow a god who is responsible for every aspect of their lives—both life and death.

Key Themes and Symbols

In works of art, Brahma is usually portrayed with four faces and four arms. The four faces symbolize the four Vedas, the ancient sacred texts of Hinduism. Brahma is often shown wearing white robes and holding a scepter, an alms bowl, a bow, and other items. Brahma is also associated with the swan, a bird that signifies justice and the ability to separate good from bad.

Brahma in Art, Literature, and Everyday Life

Because Brahma does not have nearly as many dedicated temples as other principal Hindu gods, there are fewer instances of his appearance in art.

Ralph Waldo Emerson wrote a poem titled "Brahma" in 1856, though some academics suggest that Emerson's poem refers not to Brahma but to the idea of "brahman," the Hindu belief that the divine is present in all things in the universe.

Read, Write, Think, Discuss

Using your library, the Internet, or other available resources, research the Thai god known as Phra Phrom. How is this god similar to Brahma? Are there any differences between the two?

SEE ALSO Hinduism and Mythology; Shiva; Vishnu

Brer Rabbit

Character Overview

Brer Rabbit is the main character in the Uncle Remus tales written by Joel Chandler Harris (1848–1908). As a trickster—a mischievous character known for the ability to deceive—Brer Rabbit outsmarts larger and stronger animals, such as Brer Fox and Brer Bear. Many stories about Brer Rabbit originated in African folklore and were brought to America by African slaves.

Perhaps the most famous Brer Rabbit story is the one about Brer Rabbit and the tar baby. In this tale, Brer Fox makes a life-size figure out of sticky tar and places it on the road in the hopes of catching Brer Rabbit with it. Indeed, when Brer Rabbit comes along and greets the tar baby several times without getting a reply, he gets annoyed enough to hit the tar baby. His hand gets stuck in the tar and he is unable to escape.

Brer Fox pulls Brer Rabbit out of the tar, with the intent of doing him harm. He proposes several different ways of disposing of Brer Rabbit, and Brer Rabbit makes a show of accepting each option, but adding a plea each time that Brer Fox not throw him into a nearby briar patch. Thinking that the briar patch must surely be the worst fate of all if Brer Rabbit was willing to be killed in any other way, Brer Fox flung the rabbit into the briar patch. Brer Rabbit had tricked him, however, because, as he taunts Brer Fox after escaping, "I was born and raised in the briar patch."

Nationality/Culture
African American

Pronunciation
brehr RAB-it

Alternate Names
None

Appears In
The *Uncle Remus* series

Lineage
None

Brer Rabbit in Context

After originating in African-American oral tales, Brer Rabbit became one of the main characters in the Uncle Remus books, written in the 1880s and 1890s by Southern journalist Joel Chandler Harris. The books brought the stories to a whole new audience, but also generated controversy. Since the tales were taken from African-American folklore, Harris, a white man, was accused of stealing the myths and passing them off as his own creations. Furthermore, by the mid-twentieth-century the stories' use of the dialect of the Deep South and the demeaning stereotype of the complacent Negro as seen in the character of the narrator Uncle Remus offended many people.

Key Themes and Symbols

The stories of Brer Rabbit are generally trickster tales and involve Brer Rabbit getting himself into trouble through his own selfishness or mischievous nature. He must then use his cleverness to get himself out of trouble.

Brer Rabbit in Art, Literature, and Everyday Life

Several stories of Brer Rabbit and his friends were combined and adapted into the Disney animated feature *Song of the South*, released in 1946. The characters can also be seen in the Splash Mountain attractions at both Disneyland and Walt Disney World amusement parks.

Read, Write, Think, Discuss

Some people feel that Joel Chandler Harris took the Brer Rabbit stories from African-American folklore and wrongly sold them as his own. Do you think it is acceptable for a person to write his or her own version of a folktale or myth, and then sell it? What about modern authors who create their own versions of fairy tales or Greek myths? In your opinion, do myths belong only to the culture that creates them?

SEE ALSO African Mythology; Anansi; Tricksters

Brunhilde

Character Overview

In Icelandic and German mythology, Brunhilde was a strong and beautiful princess who was cruelly deceived by her lover. Her story is told in the Edda poems of Iceland and the ***Nibelungenlied***, a German poem

Nationality/Culture
Norse

Pronunciation
BROON-hilt

Alternate Names
Brünhild, Brunhilda, Brynhildr

Appears In
The Poetic Edda, the *Nibelungenlied*

Lineage
Daughter of Budli

of the thirteenth century CE. Her name appears with many slight variations, including Brünhild, Brunhilda, or Brynhildr.

In the Icelandic version of the legend, Brunhilde was a Valkyrie—a warrior maiden of the supreme god **Odin** (pronounced OH-din). She was asked to settle an argument between two kings, and she did not support the king that Odin favored. For this, Odin punished Brunhilde by causing her to fall into an everlasting sleep surrounded by a wall of **fire**. The hero **Sigurd** (pronounced SIG-erd) crossed through the flames and woke the maiden with a kiss. They became engaged, but Sigurd left to continue his travels. Later, after receiving a magic potion that made him forget his love for Brunhilde, Sigurd married Gudrun.

Gudrun's brother Gunnar wanted Brunhilde for himself and persuaded Sigurd to help him. Gunnar was unable to reach Brunhilde because of the ring of fire that encircled the castle where she stayed. Disguising himself as Gunnar, Sigurd was able to pass through the fire and reach Brunhilde, and they married. Later Brunhilde realized she had been tricked, and arranged to have Sigurd murdered. When she learned of his death, however, she was overcome with grief and committed suicide by throwing herself on his funeral pyre, a large pile of burning wood used to cremate a dead body. In that way, she could join him in death.

In the *Nibelungenlied*, the story was slightly different. Brunhilde declared that the man she would marry must be able to outperform her in feats of strength and courage. Siegfried (Sigurd), disguised as Gunther (Gunnar), passed the test and won Brunhilde for Gunther. When she discovered the deception, she arranged for Siegfried to be killed.

Brunhilde in Context

Many scholars believe that Brunhilde is based on Queen Brunhilda of Austrasia, who ruled regions of what is now France and Germany during the sixth and seventh centuries CE. She married a king named Sigebert. Queen Brunhilda also had an ongoing feud with her brother-in-law's wife, Fredegund, who eventually hired assassins to murder Sigebert in order to gain the upper hand in a war between the brothers. Queen Brunhilda went on to control the kingdoms of Austrasia and Burgundy through her son and later her grandson, but was accused of using murder and treachery to maintain power. She was eventually condemned to

Brunhilde. © PRIVATE COL-
LECTION/© CHRIS BEETLES,
LONDON, UK/THE BRIDGE-
MAN ART LIBRARY.

death, the manner of which required her to be tied to several horses and
torn apart as they each pulled in different directions.

Key Themes and Symbols

Two of the main themes found in Brunhilde's tale are betrayal and
revenge. Odin seeks revenge on Brunhilde when she does not support
the argument of the king he favored. Later, Brunhilde seeks revenge

against Sigurd when she discovers that he deceived her into marrying him instead of his brother. Gunnar wants revenge against Sigurd because he believes Sigurd betrayed him by sleeping with Brunhilde, even though he did not.

Brunhilde in Art, Literature, and Everyday Life

Brunhilde has proven to be an especially popular character in European art and literature. The German composer Richard Wagner based part of his opera cycle *The Ring of the Nibelung* on the legend of Brunhilde. Brunhilde is a main character in the 2006 film *Dark Kingdom: The Dragon King* (released in the UK in 2004 as *Sword of Xanten*), a partial adaptation of the story of the rings of the Nibelung.

Read, Write, Think, Discuss

The legend of Brunhilde shares some similarities with the fairy tale *Sleeping Beauty*, written in 1697 by Charles Perrault and later adapted into a Disney animated film. Find and read a version of the Sleeping Beauty tale, and compare it to the legend of Brunhilde. How are the stories similar? How are they different?

SEE ALSO Sigurd; Valkyries

Buddhism and Mythology

Buddhist Mythology in Context

Buddhism, one of the major religions of the world, was founded in India in the sixth century BCE and then spread throughout Asia. Over time, many different Buddhist sects, or unique groups, have developed, each with its own variations of gods and legends. Although Buddhism has produced little mythology of its own, it has incorporated stories from mythologies of various groups that adopted the religion.

Core Deities and Characters

The roots of Buddhism can be traced to one man: Siddhartha Gautama (pronounced see-DAHR-tuh GAW-tuh-muh), a prince from a small state in northern India. Although he was a historical figure, many of the stories about him are based on legend. This has made it difficult to distinguish between fact and fiction. Yet the basic elements of Siddhartha Gautama's life story—whether real or invented—are well known, as are his religious teachings.

The son of King Suddhodana (pronounced soo-doh-DAH-nah), Gautama was born around 563 BCE. According to legend, his mother, Queen Maya, had a dream in which she was expecting a child fathered by a white elephant. Local brahmins, or holy men, interpreted the dream to mean that the queen would give birth to a great man. They said that the child would become a powerful king unless he became aware of human suffering in the world. If that happened, he would become a great holy man and savior.

Some legends say that when Gautama was born the earth shook, rivers stopped flowing, flowers fell from the sky, and a lotus flower sprang from the place where he first touched the earth. Mindful of the prophecy about his son, King Suddhodana did everything possible to shield the boy from knowledge of the outside world and human suffering. He built a palace in which his son could enjoy all of life's pleasures, and he forbade any mention of death, grief, or sickness.

One day Gautama expressed a wish to see the world outside the palace. Suddhodana agreed to take his son to a nearby town, but first he had the town cleaned up and ordered that everything unpleasant be removed. During the visit, however, Gautama saw a sick man, an old man, a beggar, and a corpse. Shocked to discover that people lived in poverty, became sick, grew old, and died, the prince realized that he knew nothing about the real world. Determined to learn the truth about the world, Gautama gave up all his possessions and left his home. He became a beggar and sought truth and understanding by denying himself all pleasures.

After six years of wandering and seeking wisdom from holy men, Gautama realized that he was no nearer truth and understanding than before. He decided to look for the truth within himself and went to the town of Bodh Gaya to sit beneath the Bodhi (pronounced BOH-dee) tree and meditate, or think deeply and spiritually. While he was meditating, the evil spirit Mara tried to tempt Gautama with beautiful women. When this failed, Mara threatened him with demons and finally threw a fiery disc at him. However, the disc turned into flowers that floated down on Gautama's head.

The Noble Eightfold Path

Buddhism describes a "noble eightfold path" to enlightenment:

1. Right view
2. Right intention
3. Right speech
4. Right action
5. Right livelihood
6. Right effort
7. Right mindfulness
8. Right concentration

After five weeks of meditation, Gautama came to understand that the only way to avoid suffering was to free oneself from all desires. At the moment he realized this, Siddhartha Gautama became the Buddha, the "enlightened one" who is free from suffering. He then began to travel and teach others how to achieve spiritual happiness. Buddha gained many followers before his death around 483 BCE.

After the death of Buddha, his followers carried Buddhist teachings throughout Asia. Within a few hundred years, Buddhism was practiced in Sri Lanka, Burma (modern-day Myanmar), Thailand, Cambodia, and most of Southeast Asia. By the 600s CE, it had spread to central Asia, China, Korea, Japan, and Tibet.

Major Myths

Buddhism teaches that all humans experience many lives and are constantly reincarnated—reborn after death into a different form of existence. The form each person takes in a new life depends on *karma*, which is the total of one's good and bad deeds in previous lives. The goal of Buddhism is to escape this cycle of death and rebirth by achieving enlightenment. When that happens, a person enters a timeless state known as *nirvana* and is free of all desire.

The original form of Buddhism, recorded in texts from about 100 BCE, is called Theravada Buddhism. Its followers believed that there would be only one Buddha in the world at any one time. Theravada Buddhism spread to Sri Lanka, Burma, and much of Southeast Asia. A later form of Buddhism, called Mahayana, taught that many Buddhas might exist at the same time. It attracted followers in China, Japan, Tibet, and Korea.

As Buddhism spread, it divided into many different sects. Each sect developed its own traditions and mythology, often based on a combination of local beliefs and deities with Buddhist teaching.

India Early Buddhism in India was influenced by Brahmanism, an early form of the Hindu religion. Both religions shared the idea of the cycle of birth and **reincarnation**, and both included Devas, traditional Indian gods, and Asuras, powerful demons.

A principal figure in Indian Buddhism was Amitabha, who was a *bodhisattva* (pronounced boh-dee-SAT-vah)—a person who had become enlightened but chose not to enter nirvana in order to help others gain enlightenment. According to legend, Amitabha was born from a lotus flower and came to the aid of Buddhists who worshipped him and pronounced his sacred name.

China Arriving in China in about 65 CE, Buddhism developed into one of that country's three most important religions, alongside Taoism and Confucianism. Buddhist gods came to be worshipped in Taoist temples and vice versa, and in some temples, the three religions were practiced side by side.

The Mahayana Buddhism practiced in China was an elaborate form of the religion, with more gods and myths than Theravada Buddhism. In the 600s CE, questions arose about certain Buddhist teachings, so a monk named Xuan Zang (also called Tripitaka) went to India to obtain copies of official scriptures. An account of his legendary trip was published in the 1500s as *Journey to the West*. In the story, the monkey god Sun Wukong and the pig god Zhu Bajie joined Xuan Zang on his journey. During the fourteen-year expedition, the three travelers had to endure many ordeals and tests of their sincerity, including fighting demons and monsters with the help of a magic stick.

Chinese Buddhists established a complex hierarchy, or ranked order of importance, for gods and goddesses. One of the more important deities was Shang Di, whose main assistant, Dongyue Dadi, was known as Great Emperor of the Eastern Peak. Under him were various departments where the souls of virtuous people worked to manage every aspect of human and animal life.

Some of the other important Buddhist gods were the Four Kings of Heaven, the Four Kings of Hell, and the kitchen god, the most important deity of the home. Another major deity was the bodhisattva Mi-Le (known in India as Maitreya), considered to be the future Buddha. Portrayed as a fat, cheerful man, Mi-Le was sometimes called the Laughing Buddha. Worshipers prayed to join him in paradise. Each district in China had its own local deity, and so did each occupation. Even the smallest details of life were controlled by various minor gods and goddesses.

In Chinese Buddhism, the bodhisattva Avalokitesvara evolved from a male figure of sympathy into Kuanyin, the goddess of mercy. Tibetans gave Avalokitesvara's wife, Tara, the title Pandaravasin, meaning "dressed in white." The Chinese translation of that title is Pai-i-Kuanyin. Chinese Buddhists apparently combined the figure of Tara with the characteristics of Avalokitesvara to create a mother goddess figure. As the one who blesses couples with children, Kuanyin appealed to the Chinese belief in ancestor worship, and she became one of the most popular and important Buddhist deities. In Japan, Avalokitesvara is worshiped in both male and female forms as the deity Kannon.

Japan Buddhism came to Japan in about 550 CE and spread quickly because of support from the Japanese royal family. Although supporters of Shinto, the native religion of Japan, at first opposed Buddhism, the two religions eventually became closely linked. Buddhist temples contained Shinto shrines, and Shinto gods (known collectively as *kami*) became Buddhist guardians. This mix of Shintoism and Buddhism continued until 1868, when the emperor declared Shinto a state religion and banned Buddhist priests and images from Shinto temples. Yet Buddhism remained popular and still has a larger following in Japan than does Shinto.

Although the various forms of Japanese Buddhism include religious ideas from India and China, they have their own mythologies and gods. One of the main deities is Amida (known in other Buddhist regions as Amitabha), ruler of a paradise called the Pure Land. He is worshipped by some Japanese sects as the savior of humankind. Kannon—a bodhisattva known elsewhere as Kuanyin and Avalokitesvara—is the protector of children, women in childbirth, and dead souls. Another

This relief sculpture from a temple in Indonesia shows the temptation of Buddha by the women of Mara. © CHARLES & JOSETTE LENARS/CORBIS.

popular deity, the bodhisattva Jizô, protects humans and rescues souls from **hell**. He is often described as a gentle monk who wanders through the land of the dead bringing light and comfort to the souls imprisoned there.

Tibet Buddhism reached Tibet from India in the 600s CE and gradually absorbed native religious practices, creating a unique form of Buddhism. Tibetan Buddhists worship many groups of Buddhas, gods, and bodhisattvas. They also believe in the existence of numerous demons and evil spirits.

According to Tibetan Buddhists, the world goes through an endless cycle of creation and decay, and a new Buddha appears in each world age to teach Buddhist principles. Legend says that one of these Buddhas, Amitabha, ordered a bodhisattva named Avalokitesvara to bring Buddhism to Tibet. At the time, only animals and ogres—large, fearsome creatures—lived there. Avalokitesvara produced a monkey and sent it to meditate in Tibet. The monkey was approached by a female ogre in the form of a beautiful woman, who offered to be his wife. The two had children, but they were covered with hair and had tails. Avalokitesvara sent the children to a forest to mate with other monkeys. He returned a year later and discovered many offspring. When Avalokitesvara gave these creatures food they turned into human beings, and he was then able to convert them to Buddhism.

Key Themes and Symbols

A major theme in Buddhism is the notion of *maya*, or illusion. Humans believe that their egos and bodily forms are reality, but Buddhism teaches that they are, in fact, just an illusion. Moreover, they are what keep humans entangled in the cycle of birth and rebirth. In order to break out of that cycle and achieve true spiritual liberation, humans must see through the illusion of materiality and ego-consciousness, and embrace the true reality of the divine.

Both the Bohdi tree and the lotus flower symbolize enlightenment in Buddhism. Another prominent symbol is the dharmacakra (pronounced dar-mah-CAK-rah), the "eight-spoked wheel" which represents the "eightfold path" of Buddhism.

Buddhist Mythology in Art, Literature, and Everyday Life

Because Buddhism has spread across so many regions of Asia, there are countless examples of Buddhist art to be found in countries like China, Japan, and Tibet. In India, the land where Buddhism began, examples of Buddhist art are much rarer, as the country is predominantly Hindu and Muslim.

Some Buddhist concepts found their way into Western art and literature in the mid-nineteenth century as Europe and the United States increased trade with Asia. One important export from Asia, in addition to spices and tea, was the drug opium. The phrase "kicking Buddha's gong" eventually came to be slang for using opium, which was popular in Europe and America through the nineteenth and early twentieth centuries. Over time, the West became interested in Asia for more than just opium, spices, and tea. The Buddhist philosophy interested many

Giant Buddhas

Perhaps the greatest example of Buddhism in art was the giant Buddha sculptures of Bamyan in Afghanistan. The two sculptures, each standing over one hundred feet tall, were carved into sandstone cliff walls in the sixth century CE. Details were added using mud plaster, and the statues were originally brightly painted. Being carved from soft sandstone, the statues lost a great deal of their original detail and form due to centuries of erosion by wind and rain. In 2001, the Taliban, an extremist Islamic political party that controlled Afghanistan, destroyed much of what remained of the giant Buddha statues. The giant statues were blasted with dynamite and tank mortars for nearly a month to ensure their destruction.

The Giant Buddhas (2005), a documentary by Christian Frei, details the history of the Bamyan Buddhas and their destruction at the hands of the Taliban. The film was nominated for the Grand Jury Prize at the 2006 Sundance Film Festival.

free-thinkers in the nineteenth century, including the American Transcendentalists, who sought alternatives to the dominant Western worldview. The writings of American poet Walt Whitman and social maverick Henry David Thoreau (author of *Walden*, 1854) both show the influence of Buddhism.

German author Herman Hesse introduced many Westerners to Buddhism with his 1922 novel *Siddhartha*, which was based on the spiritual journey of Siddhartha Gautama. The branch of Buddhism known as Zen Buddhism attracted the attention of the Beat generation writers of the 1950s, and featured prominently in Jack Kerouac's 1958 novel *The Dharma Bums*. Novelist J. D. Salinger's work, including *The Catcher in the Rye* (1951) and *Raise High the Roofbeams, Carpenters* (1963), also reveals the author's interest in Zen Buddhism.

The novel *Siddhartha* and Buddhist teachings in general became particularly popular in the United States during the countercultural movement of the 1960s and 1970s, when, again, Buddhism was seen as an alternative to what many perceived as a violent, consumerist Western culture. Robert M. Pirsig's 1974 book *Zen and the Art of Motorcycle Maintenance: An Inquiry into Values* became one of the bestselling books of philosophy of all time.

Read, Write, Think, Discuss

Many prominent American celebrities have converted to Buddhism in adulthood. Examples include actors Keanu Reeves, Uma Thurman, and Mark Wahlberg, as well as singer Tina Turner. Among the general American population, however, adult conversion to Buddhism remains fairly rare. Why do you think celebrities might be more interested in Buddhism than the general population?

SEE ALSO Brahma; Chinese Mythology; Devils and Demons; Flowers in Mythology; Hinduism and Mythology; Japanese Mythology; Reincarnation

Where to Learn More

African

Altman, Linda Jacobs. *African Mythology.* Berkeley Heights, NJ: Enslow Publishers, 2003.

Ardagh, Philip, and Georgia Peters. *African Myths & Legends.* Chicago: World Book, 2002.

Giles, Bridget. *Myths of West Africa.* Austin, TX: Raintree Steck-Vaughn, 2002.

Husain, Shahrukh, and Bee Willey. *African Myths.* 1st ed. North Mankato, MN: Cherrytree Books, 2007.

Lilly, Melinda. *Spider and His Son Find Wisdom: An Akan Tale.* Vero Beach, FL: Rourke Press, 1998.

Lilly, Melinda. *Warrior Son of a Warrior Son: A Masai Tale.* Vero Beach, FL: Rourke Press, 1998.

Lilly, Melinda. *Zimani's Drum: A Malawian Tale.* Vero Beach, FL: Rourke Press, 1998.

Schomp, Virginia. *The Ancient Africans.* New York: Marshall Cavendish Benchmark, 2008.

Seed, Jenny. *The Bushman's Dream: African Tales of the Creation.* 1st American ed. Scarsdale, NY: Bradbury Press, 1975.

Anglo-Saxon/Celtic

Ardagh, Philip, and G. Barton Chapple. *Celtic Myths & Legends.* Chicago: World Book, 2002.

Crossley-Holland, Kevin, and Peter Malone. *The World of King Arthur and His Court: People, Places, Legend, and Lore.* New York: Dutton Children's Books, 2004.

Hicks, Penelope, and James McLean. *Beowulf.* New York: Kingfisher, 2007.

Lister, Robin, Alan Baker, and Sir Thomas Malory. *The Story of King Arthur.* Boston: Kingfisher, 2005.

Martell, Hazel Mary. *The Celts.* 1st American ed. New York: Peter Bedrick, 2001.

Morris, Gerald. *The Lioness & Her Knight.* Boston: Houghton Mifflin, 2005.

Whittock, Martyn J. *Beliefs and Myths of Viking Britain.* Oxford: Heinemann, 1996.

Williams, Marcia, ed. *Chaucer's Canterbury Tales.* London: Walker, 2008.

Asian/Pacific

Behnke, Alison. *Angkor Wat.* Minneapolis: Twenty-First Century Books, 2008.

Carpenter, Frances. *Tales of a Korean Grandmother.* Boston: Tuttle Pub., 1973.

Coburn, Jewell Reinhart. *Encircled Kingdom: Legends and Folktales of Laos.* Rev. ed. Thousand Oaks, CA: Burn, Hart, 1994.

Coulson, Kathy Morrissey, Paula Cookson Melhorn, and Hmong Women's Project (Fitchburg, MA). *Living in Two Worlds: The Hmong Women's Project.* Ashburnham, MA: K. M. Coulson and P. C. Melhorn, 2000.

Dalal, Anita. *Myths of Oceania.* Austin, TX: Raintree Steck-Vaughn, 2002.

Green, Jen. *Myths of China and Japan.* Austin, TX: New York: Raintree Steck-Vaughn Publishers, 2002.

Htin Aung, U., G. Trager, and Pau Oo Thet. *A Kingdom Lost for a Drop of Honey, and Other Burmese Folktales.* New York: Parents' Magazine Press, 1968.

Kanawa, Kiri Te. *Land of the Long White Cloud: Maori Myths, Tales, and Legends.* 1st U.S. ed. New York: Arcade Pub., 1989.

Sakairi, Masao, Shooko Kojima, and Matthew Galgani. *Vietnamese Fables of Frogs and Toads.* Berkeley, CA: Heian International, 2006.

Sakairi, Masao, Shooko Kojima, and Matthew Galgani. *Vietnamese Tales of Rabbits and Watermelons.* Berkeley, CA: Heian International, 2006.

Egyptian

Ardagh, Philip, and Danuta Mayer. *Ancient Egyptian Myths & Legends.* Chicago: World Book, 2002.

Broyles, Janell. *Egyptian Mythology.* 1st ed. New York: Rosen Pub. Group, 2006.

Cline, Eric H., and Jill Rubalcaba. *The Ancient Egyptian World.* California ed. New York: Oxford University Press, 2005.

Gleason, Katherine. *Ancient Egyptian Culture.* New York: Newbridge Educational Pub., 2006.

Kramer, Ann. *Egyptian Myth: A Treasury of Legends, Art, and History.* Armonk, NY: Sharpe Focus, 2008.

Kudalis, Eric. *The Royal Mummies: Remains from Ancient Egypt.* Mankato, MN: Capstone High-Interest Books, 2003.

McCall, Henrietta. *Gods & Goddesses in the Daily Life of the Ancient Egyptians.* Columbus, OH: Peter Bedrick Books, 2002.

Mitchnik, Helen. *Egyptian and Sudanese Folk-Tales.* New York: Oxford University Press, 1978.

Schomp, Virginia. *The Ancient Egyptians.* New York: Marshall Cavendish Benchmark, 2008.

Wyly, Michael J. *Death and the Underworld.* San Diego, CA: Lucent Books, 2002.

Greek/Roman

Bingham, Jane. *Classical Myth: A Treasury of Greek and Roman Legends, Art, and History.* Armonk, NY: M. E. Sharpe, 2008.

Hepplewhite, Peter, and Mark Bergin. *The Adventures of Perseus.* Minneapolis, MN: Picture Window Books, 2005.

Lister, Robin, Alan Baker, and Homer. *The Odyssey.* Reformatted ed. Boston: Kingfisher, 2004.

McCarty, Nick, Victor G. Ambrus, and Homer. *The Iliad.* Reformatted ed. Boston: Kingfisher, 2004.

Mellor, Ronald, and Marni McGee. *The Ancient Roman World.* New York: Oxford University Press, 2005.

Roberts, Russell. *Athena.* Hockessin, DE: Mitchell Lane Publishers, 2008.

Roberts, Russell. *Dionysus.* Hockessin, DE: Mitchell Lane Publishers, 2008.

Roberts, Russell. *Zeus.* Hockessin, DE: Mitchell Lane Publishers, 2008.

Schomp, Virginia. *The Ancient Romans.* New York: Marshall Cavendish Benchmark, 2008.

Spires, Elizabeth, and Mordicai Gerstein. *I Am Arachne: Fifteen Greek and Roman Myths.* New York: Frances Foster Books, 2001.

Whiting, Jim. *The Life and Times of Hippocrates.* Hockessin, DE: Mitchell Lane Publishers, 2007.

Hindu

Choudhury, Bani Roy, and Valmiki. *The Story of Ramayan: The Epic Tale of India.* New Delhi: Hemkunt Press; Pomona, CA: Distributed in North America by Auromere, 1970.

Dalal-Clayton, Diksha, and Marilyn Heeger. *The Adventures of Young Krishna: The Blue God of India.* New York: Oxford University Press, 1992.

Ganeri, Anita. *The* Ramayana *and Hinduism*. Mankato, MN: Smart Apple Media, 2003.

Ganeri, Anita, and Carole Gray. *Hindu Stories.* Minneapolis: Picture Window Books, 2006.

Ganeri, Anita, and Tracy Fennell. *Buddhist Stories.* Minneapolis: Picture Window Books, 2006.

Husain, Shahrukh, and Bee Willey. *Indian Myths.* London: Evans, 2007.

Kipling, Rudyard. *The Jungle Book.* New York: Sterling Pub., 2008.

Parker, Vic, and Philip Ardagh. *Traditional Tales from India.* Thameside Press; North Mankato, MN: Distributed in the United States by Smart Apple Media, 2001.

Sharma, Bulbul. *The* Ramayana *for Children*. Penguin Global, 2004.

Staples, Suzanne Fisher. *Shiva's Fire.* 1st ed. New York: Farrar Straus Giroux, 2000.

Judeo-Christian

Geras, Adele. *My Grandmother's Stories: A Collection of Jewish Folk Tales.* New York: Alfred A. Knopf, 2003.

Kimmel, Eric A., and John Winch. *Brother Wolf, Sister Sparrow: Stories about Saints and Animals.* 1st ed. New York: Holiday House, 2003.

Schwartz, Howard, and Barbara Rush. *The Diamond Tree: Jewish Tales from Around the World.* 1st Harper Trophy ed. New York: HarperTrophy, 1998.

Schwartz, Howard, and Stephen Fieser. *Invisible Kingdoms: Jewish Tales of Angels, Spirits, and Demons.* 1st ed. New York: HarperCollins Publishers, 2002.

Self, David, and Nick Harris. *Stories from the Christian World.* Englewood Cliffs, NJ: Silver Burdett Press, 1988.

Senker, Cath. *Everyday Life in the Bible Lands.* North Mankato, MN: Smart Apple Media, 2006.

Taback, Simms. *Kibitzers and Fools: Tales My Zayda (Grandfather) Told Me.* New York: Puffin, 2008.

Native American

Ardagh, Philip, and Syrah Arnold. *South American Myths & Legends.* Chicago: World Book, 2002.

Berk, Ari, and Carolyn Dunn Anderson. *Coyote Speaks: Wonders of the Native American World.* New York: Abrams Books for Young Readers, 2008.

Brown, Virginia Pounds, Laurella Owens, and Nathan H. Glick. *Southern Indian Myths and Legends.* Birmingham, AL: Beechwood Books, 1985.

Curry, Jane Louise. *The Wonderful Sky Boat and Other Native American Tales from the Southeast.* New York: Margaret K. McElderry, 2001.

Monroe, Jean Guard, and Ray A. Williamson. *They Dance in the Sky: Native American Star Myths.* Award ed. Boston: Houghton Mifflin, 1993.

Parker, Victoria. *Traditional Tales from South America.* North Mankato, MN: Thameside Press. Distributed in the United States by Smart Apple Media, 2001.

Philip, Neil. *The Great Mystery: Myths of Native America.* New York: Clarion Books, 2001.

Pijoan, Teresa. *White Wolf Woman: Native American Transformation Myths.* 1st ed. Little Rock, AR: August House Publishers, 1992.

Ramen, Fred. *Native American Mythology.* 1st ed. New York: Rosen Central, 2008.

Schomp, Virginia. *The Native Americans.* New York: Marshall Cavendish Benchmark, 2008.

Vogel, Carole G. *Weather Legends: Native American Lore and the Science of Weather.* Brookfield, CT: Millbrook Press, 2001.

Near Eastern/Islamic

Ganeri, Anita. *Islamic Stories.* 1st American ed. Minneapolis, MN: Picture Window Books, 2006.

Grimal, Pierre. *Stories from Babylon and Persia.* Cleveland, OH: World Pub, 1964.

Ibrahim, Abdullahi A. *Enuma Elish.* Austin, TX: Steck-Vaughn Co., 1994.

Jabbari, Ahmad. *Amoo Norooz and Other Persian Folk Stories.* Costa Mesa, CA: Mazda Publishers, 2000.

León, Vicki. *Outrageous Women of Ancient Times.* New York: Wiley, 1998.

Marston, Elsa. *Figs and Fate: Stories about Growing Up in the Arab World Today.* 1st ed. New York: George Braziller, 2005.

Marston, Elsa. *Santa Claus in Baghdad and Other Stories about Teens in the Arab World.* Bloomington: Indiana University Press, 2008.

McCaughrean, Geraldine. *Gilgamesh the Hero.* Oxford: Oxford University Press, 2002.

Podany, Amanda H., and Marni McGee. *The Ancient Near Eastern World.* New York: Oxford University Press, 2005.

Schomp, Virginia. *The Ancient Mesopotamians.* New York: Marshall Cavendish Benchmark, 2008.

Walker, Barbara K. *Turkish Folk-Tales.* Oxford: Oxford University Press, 1993.

Norse/Northern European

Andersen, H. C., Diana Frank, Jeffrey Frank, Vilhelm Pedersen, and Lorenz Frolich. *The Stories of Hans Christian Andersen: A New Translation from the Danish.* Durham: Duke University Press, 2005.

Ardagh, Philip, and Stephen May. *Norse Myths & Legends.* Chicago: World Book, 2002.

Branford, Henrietta, and Dave Bowyer. *The Theft of Thor's Hammer.* Crystal Lake, IL: Rigby Interactive Library, 1996.

D'Aulaire, Ingri, and Edgar Parin. *D'Aulaires' Book of Norse Myths.* New York: New York Review of Books, 2005.

Evan, Cheryl, and Anne Millard. *Usborne Illustrated Guide to Norse Myths and Legends.* London: Usborne, 2003.

Jones, Gwyn, and Joan Kiddell-Monroe. *Scandinavian Legends and Folk-Tales.* New ed. Oxford: Oxford University Press, 1992.

Osborne, Mary Pope. *Favorite Norse Myths.* New York: Scholastic, 2001.

Porterfield, Jason. *Scandinavian Mythology.* New York: Rosen Central, 2008.

Web Sites

American Folklore. http://www.americanfolklore.net/ (accessed on June 11, 2008).

The British Museum: Mesopotamia. http://www.mesopotamia.co.uk/menu.html (accessed on June 11, 2008).

The Camelot Project at the University of Rochester. http://www.lib.rochester.edu/CAMELOT/cphome.stm (accessed on June 11, 2008).

Common Elements in Creation Myths. http://www.cs.williams.edu/~lindsey/myths (accessed on June 11, 2008).

Egyptian Museum Official Site. http://www.egyptianmuseum.gov.eg/ (accessed on June 11, 2008).

Internet History Sourcebooks Project. http://www.fordham.edu/halsall/ (accessed on June 11, 2008). Last updated on December 10, 2006.

Iron Age Celts. http://www.bbc.co.uk/wales/celts/ (accessed on June 11, 2008).

Kidipede: History for Kids. http://www.historyforkids.org/ (accessed on June 11, 2008).

Mythography. http://www.loggia.com/myth/myth.html (accessed on June 11, 2008). Last updated on April 17, 2008.

National Geographic. http://www.nationalgeographic.com/ (accessed on June 11, 2008).

NOVA Online: The Vikings. http://www.pbs.org/wgbh/nova/vikings/ (accessed on June 11, 2008).

Perseus Project. http://www.perseus.tufts.edu/ (accessed on June 11, 2008).

Sanskrit Documents. http://sanskritdocuments.org/ (accessed on June 11, 2008). Last updated on February 2, 2008.

United Nations Educational, Scientific and Cultural Organization. http://portal. unesco.org/ (accessed on June 11, 2008).

World Myths & Legends in Art. http://www.artsmia.org/world-myths/artbyculture/index.html (accessed on June 11, 2008).

Index

Italic type indicates volume number; **boldface** type indicates main entries and their page numbers; (ill.) indicates photos and illustrations.

A

Aborigines, *1:* 144–49
    assimilation, *2:* 317
    creation stories, *1:* 147; *2:* 315–17
    Dreamtime, *1:* 145–49; *2:* 320–22, 321 (ill.);
      5: 888
    floods, *2:* 390–91
    giants, *3:* 433–34
    serpents and snakes, *5:* 931
Abraham, *5:* 906
Achilles, *1:* **1–4**; *2:* 272; *3:* 530, 568–71
    Aeneas, provoked to join Trojan War, *1:* 12
    Agamemnon, feud with, *1:* 39–40;
      3: 489
    Amazon queen Penthesilea, killed by, *1:* 54
    Apollo, helped to kill, *1:* 92
    Balder, similar to, *1:* 166–67
    Chiron, teacher of, *2:* 221
    and Hector, *3:* 489–90
    Hephaestus, made armor for, *3:* 508
    Hera, protector of, *3:* 513
    Odysseus, encounters with, *4:* 774, 780
Achilles' heel, *1:* 1, 3
Acoetes, *2:* 311
Acrisius (King), *2:* 286, 287; *4:* 826, 829
Acropolis, *1:* 133–34
Actaeon, *1:* 111
The Acts of King Arthur and His Noble Knights
  (Steinbeck), *1:* 119
Adad, *5:* 923

Adam and Eve, *1:* **4–8**, 6 (ill.), 77; *2:* 260
    Cain and Abel, *1:* 5; *2:* 203
    cherubim, *2:* 230, 231
    fruit appearing in the myth of, *2:* 409, 410
    Garden of Eden, *2:* 331–33
    refusal of a jinn to bow down to, *3:* 425
    impact of sin on the rose, *2:* 396
    Lilith, first wife of Adam, *3:* 646–48, 647 (ill.)
    Satan, as tempter of, *5:* 910
Adam's rib, *1:* 5, 6–7
Adapa, *5:* 925
Adaro, *4:* 689
Adilgashii. See Skinwalkers
"Adonais" (Shelley), *1:* 11
Adonis, *1:* **8–11**, 10 (ill.), 86; *3:* 555
    association with the anemone flower, *2:* 393
    similar to Egyptian myth, *3:* 588
    similar to Semitic myth, *1:* 87; *2:* 296 (ill.),
      398; *5:* 924
The Adventures of Baron Munchausen (film), *1:* 88;
  3: 510
The Adventures of Robin Hood (film), *3:* 535;
  5: 893, 893 (ill.)
The Adventures of Sharkboy and Lavagirl in 3-D
  (film), *4:* 820
Aeëtes (King), *1:* 101
Aegeus, *4:* 682; *5:* 980, 981
Aegisthus, *1:* 38, 40–41; *2:* 208, 348
Aeneas, *1:* **11–16**, 15 (ill.), 135; *2:* 271 (ill.);
  5: 898–99
    Cerberus, *2:* 223

D

H

I

M

O

S

W

X